Images of Modern America

DETROIT'S GRAND RIVER & GREENFIELD NEIGHBORHOOD

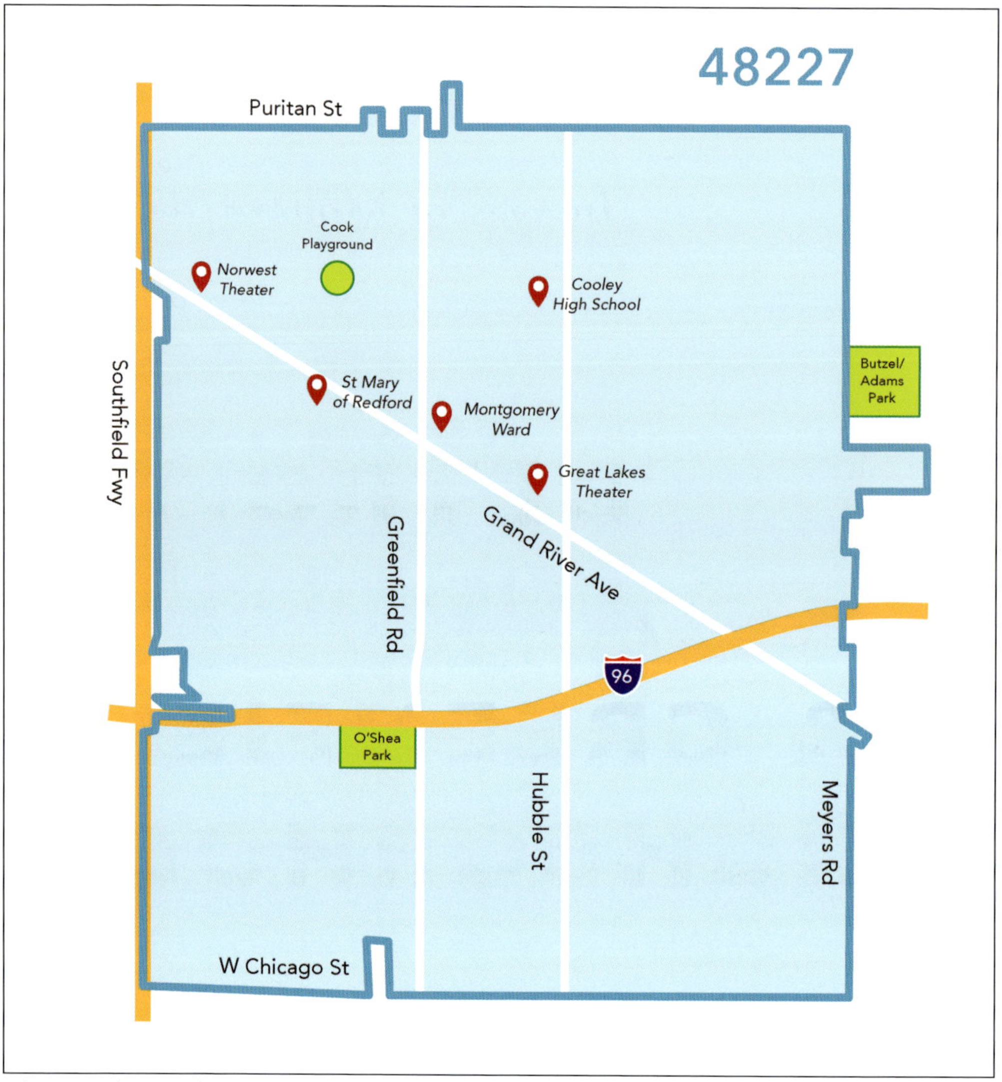

This map depicts the Grand River and Greenfield neighborhood, within the 48227 postal code. Some landmarks from the area's heyday are included, as well as some that still exist today. The neighborhood and the contents of this book are bound by Puritan Street, the Southfield Freeway, West Chicago Street, and Meyers Road. (Courtesy of Capelle Gabriel.)

Front Cover: Children gather on Winthrop Street for a possible impromptu sidewalk parade. (Courtesy of Marianne Szymanski.)

Upper Back Cover: Students stream out of Cooley High School. (Courtesy of Wayne State University, Walter P. Reuther Library.)

Lower Back Cover (from left to right): Children enjoy Popsicles on a backyard porch in summertime (author's collection); kids on Monte Vista Street help with a hands-on car wash (author's collection); a batter stands at the plate at Butzel Field while girls leave the outdoor pool house in the background (author's collection).

Images of Modern America

DETROIT'S GRAND RIVER & GREENFIELD NEIGHBORHOOD

Joseph McCauley

ARCADIA
PUBLISHING

ISBN 978-1-4671-2983-1

Published by Arcadia Publishing
Charleston, South Carolina

Printed in the United States of America

Library of Congress Control Number: 2018936306

For all general information, please contact Arcadia Publishing:
Telephone 843-853-2070
Fax 843-853-0044
E-mail sales@arcadiapublishing.com
For customer service and orders:
Toll-Free 1-888-313-2665

Visit us on the Internet at www.arcadiapublishing.com

To my wife, Grace Colette McCauley, who has loved and believed in me when no one else did, and to my high school journalism teacher, Betty Griffin.

Contents

Acknowledgments

This book was created with the help and generosity of many people I have met or corresponded with over many years. Their photographs, stories, and friendship have made this small neighborhood history possible.

Having grown up in the area, I have a special bond with many contributors, and hope I have made a decent representation of our childhood and early adulthood in the 1950s, 1960s, 1970s, and beyond.

Special thanks to Sam Allen, Joanne Rumford, Kathlyn Snow, Jim Strohman, Christine Tishler Davies, Joe Panacki, Kathy Weber, Amina Fakir, Marilyn Hardy, Michael Koch, Jim Burke, the Sloan family, the Hoban family, the Haas family, Jayne Marts Schmelzer Chrzan, Kathy Weber Wolfe Videcoq, the Szymanski family, Douglas Gordon, Nora Manning, Capelle Gabriel, Pete Anton, Mike Licata, Jake Frumm, H.B. Craig II, Hugh Groff, Dave Bobrowski, Brian Quinn, Renee Amiot, the Immaculate Heart of Mary sisters—especially Sr. Patrice Selby and Sr. Theresa Milne—and the 3,325 members of the Facebook page If You Live or Grew Up near Grand River and Greenfield. Finally, thanks to all the people who shared photographs.

I could not have completed this book without the assistance of Fr. Charles Morris, St. Mary of Redford administrator; Dr. Nathan Kelber; the Detroit Historical Society; Elisabeth Clemons, Wayne State University Reuther Library's Virtual Motor City; the Detroit Public Library; the Burton Collection; Florence Combes at Zuma Press Licensing for the *Detroit Free Press* and *Detroit News*; Kate Meyer at History of Living Farms; Historical Images; Kevin Bunce, coordinator for Ferris State Alumni Relations; the *Detroit Almanac*; the *Detroit Free Press*; Chaney Library librarians; Mark Drane, American Institute of Architects (AIA); and LEED AP Principal Rogvoy Architects.

Unless attributed otherwise, all images appear courtesy of the author's personal collection.

INTRODUCTION

It is easy to go about life in a neighborhood unaware of its historical significance. Around Grand River Avenue and Greenfield Road, the gateway to neighborhood history is typically learning of Henry Ford's romance with Clara Jane Bryant, whose family farm once sat where the Montgomery Ward was located at the crux of the neighborhood's defining intersection.

In the early 1900s, this area was considered the suburbs before it was developed as it exists today. Greenfield Township was annexed by the City of Detroit in the mid-1920s. St. Mary Cemetery made way for a wider Grand River Avenue, and farmlands were sold and developed to build houses for people flocking to Detroit.

For the most part, this community has been a middle-class example of the American Dream. The Roaring Twenties created wealth and attracted people from rural areas to the Motor City, where Henry Ford was promising automobile workers an unheard-of $5 a day.

No city grew faster than Detroit did between 1910 and 1930. The city went from the ninth-largest in the United States with 465,766 citizens in 1910 to the fourth-largest with 1,568,662 people in 1930.

The relatively flat land and local banks, flush with auto industry cash, propelled home building out to the city limits and beyond. In 1925, voters approved annexing the eastern two-thirds of Redford to Detroit. The Grand River and Greenfield neighborhood was part of that city expansion.

Schools surrounded residences in the space bordered by Puritan Road to the north, Southfield Freeway to the west, West Chicago Street to the south, and Meyers Road to the east. Parochial and public schools within the neighborhood have been considered some of the best in the city, and although many have closed or changed names, some are included in this work. Their alumni still talk proudly of their days growing up here.

Several religious denominations are represented as well. St. Mary of Redford was the largest Catholic parish in the city and grew so large that two other parishes (Mother of Our Savior and Our Lady Queen of Hope) spun off from the original congregation. Holy Cross Lutheran Missouri Synod Church and School was just one block from the intersection of Grand River Avenue and Greenfield Road. Pastor Armin W. Born served the parish for over 30 years. St. Paul's Memorial Episcopal, Hope Presbyterian, Strathmoor Methodist, Evangelical United Brethren, and Bushnell Congregational Churches also served the faithful, and the church buildings (except for St. Paul's) are still intact and being used today.

Whether it was washing the family car, swimming at Butzel Pool, playing ball at the sandlot, riding bikes, or stopping off for a beer, there was always something to do in the neighborhood. The "Fun and Games" and "Neighborhood" chapters include some familiar sights and a few friendly faces.

"Our Downtown and All Around" explores the businesses along Grand River Avenue. Locals could pick up popcorn near the entrances to Montgomery Ward and S.S. Kresge, attend a class at Wendy Ward's Charm School, get a comic or soda at Cunningham's Drug Store, enjoy a burger at Big Boy's, have a sundae at Sanders, buy some clothes from a variety of women's and men's clothiers, slip into a new pair of shoes, exchange light bulbs, redeem green stamps, or go roller skating, all within a few blocks.

Residents always found reasons for having a party or celebration, whether it was a family birthday party, American Legion parades on Memorial Day, Fourth of July fireworks, a dance class, a Knights of Columbus gathering, trick-or-treating on Halloween, dying Easter eggs, participating in J.C. Penney's back-to-school parade, or celebrating the holidays over Christmas and New Year's.

The neighborhood had plenty of famous sons and daughters who either grew up nearby or who blessed us with their presence from time to time. A beauty queen (Amina Fakir), football stars (Jack Clancy and Fred Arbanas), future actors (Brian Mallon and Linda Gehringer), hockey stars (Doug and Gordie Roberts), a labor leader (James Hoffa Jr.), and a pizza magnate and sports team owner (Mike Ilitch) grew up around the neighborhood and in area classrooms.

Many white people who grew up in Detroit's heyday were shocked when the 1967 Detroit riots unfolded not far from their houses. In hindsight, the black community pointed to discontent even before the 1943 riots. Housing shortages, discrimination in all walks of life, and distrust in the police department eventually erupted in July 1967.

Many families were attracted to the bigger spaces of suburban living. The threat of school busing (to integrate schools, courts required some students to go to schools outside their neighborhoods), real estate block busting (realtors often used scare tactics to get white residents to sell their houses), distrust between the races, upheaval surrounding the Vietnam War, and divisive politics made many people want to flee the city for a security they felt was possible in the suburbs.

Schools and churches held on as long as they could, but dwindling enrollment forced many to close in the 1980s and 1990s. Others were bought by groups or churches that represented the changing demographics of the neighborhood.

All the old businesses along Grand River Avenue and Greenfield Road from the 1950s, 1960s, and 1970s are gone. Many of the buildings are, too. However, many strip malls have replaced them, and they seem to be thriving.

The Grand River and Greenfield neighborhood is one of seven neighborhoods that the City of Detroit has targeted for urban renewal. So far, much work has been done to remove vacant properties.

There is a sense of hope and pride now that the Detroit downtown area is thriving. Residents of the Grand River and Greenfield neighborhood are looking forward to that success spilling over to their section of the city.

The Crary–St. Mary's Community Council (CSCC) is a nonprofit community group of block clubs, businesses, and churches in the area that has been active since 1972. It carries on the pioneering fight that made the former residents so proud of the neighborhood.

One

Rustics to City Slickers

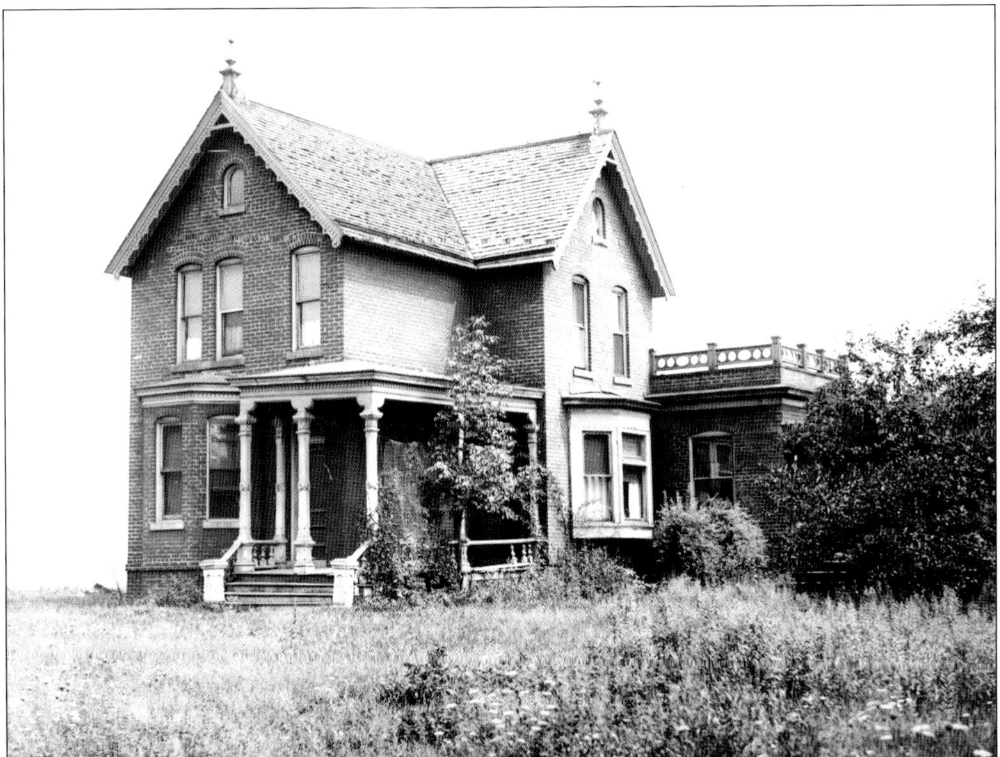

The area around Grand River Avenue and Division Road (later Greenfield Road) in Greenfield Township was mostly rural, with scattered small farms. Clara Jane Bryant was born on the family farm in 1866. She met Henry Ford in 1886 at the Bryants' new brick home on Monnier Road (a mile or so away) and married him two years later in the front parlor. Detroit was expanding, and Division Road marked the western border of the city limits. Redford Township was to the west. (Courtesy of *Detroit News*/Zuma Press.)

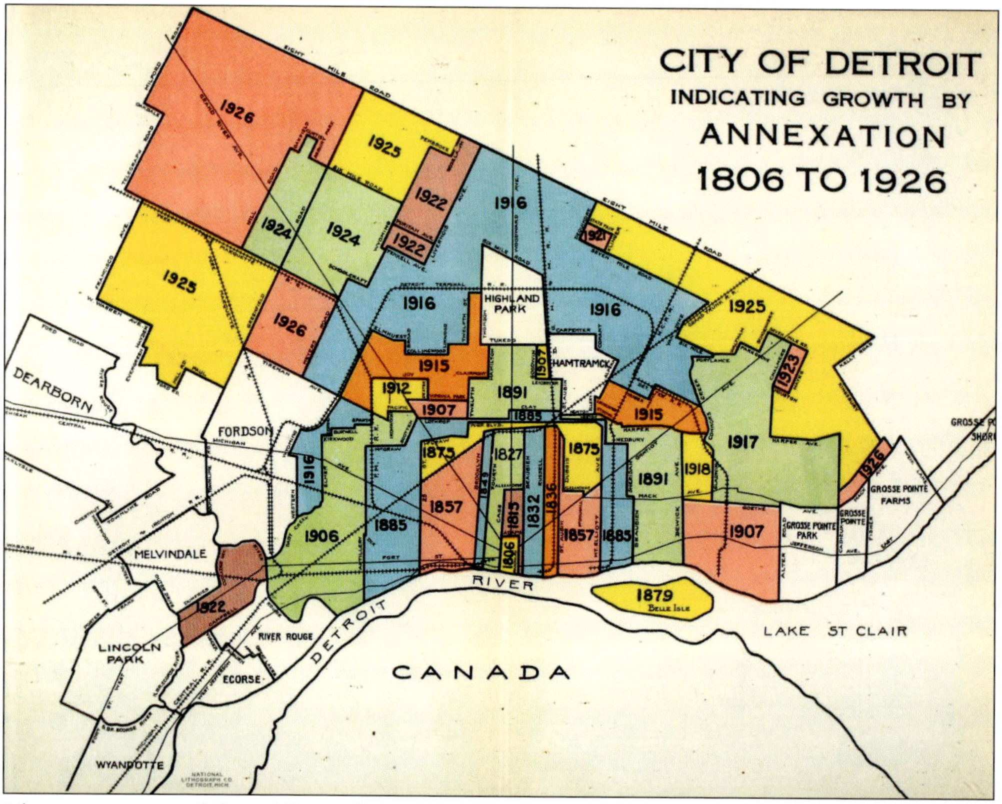

The intersection of Grand River Avenue and Greenfield Road has been an important spot for business, culture, and religion for over 174 years. In 1821, Lewis Cass and Soloman Sibley negotiated a treaty with the Ottawa, Chippewa, and Potawatomi tribes for them to give up land south of the north bank of the Grand River in western Michigan. The treaty permitted a military road (Grand River Avenue) that ran 115 miles from there to downtown Detroit. Many farmers brought their crops into Detroit along Grand River Avenue in what became Greenfield Township. From 1875 until 1926, Detroit annexed different sections of Greenfield Township until the township ceased to exist. (Courtesy of Wayne County, Michigan.)

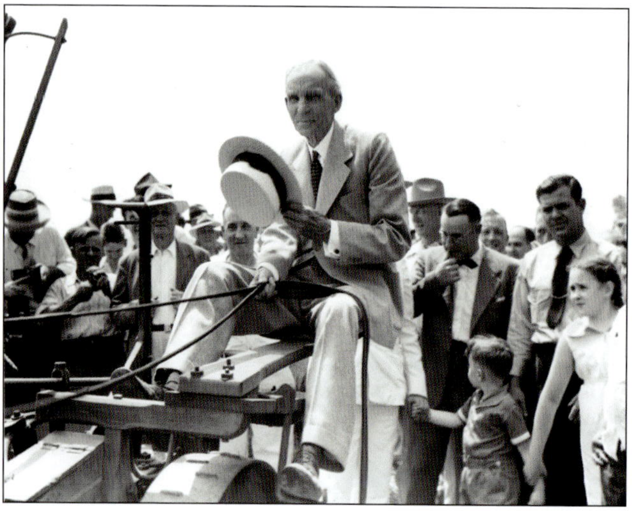

Henry Ford was known for more than mass producing automobiles. His Fordson Model F was a small, lightweight, mass-produced, affordable tractor that an average farmer could own. It was produced in 1917 for $750. Government tests showed that local farmers spent less per acre plowing with a Fordson Model F tractor than feeding eight horses and paying two drivers in a year. Henry Ford and his son Edsel (hence "Fordson") built 500,000 tractors by 1925. (Courtesy of the *Detroit Free Press*/Zuma Press.)

St. Mary's Church and Cemetery were on the southeast corner of Grand River Avenue and Division Road in 1843. The church moved five blocks west into Redford Township in the 1850s. Parishioners Michael J. Marclay (left) and Gerald "Darby" Sheehan stand in front of the third St. Mary's of Redford Church building in 1915. Previous churches were burned down by intolerant people.

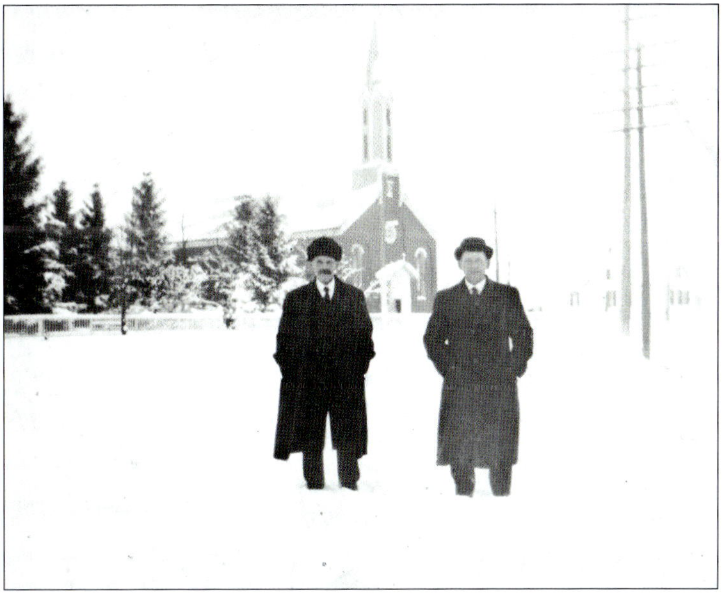

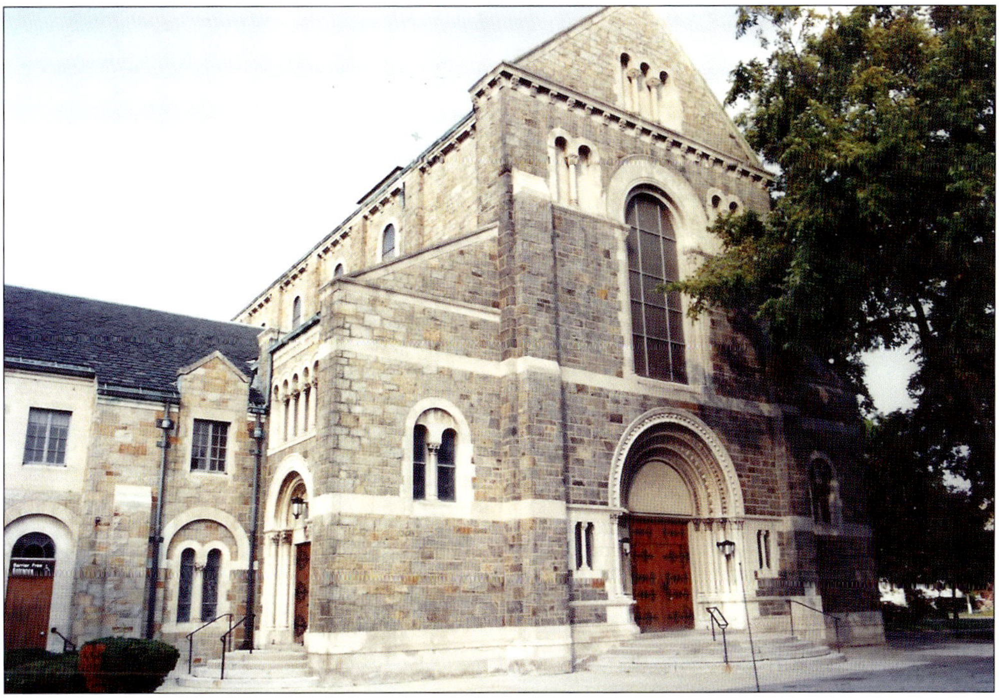

The fourth and present St. Mary's of Redford Church had its ground breaking on May 1, 1925. Boston designer Ralph Adams Cram, with the Detroit architectural firm of McGrath and Dohmen, drew inspiration for the new church from cathedrals in southern France. Talbot-Meier Inc. was the general contractor for the church, which opened in the fall of 1926. A new parish rectory, on the right, created one integrated structure. The new church sat behind the old church and rectory, which were torn down in September 1927.

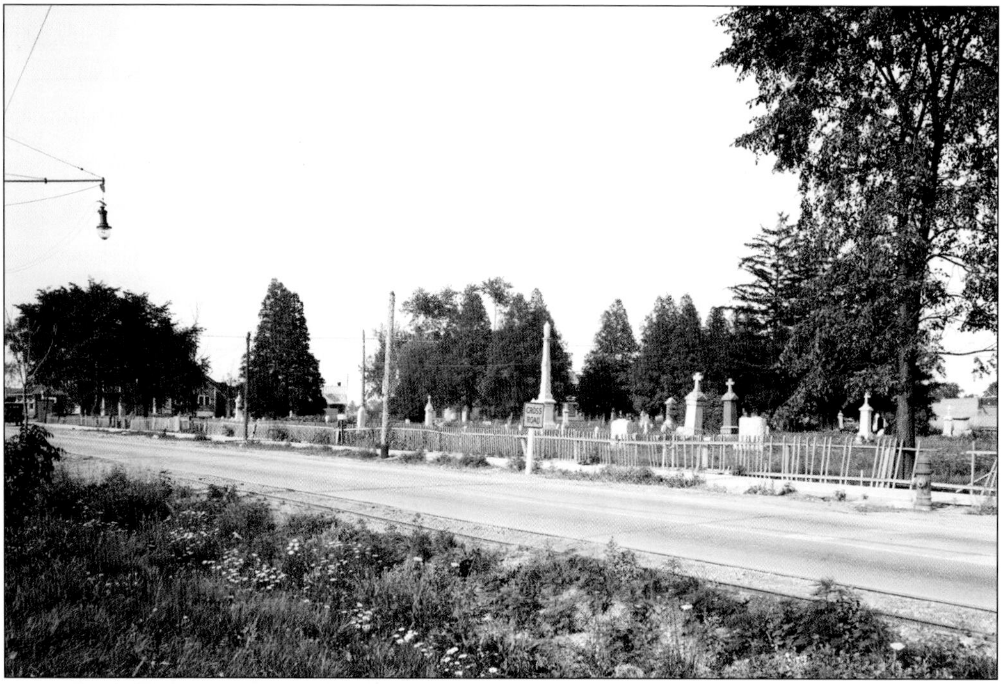

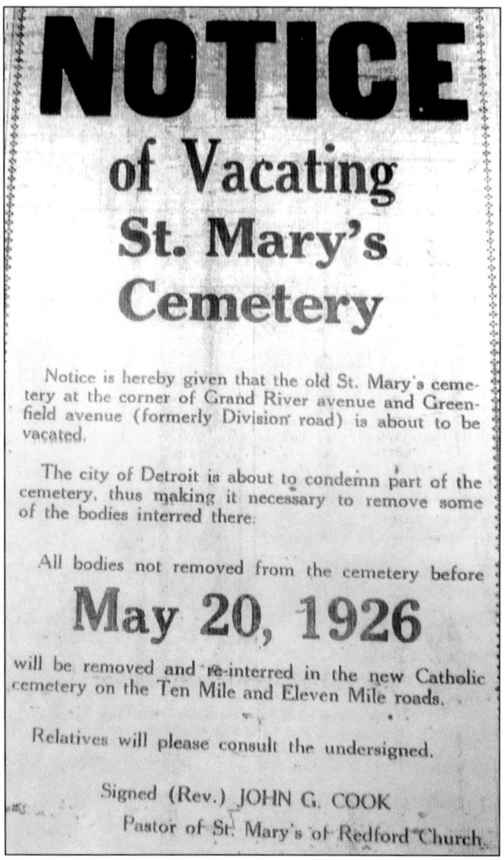

NOTICE

of Vacating

St. Mary's

Cemetery

Notice is hereby given that the old St. Mary's cemetery at the corner of Grand River avenue and Greenfield avenue (formerly Division road) is about to be vacated.

The city of Detroit is about to condemn part of the cemetery, thus making it necessary to remove some of the bodies interred there.

All bodies not removed from the cemetery before

May 20, 1926

will be removed and re-interred in the new Catholic cemetery on the Ten Mile and Eleven Mile roads.

Relatives will please consult the undersigned.

Signed (Rev.) JOHN G. COOK

Pastor of St. Mary's of Redford Church.

After the City of Detroit condemned 12 feet of the St. Mary's Cemetery to make room for improvements to Division Road in 1926, the St. Mary's of Redford Parish decided to remove all of the bodies buried there and take them to another site. Crowds of onlookers and relatives watched gravediggers take out coffins. All the bodies had been buried there for over 25 years. (Courtesy of Wayne State University, Reuther Library.)

Most of the deceased were moved to the new Catholic Holy Sepulchre Cemetery on Eleven Mile Road near Franklin Road. St. Mary's Cemetery was surrounded by hundreds of homes and businesses. While bodies were removed, city workers were digging and laying water pipes within 10 feet of the graves. (Courtesy of *Redford Record*.)

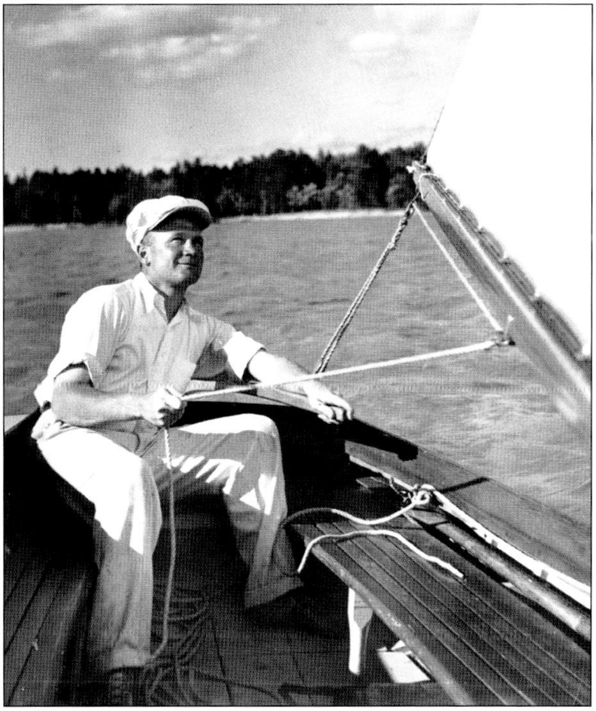

Rev. Edward J. Hickey was the chancellor of the Detroit archdiocese from 1938 to 1951. Hickey was a graduate of the Harvard Business School before he became a priest. He helped negotiate the diocese out of default in the Depression. He became a monsignor and the head of St. Mary's of Redford Parish in 1951. Under his guidance, the parish became the largest in Detroit. (Courtesy of the *Detroit Free Press*/Zuma Press.)

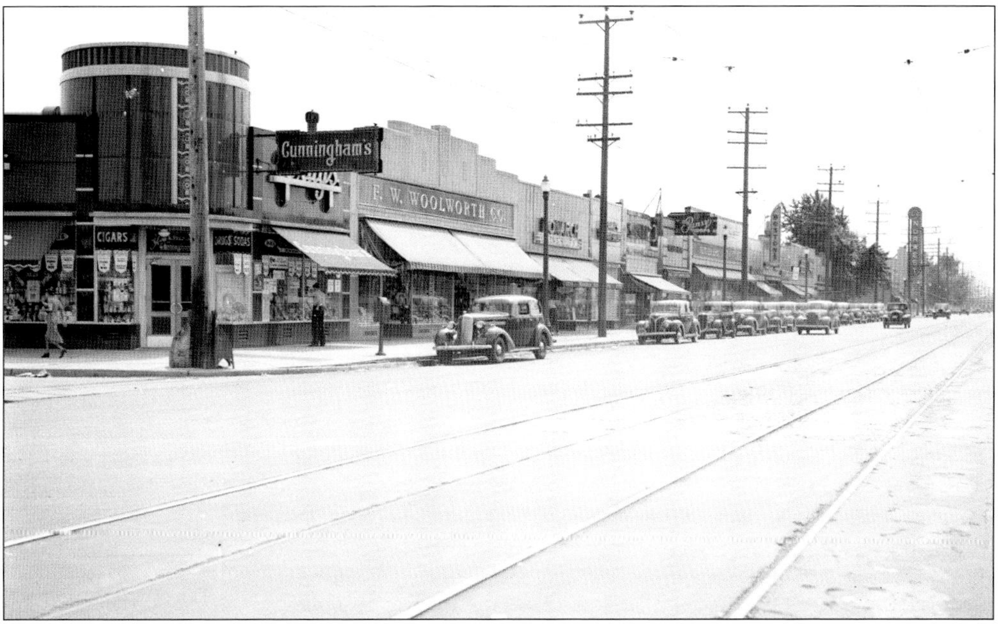

Located one mile northwest of the intersection of Grand River Avenue and Greenfield Road, the Norwest Theater (far right), at 17630 Grand River Avenue, was a landmark in the neighborhood from 1936 until 2000. The theater opened on May 21, 1936, and had 1,366 seats. It had air-conditioning and specially designed seats. The theater was built by United Detroit Theaters and was part of a citywide expansion program. Cunningham's Drug Store and the F.W. Woolworth store seen here were relocated one mile east in the late 1940s and early 1950s. (Courtesy of Wayne State University, Reuther Library.)

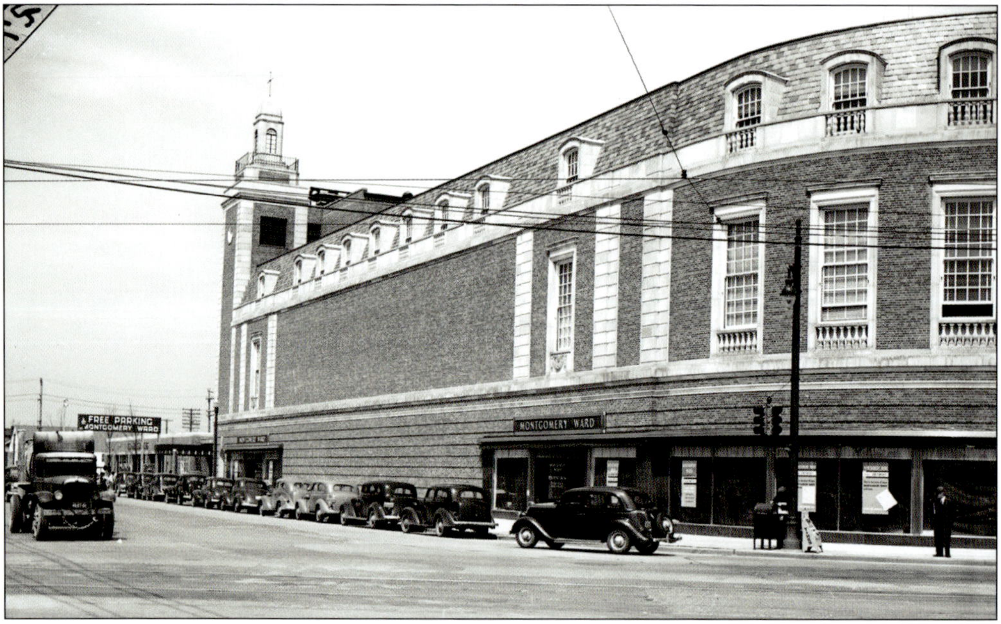

In 1939, ground was broken for a $1.2-million Montgomery Ward department store at 15400 Grand River Avenue. The three-floor Greco-Roman retail store, the largest Ward's store in the country, had parking for 1,200 automobiles. There was also a car servicing department attached to the main building. The George A. Fuller construction company built the store, which employed 250 people when it opened. (Courtesy of Wayne State University, Reuther Library.)

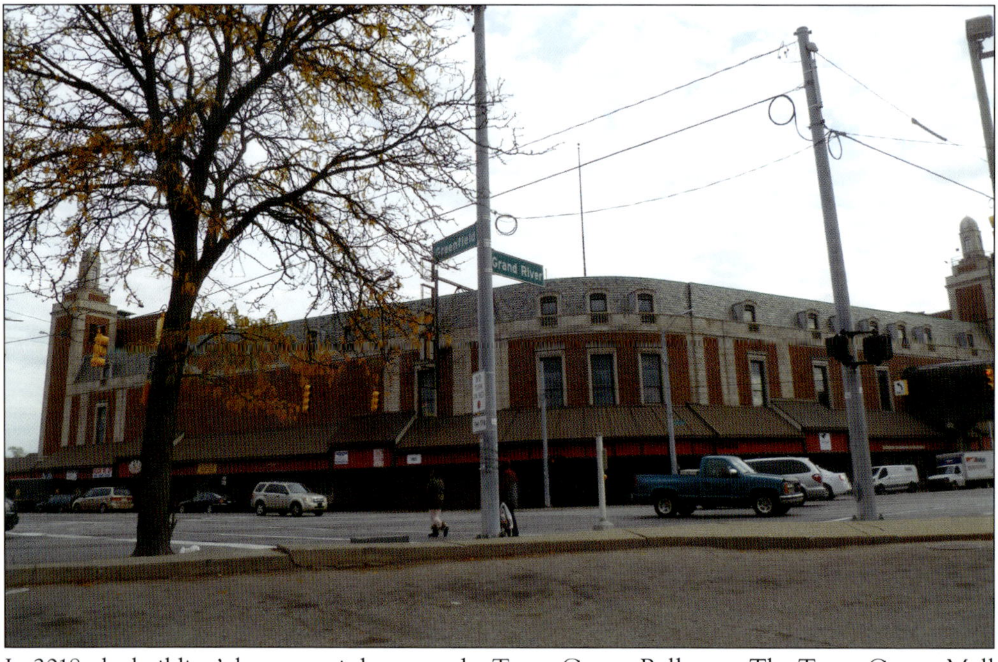

In 2018, the building's basement is home to the Tower Center Ballroom. The Tower Center Mall is on the main floor and houses jewelry, hair care, and nail care shops along with a real estate academy. Some artists are located on the upper level. Minnesota Fats once played pool with local kids in the basement. Chubby Checker held a limbo contest in the parking lot in 1963.

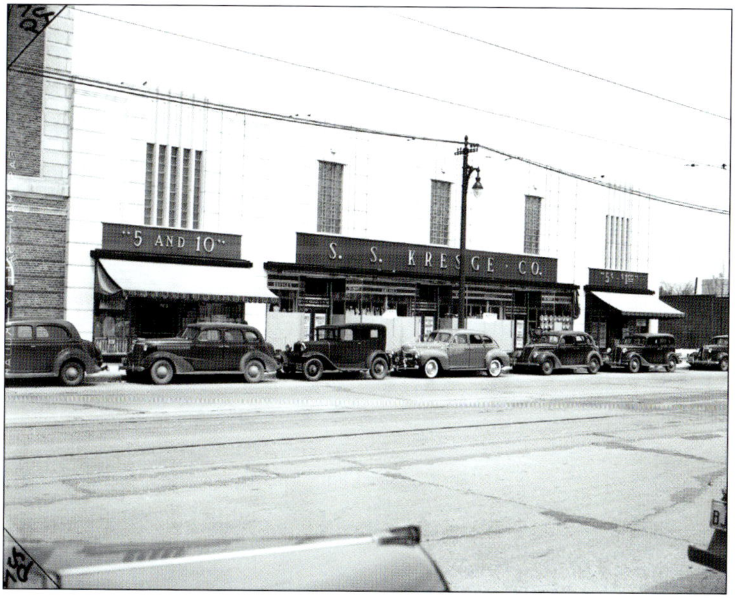

This S.S. Kresge Company department store was built next to the Montgomery Ward store and formally opened on May 16, 1940. It was the largest store in the Kresge chain, with 16,000 square feet of sales area and a frontage of 110 feet on Grand River Avenue. It had a lunch counter and later a cafeteria. (Courtesy of Wayne State University, Reuther Library.)

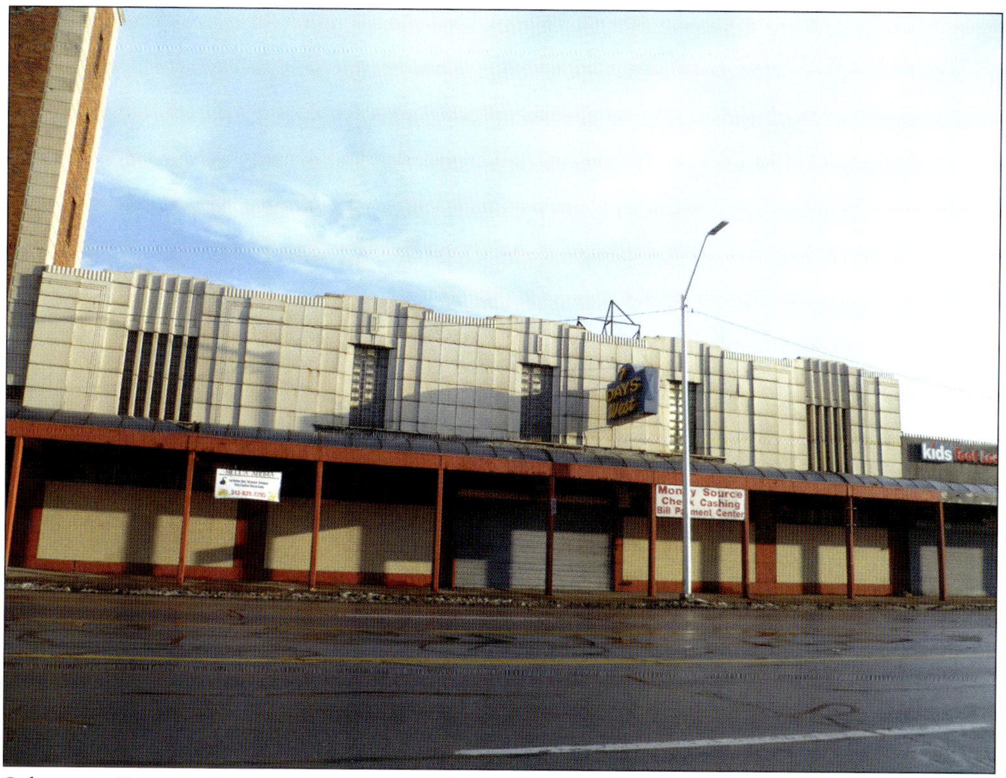

Sebastian Spering Kresge was born on July 31, 1867, and was president of his company until 1925. After he stepped down as president, he continued as chairman of the board until shortly before he died in 1966. He donated about $175 million to his foundation, which promoted the well-being of mankind. Many Detroit S.S. Kresge stores became K-Marts in the 1960s, and most moved to the suburbs. The Grand River store is now home to a variety of low-cost clothing and jewelry merchants.

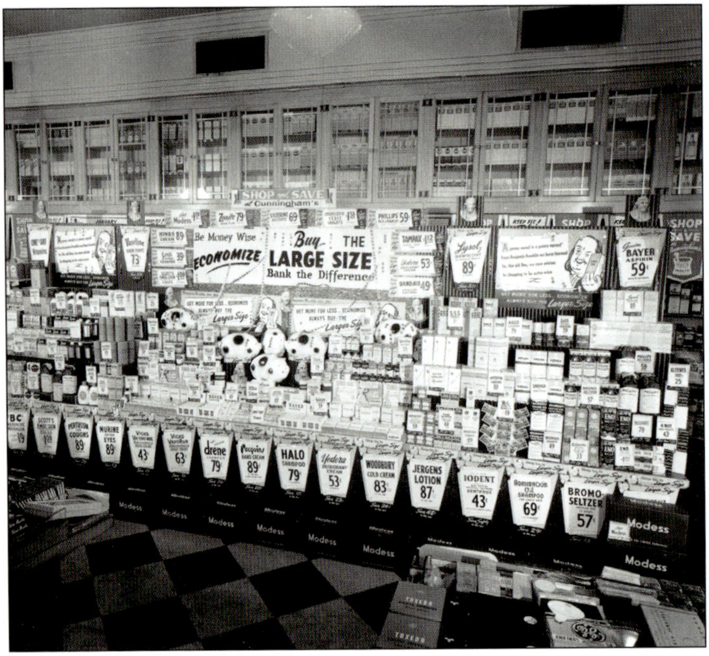

Cunningham Drug Co. opened its 99th store on the northwest corner of Grand River Avenue and Greenfield Road in 1940. The store, designed by architect Charles N. Agree, occupies 110 feet on Greenfield Road and 28 feet on Grand River Avenue. The drugstore chain was founded in 1889 by Andrew Cunningham. By 1959, after a merger with Broward Drug of Fort Lauderdale and Kinsel Drug Co. of Detroit, Cunningham became the largest drugstore chain in Michigan.

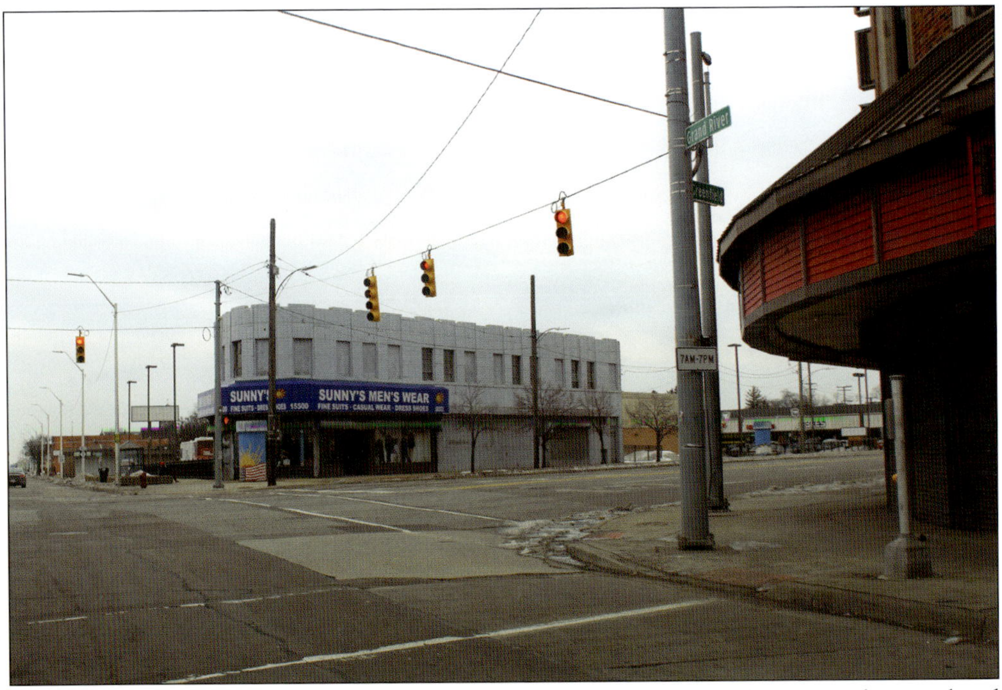

The green and cream exterior of Cunningham Drug Co. featured porcelain enamel on steel and structural glass brick. The soda fountain had seating for 35, with a low counter and chair-length stools. The store was air-conditioned, with fluorescent lighting used for window displays and illumination. Located at 15500 Grand River Avenue, the building has been a shoe store and Sunny's Men's Wear since Cunningham went out of business in the 1980s.

Owen Emmons was a baseball star in high school and a coach before he joined the Detroit schools in 1921 as an assistant principal at Southwestern High School. He was then Detroit superintendent of health education and principal of Strathmoor High School before he became principal of Cooley High School in 1928. Cooley High School was built in a former cow pasture as the population of Detroit reached past Greenfield Road and Fenkell Avenue. Emmons had a voice in choosing Cooley's Spanish Renaissance architecture. (Courtesy of the *Detroit Free Press*/Zuma Press.)

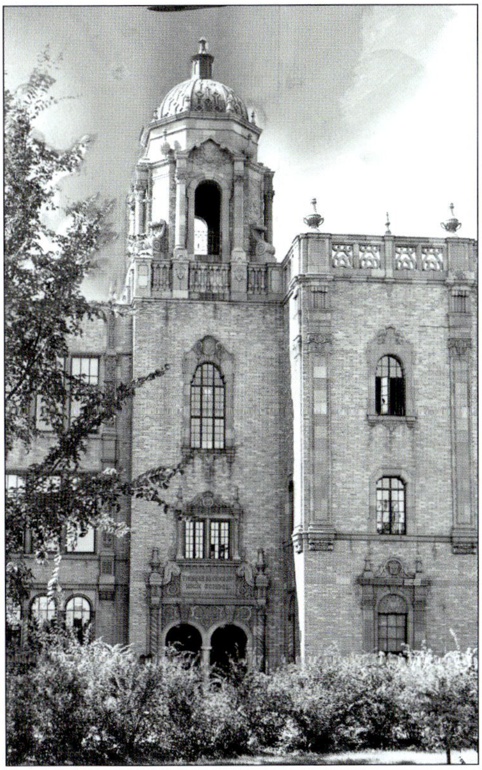

Owen Emmons was the principal at Cooley High School for 33 years (from the fall of 1928 until June 12, 1961). Cooley High School, at 15055 Hubbell Road, had attendance grow from 1,570 students in 1928 to 3,750 in 1932. During Emmons's tenure, Cooley High School had one of the most successful interscholastic athletic programs in Michigan. The three-story building was one of the more ornate structures operated by Detroit Public Schools.

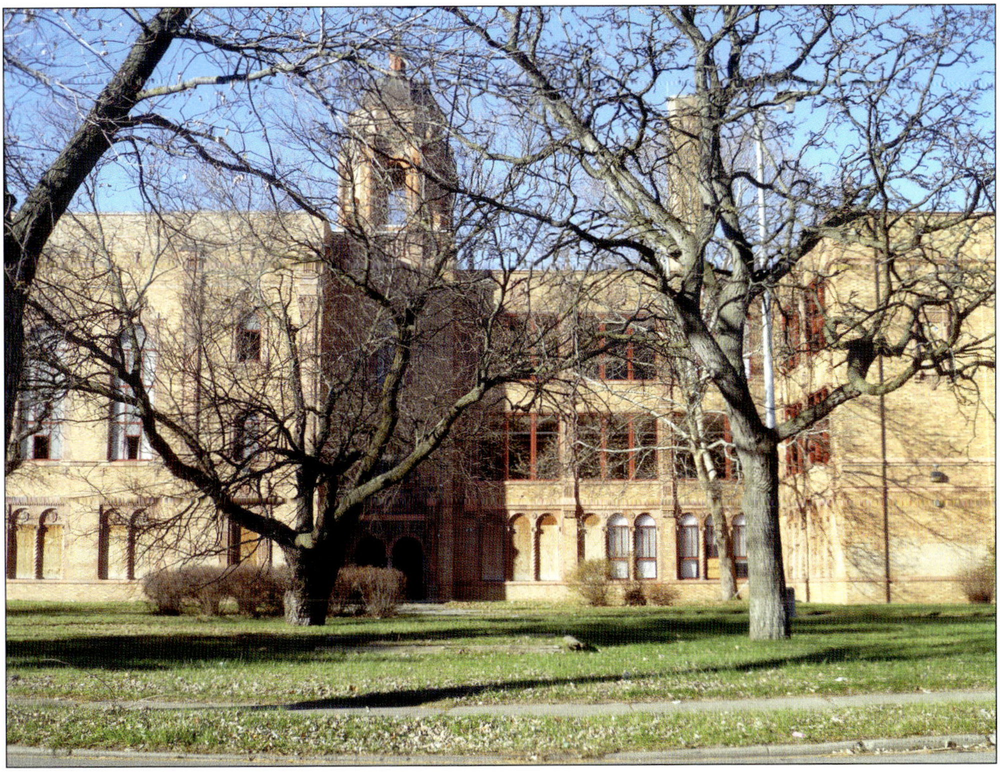

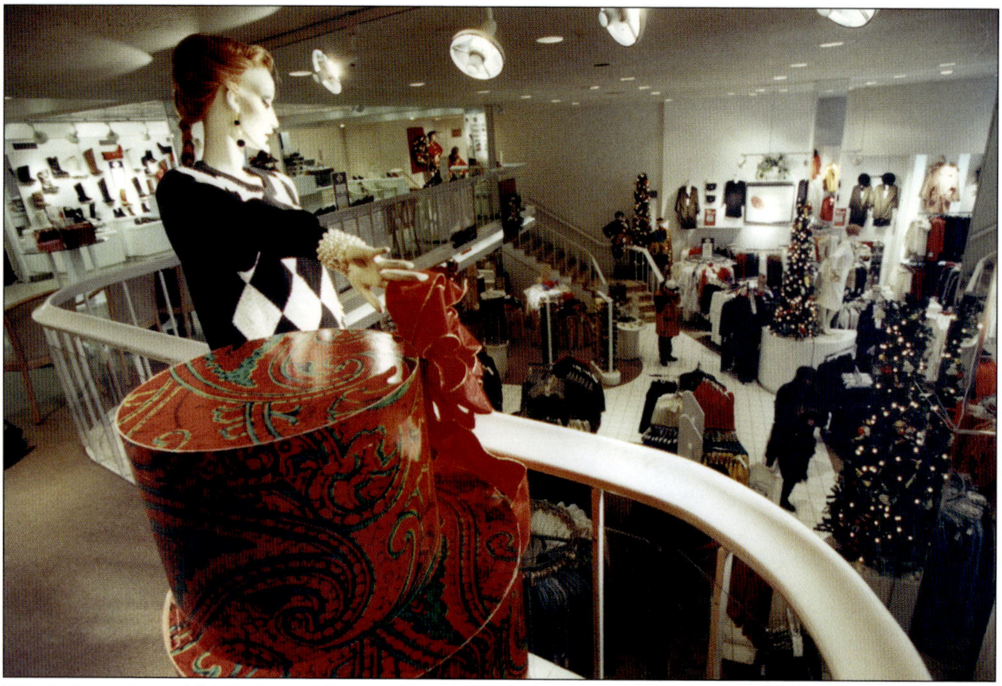

Winkelman's, at 15360 Grand River Avenue, was built and leased from Venton Realty Co. in 1941. Charles N. Agree was the architect of the air-conditioned store. Fluorescent lighting was employed throughout the interior and in the windows. It was one of the first stores to have windows displaying merchandise in both the front and back. The back windows faced the parking lot.

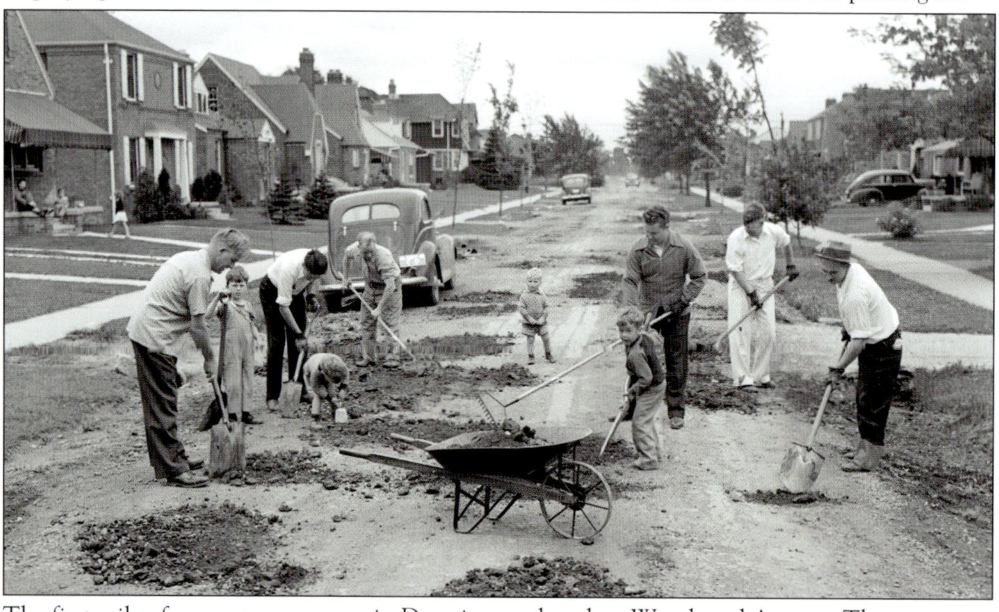

The first mile of concrete pavement in Detroit was placed on Woodward Avenue. The pavement stretched from Six Mile Road to Seven Mile Road and was laid in 1909 for $14,000. Woodward Avenue would later be one of the first streets to have a painted center line and an electric traffic signal. The side streets remained mostly dirt roads. Here, residents on Rutherford Street pitch in to repair their own street in 1939.

Two

School Days

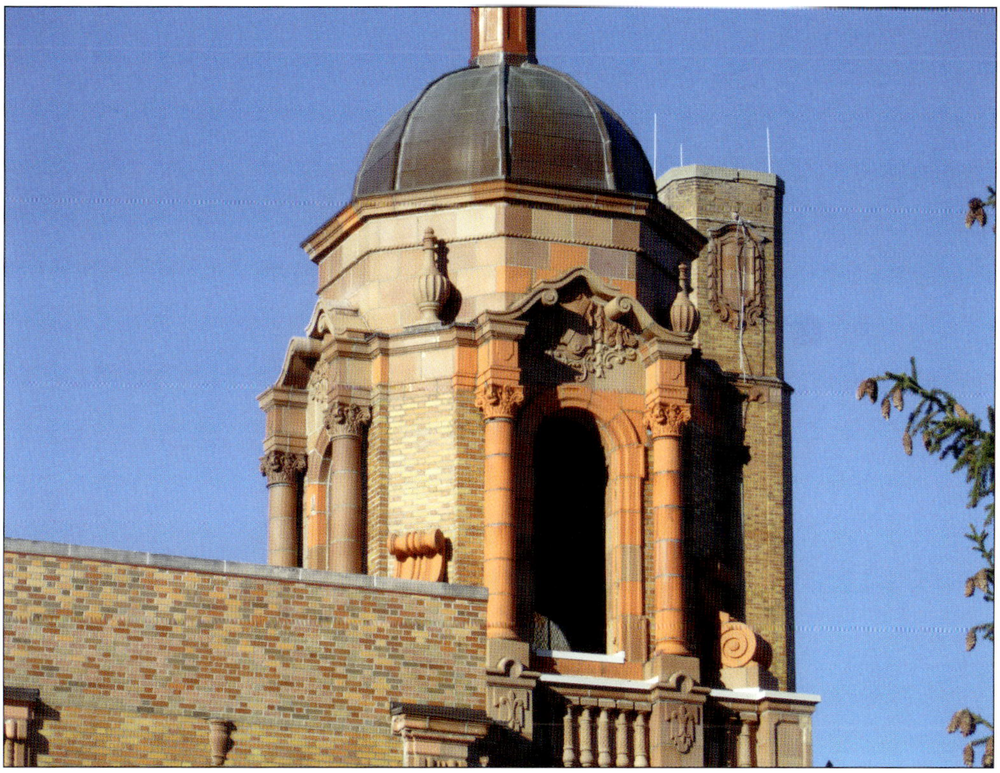

No one had to walk five miles uphill through the snow to get to school in this neighborhood. Public and parochial schools were close to just about everyone who lived in the 48227 postal zone. Cooley and St. Mary's of Redford were the high schools, and Edison, Burns, Dossin, Cadillac, Monnier, Cerveny, Holy Cross, Our Lady Queen of Hope, Edgar Guest, and Mother of Our Savior were just some of the elementary and middle schools nearby.

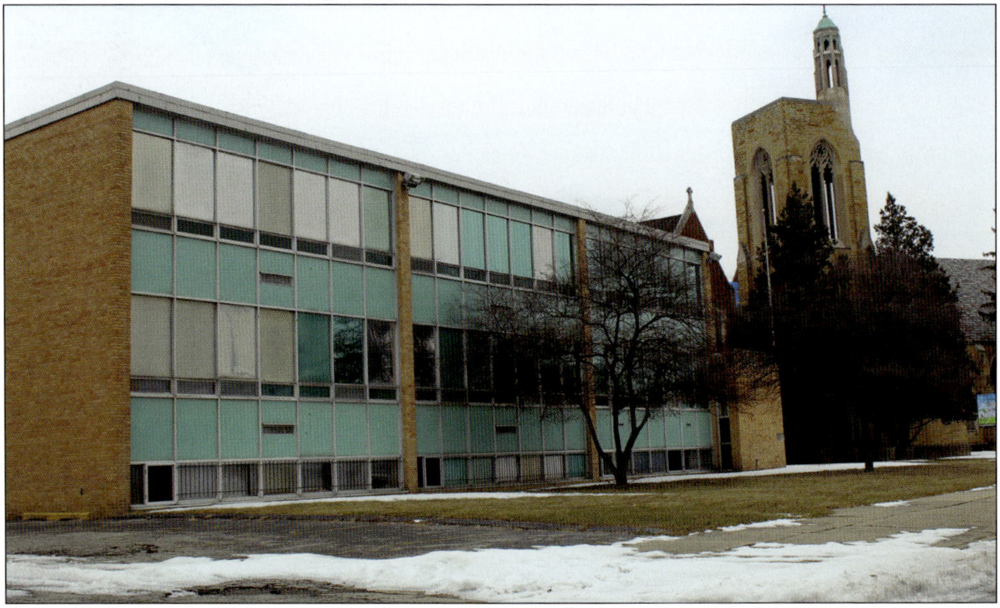

Holy Cross Lutheran School was built at 14213 Whitcomb Avenue in 1958. It adjoined the Lutheran church, Missouri Synod, on the corner of Grand River and Whitcomb Avenues. The school had nine classrooms on two levels and cost $290,000. There were eight teachers on the faculty. The school was built on the sixth anniversary of the church's dedication in 1952. The building is now home to the Oak Park Academy Whitcomb campus, with 247 students in sixth through eighth grades. Holy Cross had kindergarten through eighth grade in 12 rooms and expanded to 10 full-time teachers and two part-time teachers. The school was known for a number of science fair winners and for its music programs. Students wore uniforms, and discipline was stressed. There was also a cafeteria and gymnasium.

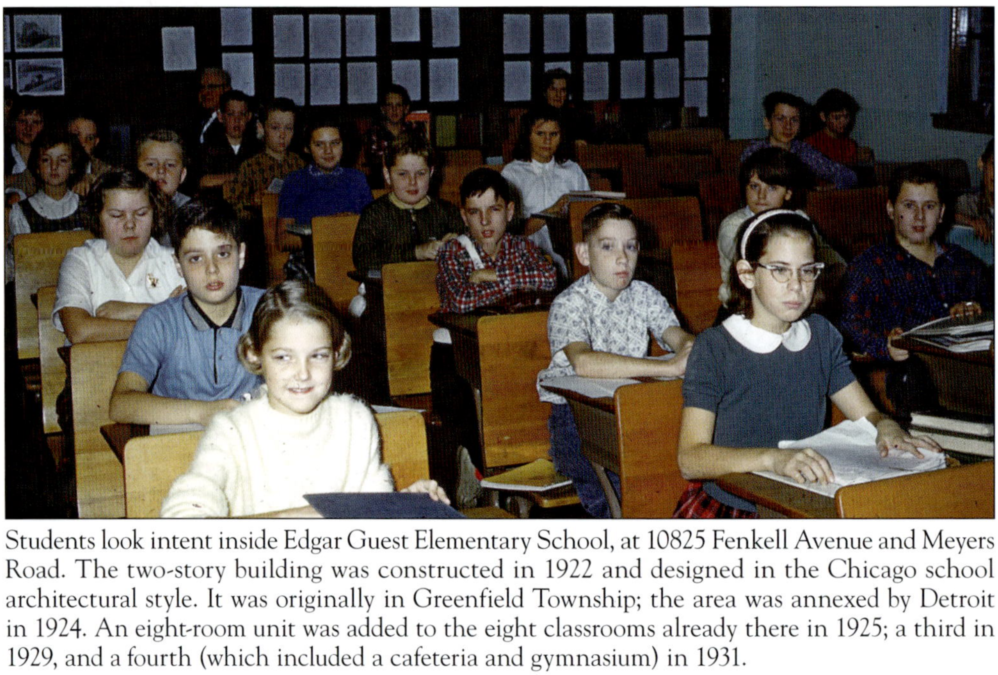

Students look intent inside Edgar Guest Elementary School, at 10825 Fenkell Avenue and Meyers Road. The two-story building was constructed in 1922 and designed in the Chicago school architectural style. It was originally in Greenfield Township; the area was annexed by Detroit in 1924. An eight-room unit was added to the eight classrooms already there in 1925; a third in 1929, and a fourth (which included a cafeteria and gymnasium) in 1931.

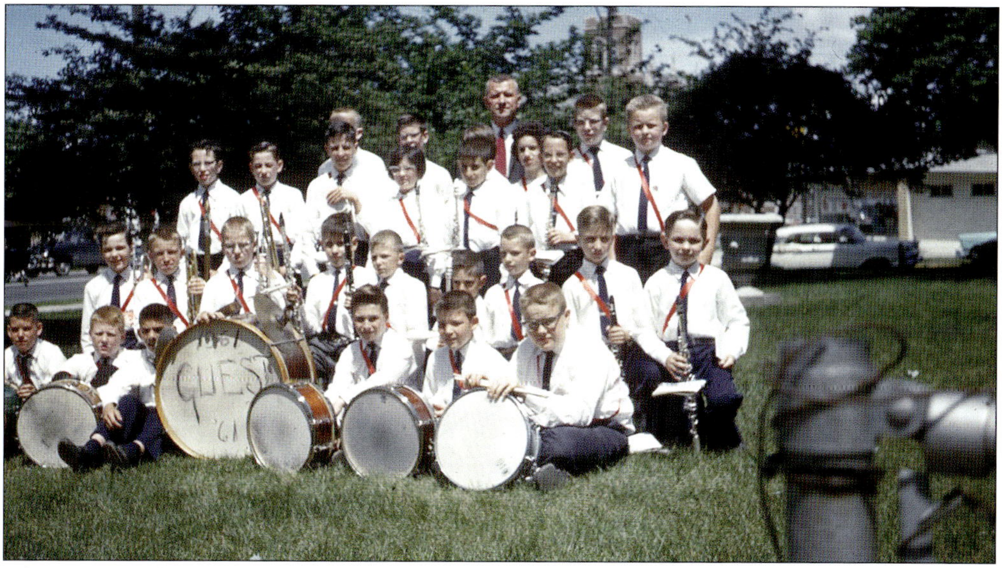

Edgar Guest Elementary School band members gather on the front lawn in 1961. The school was named after a popular English-born American in the early 20th century. Guest wrote for the *Detroit Free Press* and became known as the people's poet. In 2001, the school was renamed Mary McLeod Bethune Elementary School to reflect the greater African American influence in the neighborhood. It closed in 2010 due to low enrollment.

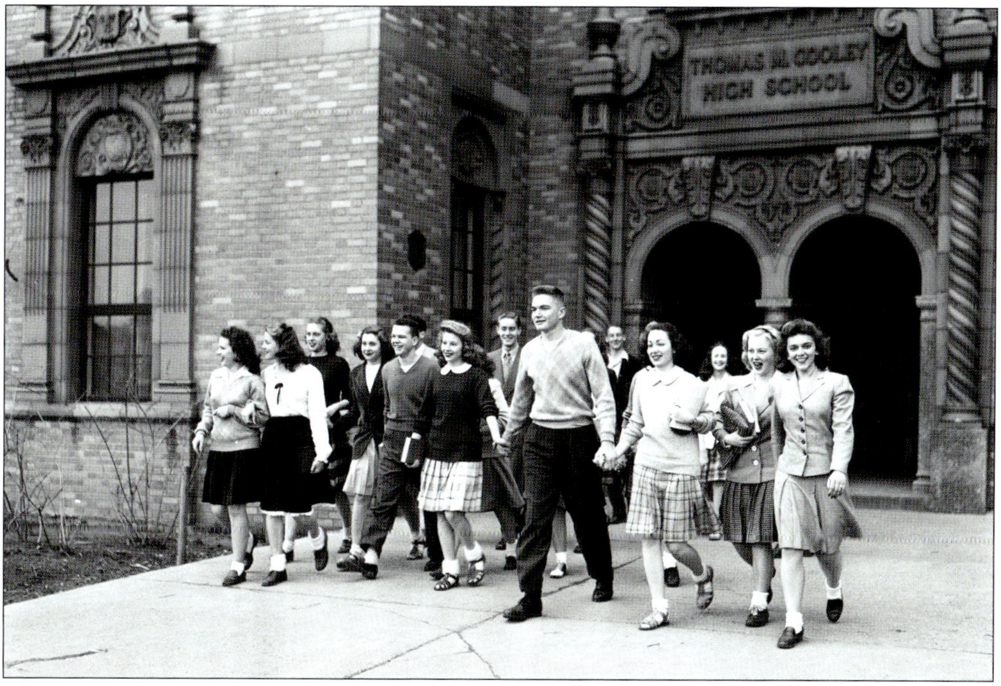

Thomas M. Cooley High School opened in September 1928 and cost $753,270 to build. It was designed by Donaldson and Meier in the Spanish baroque style and was considered an architectural masterpiece. Cooley's floor plan put classrooms in outer wings and connected them in the center to the auditorium, library, offices, and athletic facilities. Thomas M. Cooley had been chief justice of the Michigan Supreme Court from 1864 to 1885.

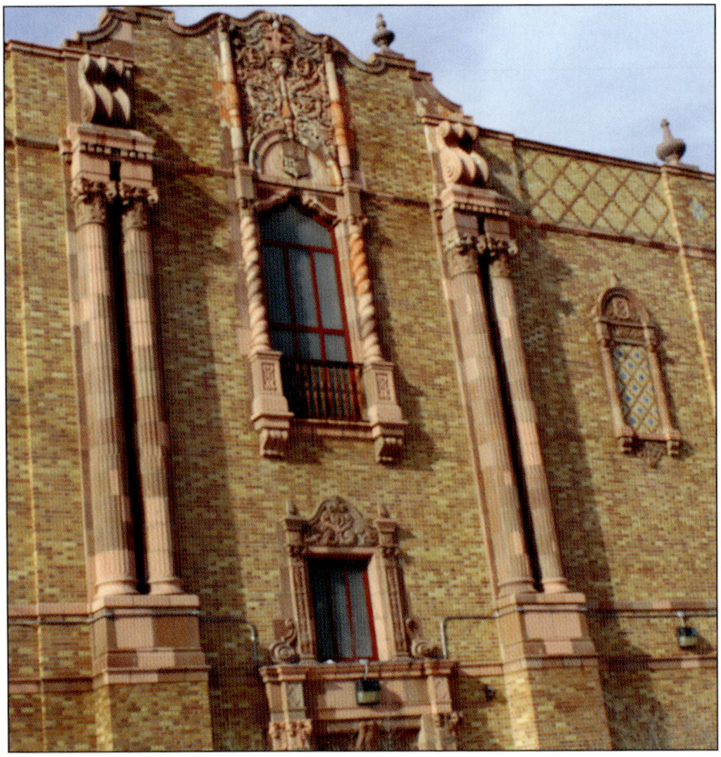

In 1961, enrollment grew to over 3,400 students, which made Cooley one of the biggest schools in Detroit. However, as black attendance went from one percent in 1961 to 52 percent in 1968, enrollment started to decline. By 2010, there were barely 1,000 students, and the 83-year-old building had high maintenance costs. In spite of protests by students and alumni, Cooley was closed in June 2010.

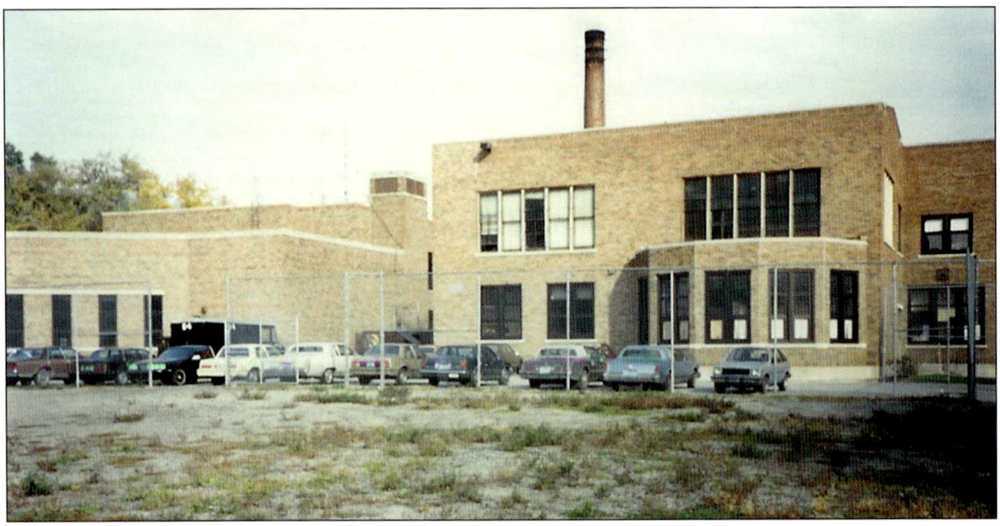

Cadillac Middle School was built in 1919 at 15125 Schoolcraft Road, between Sussex and Coyle Streets. It was a two-story building designed in a modern Renaissance style. The school was named after Antoine de la Mothe Cadillac, a French explorer who founded and settled Fort Pontchartrain, which became Detroit. Its main features included the bay windows and stone columns between each of the window sets, which were topped with friezes made of Pewbaic Pottery glazed tiles. The U-shaped floor plan included administrative offices, classrooms, a gymnasium, and a cafeteria. The school averaged 700 students from kindergarten through eighth grade. At one point, trailers housed temporary classrooms for the overflow of students. In 2007, the school closed due to a 60-percent decline in enrollment (down to 400 students) and high maintenance costs.

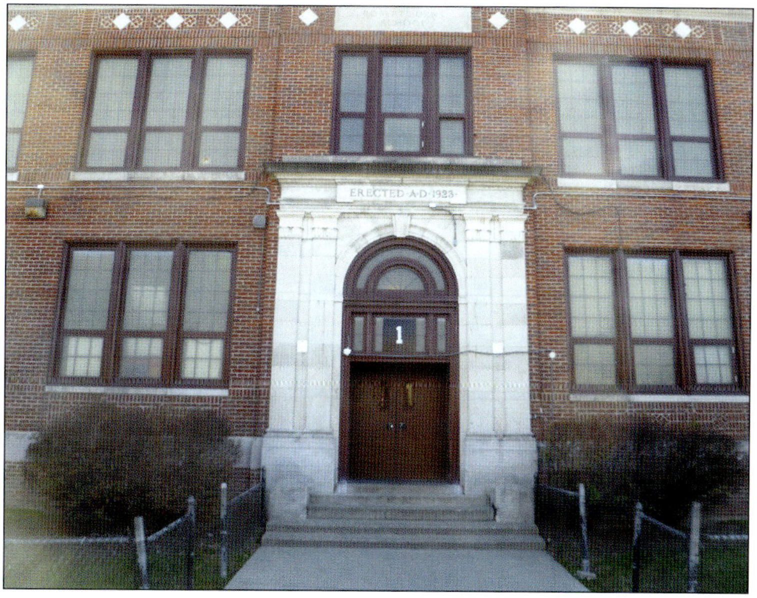

Burns Elementary School, at 14350 Terry Street, served as a partial high school in 1926 with 350 students enrolled in ninth and 10th grades. This caused the Detroit Board of Education to plan Cooley High School. The Robert Burns School now hosts pre-kindergarten through eighth grade, with 427 students and a 17-to-1 teacher-student ratio.

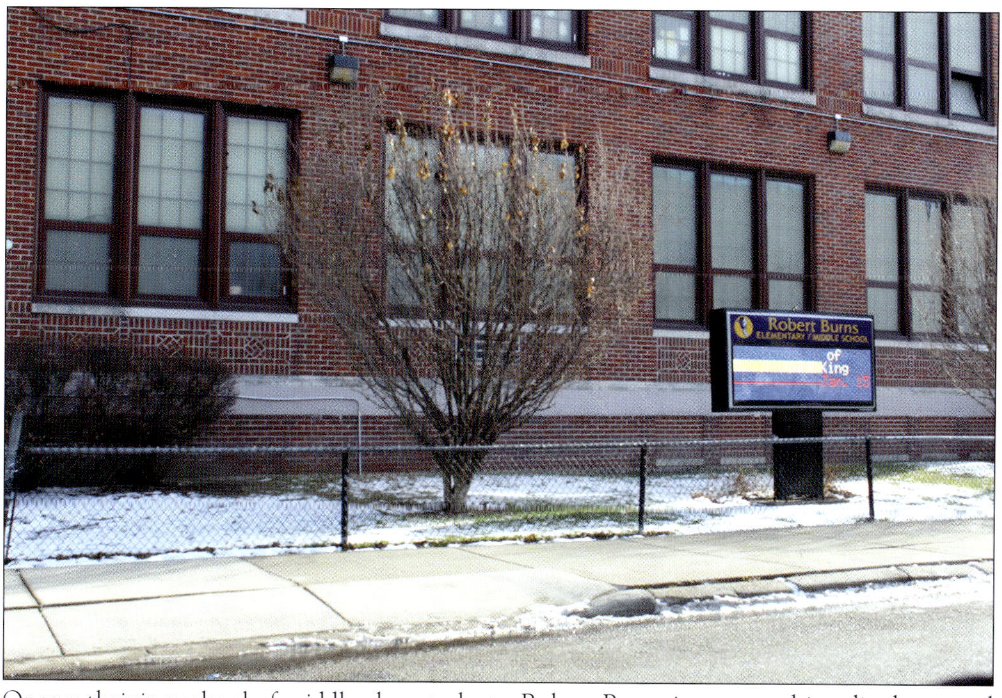

Once a thriving school of middle-class students, Robert Burns is now teaching disadvantaged children. The school has computer laboratories with more than 25 computers, with smart boards and projectors as well. It also provides classes in mathematics, information technology, reading, and arts. Robert Burns Elementary serves hot lunches and provides after-school tutoring.

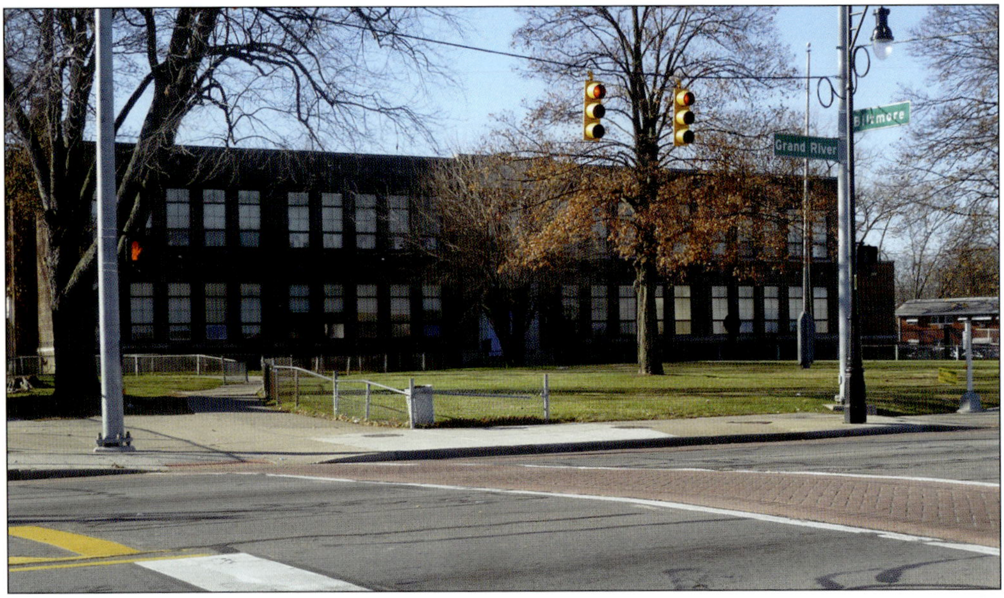

Thomas Edison School, at 17045 Grand River Avenue, is for kindergarten through fifth grade. It is among the highest rated in the Excellent Schools Detroit "5 Essentials" most likely to aid learning and boost attendance and ACT scores. It offers technology in every classroom, art, music, and physical education, a school nurse, and a fresh fruits and vegetables initiative. The school was originally administered by Redford Union in 1925; it was bought by the Detroit Board of Education in 1926 and renamed Thomas Edison in 1929.

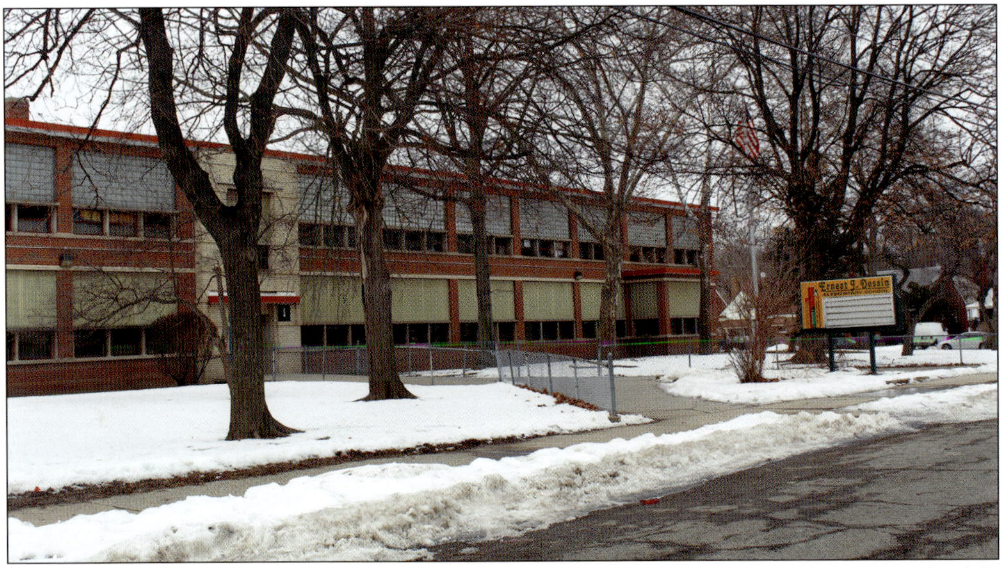

The Ernest J. Dossin Elementary-Middle School is embedded in the neighborhood at 16650 Glendale Street. The school is named after a grandson of Belgian immigrants. Dossin, who began Dossin Food Products in the early 1900s, was followed by three sons who branched out into hydroplane racing in the 1940s. All classrooms at the school are equipped with the latest technology, and the school offers a Media Club, Garden Club, Accelerated Reading/Math Club, and Robotics/Science Club. A Michigan Department of Human Services worker is on-site. Neighbors are invited to plant fruits and vegetables in the community garden.

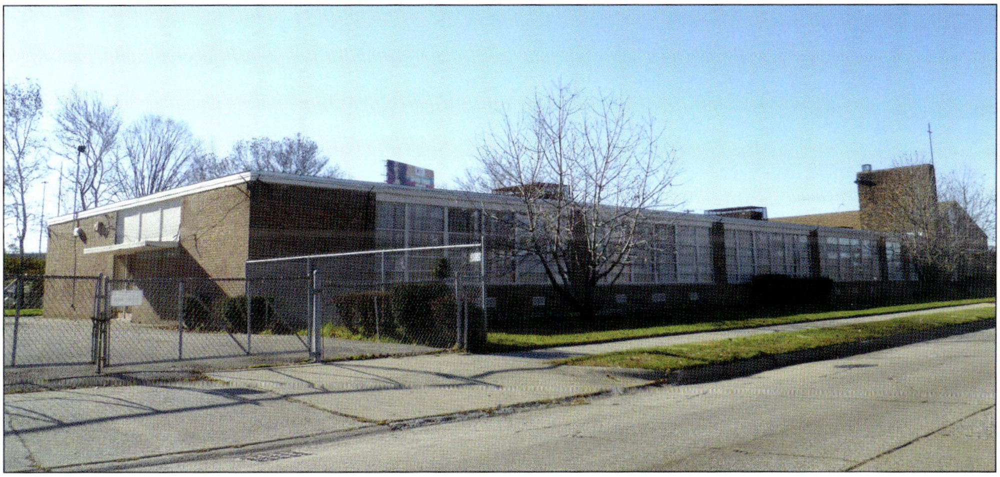

Our Lady Queen of Hope, at 17701 Glendale Street, was built in 1955 as a satellite of St. Mary's of Redford Parish. The school started with three Immaculate Heart of Mary sisters teaching grades one through four. The next year, two lay teachers were added, and they all taught 269 students in first through seventh grades. First- and second-graders had half days because of the huge enrollment. Eighth grade was added in 1957. By the fall of 1959, there were 390 students. May 1963 saw the first May crowning in the newly built outdoor shrine.

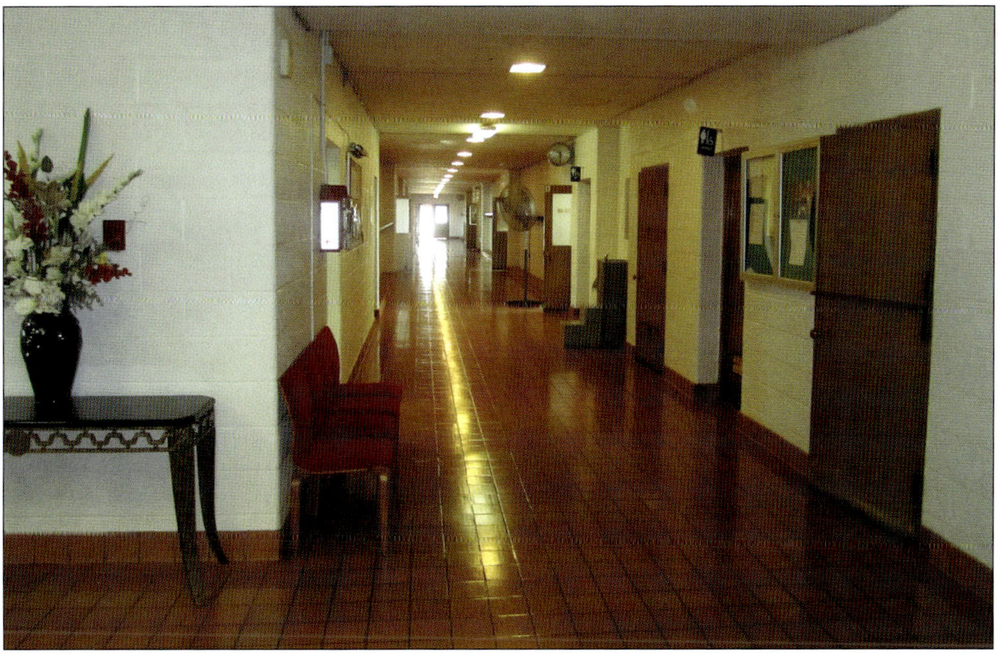

Parishioners were delighted in June 1965 when Our Lady Queen of Hope became a separate parish, just as 50 eighth-graders were graduating. The French, science, and mathematics programs used TV sets, and the library grew by adding filmstrips and records to its collection. Enrollment decreased from 420 in 1962 to 313 during the 1970–1971 school year. Despite fundraising efforts from students, teachers, and parents to keep the school open, it closed at the end of the 1976–1977 school year. The Gethsemane Apostolic Church now owns the building.

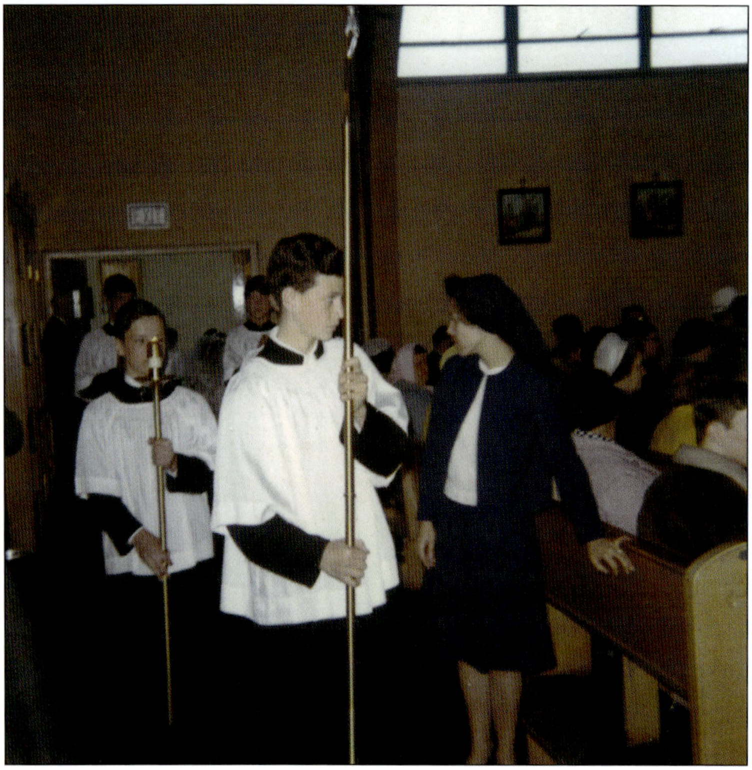

Mother of Our Savior School, at 13220 Greenfield Road, opened in 1953 with four Immaculate Heart of Mary sisters teaching 212 children in four classrooms. The school and adjacent chapel were created because nearby St. Mary's of Redford was overflowing with parishioners and their students. By 1956, four more classrooms were added, as well as a basement cafeteria/meeting room. Sister Veronica (Patricia Dreffs) is shown with altar boys in the church.

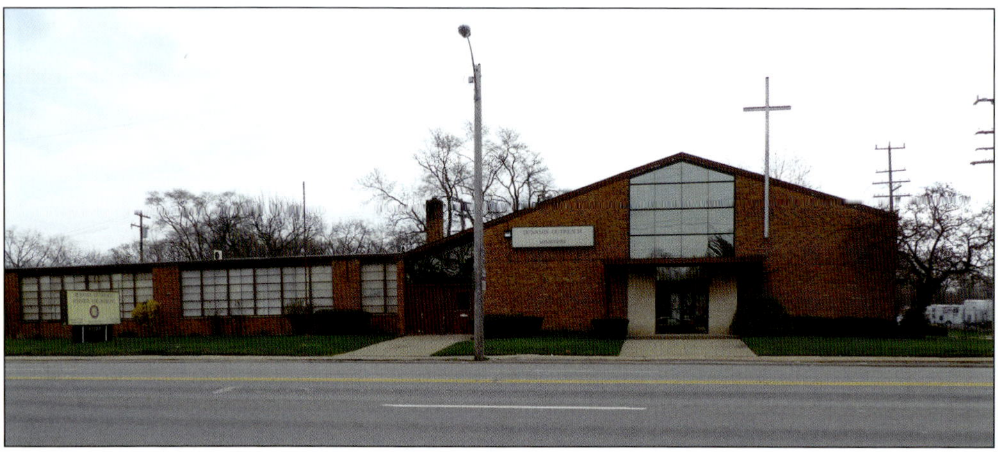

Mother of Our Savior became a parish in 1959, and 389 students were enrolled in first through eighth grades. The Service Girl and Safety Boy Program offered students a chance to develop thoughtfulness for the needs of others. The Junior Great Books Program was also well received by students. The boys' softball team won the St. Mary's of Redford Dad's Club trophy in 1961 and 1963. Due to declining enrollment, the school closed in 1972. A Birth-to-Five Head Start Development Center is now housed there.

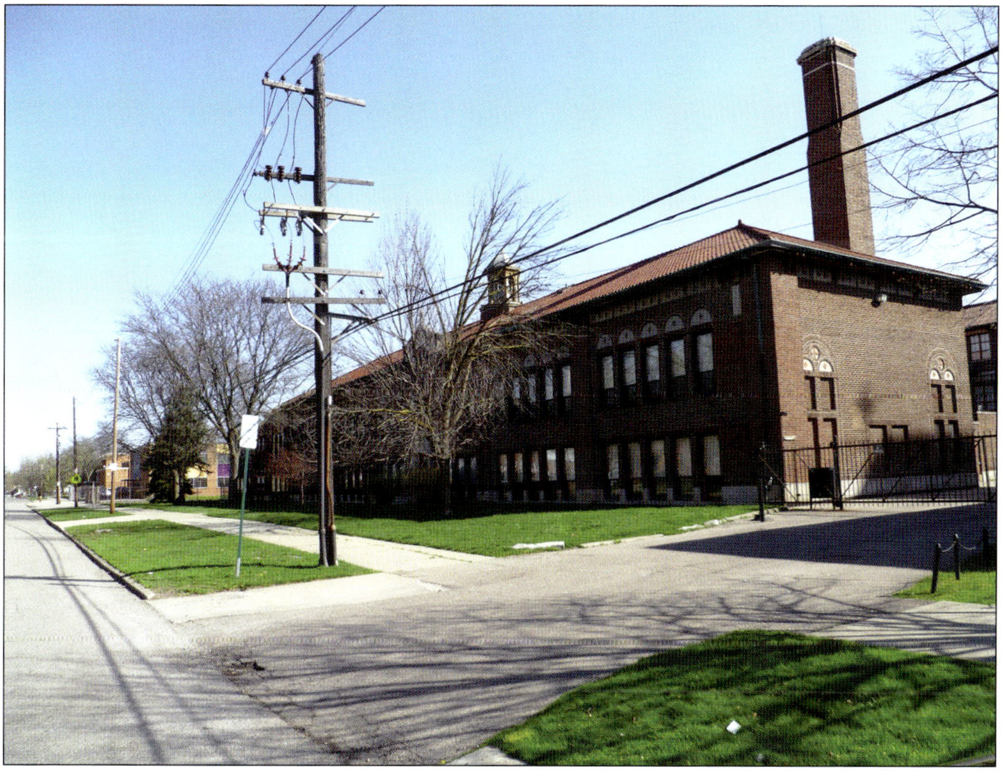

The first St. Mary's of Redford parish school at 14751 Mansfield Street was built and occupied in April 1920. The new school faced St. Mary's Avenue and had six classrooms, offices, and an auditorium. Surrounding farmland was subdivided and turned into residential housing tracts. A second wing of the school with 12 rooms was built in 1925. Elementary school enrollment for the 1925–1926 school year was 570 students.

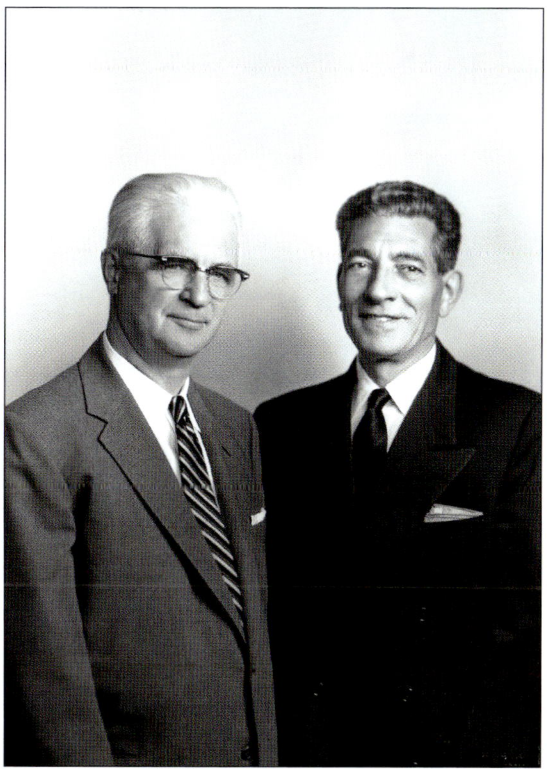

St. Mary's of Redford High School had 747 students in 1925. The 1943–1944 school year had 576 high school students sharing a building with 1,055 elementary students. By 1962, a separate high school was being built north of the gymnasium. Designed by the architectural firm Giffels and Rossetti, the building accommodated 750 senior, junior, and sophomore students. Raymond Giffels (left) and Louis Rossetti (right) also developed Cobo Hall and had one of the largest architecture firms in the United States in the 1950s.

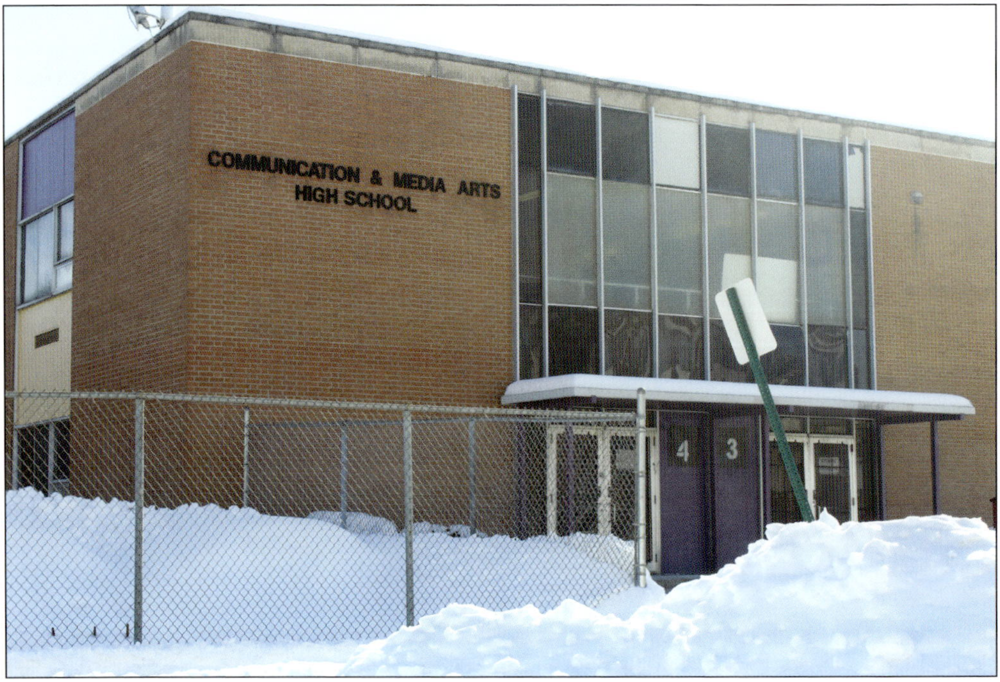

The new St. Mary's of Redford School had 13 rooms by the spring of 1963. A gymnasium was added in 1969, but declining enrollment caused the school to close in 1992. It is now home to the recently renovated Communication and Media Arts High School, run by the City of Detroit.

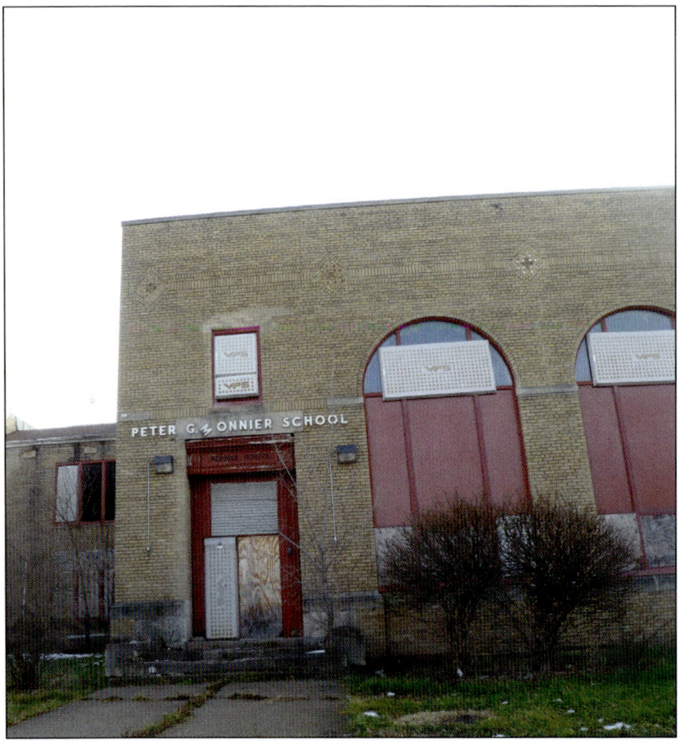

Peter Monnier Elementary School was built in 1923 and named after a local Civil War hero who donated the land for the school. Located at 13600 Ward Avenue near Schoolcraft Road, Monnier School was a two-story building designed in an Italian Romanesque style. The school had a combined gymnasium and auditorium that had unique raised seating above each side of the stage and gym floor. Monnier averaged 500 students from kindergarten through sixth grade. The school mascot was a bulldog. Monnier closed in 2007.

Three

PLACES OF WORSHIP

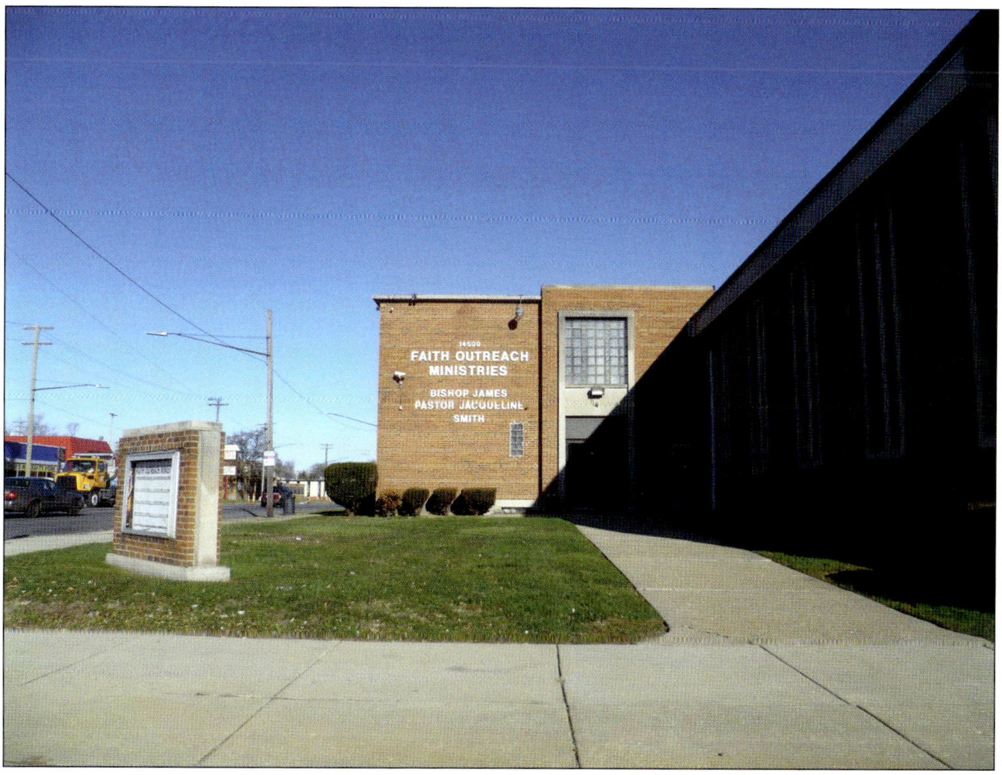

There was an amazing number of places for people to practice their faiths in the Grand River and Greenfield neighborhood. Besides the largest Catholic parish in Detroit (St. Mary's of Redford), the neighborhood had Lutheran Holy Cross Church, St. Paul's Memorial Episcopal Church, Hope Presbyterian Church, Strathmoor Methodist Church, and Bushnell Congregational Church, among others. Many businesses were closed on Sundays in the 1950s and 1960s.

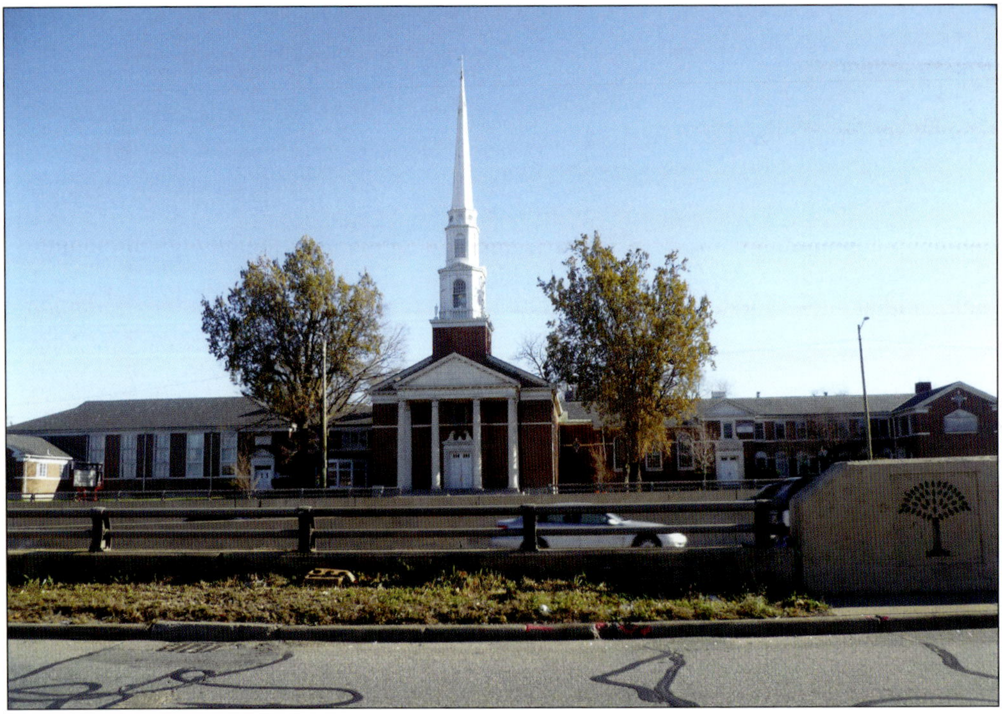

Bushnell Congregational Church was named after Horace Bushnell (1802–1876), a Congregational minister and theologian from Hartford, Connecticut. In 1924, the Detroit Council of Churches asked Rev. Irving W. Stuart, superintendent of the Detroit Congregational Union, to start a Congregational church in a rural section of land that had recently been annexed by the city from Redford Township. By 1925, a group of 40 people were meeting at a newly constructed District 2 School on Grand River Avenue. Eventually, a permanent church was built at 15000 Southfield Freeway (then Mill Road) for $75,000.

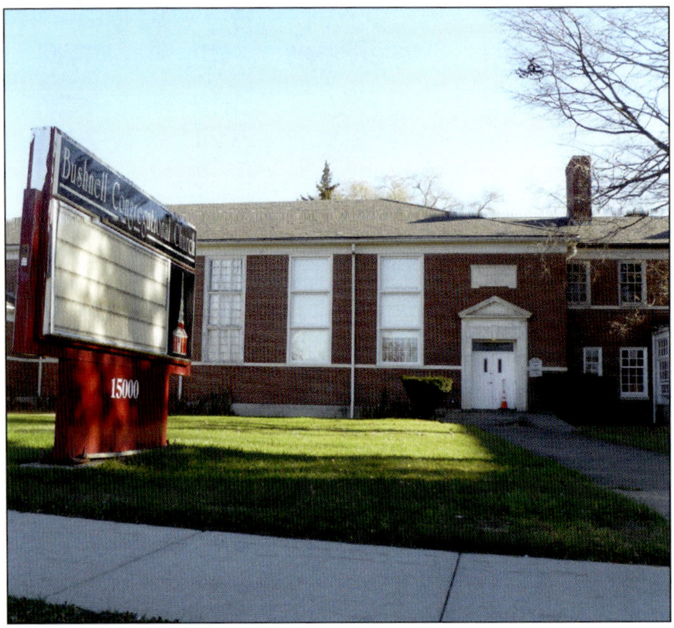

A fellowship hall was added to Bushnell in 1948. It is used for community meetings and events, and includes a large kitchen and stage. Extra offices and classrooms were added along with an educational wing in 1953. The final addition occurred in 1958, and the membership peaked at 2,650. The church has long been involved in social issues like the civil rights movement. Membership was in decline, but although there has been a Bushnell West established in Novi, Michigan, the current church has added new members and has voted to remain in Detroit.

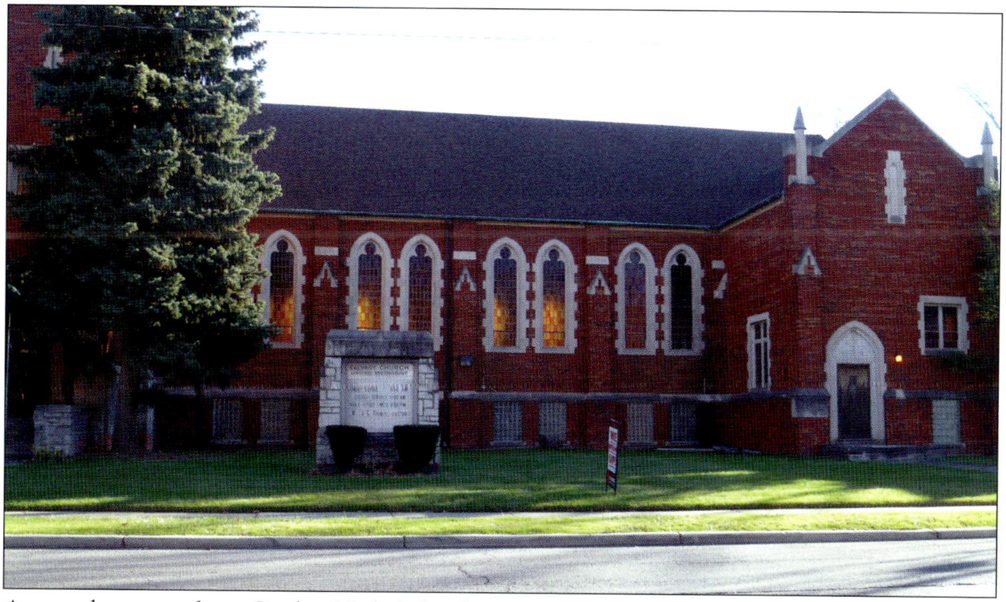

Across the street from Cooley High School at 15050 Hubbell Street, the Evangelical United Brethren Church was a neo-Gothic building constructed in 1954. The $230,000 sanctuary was dedicated in March 1955 and sat 500 people. The church became the Calvary United Methodist Church in 1968, when the United Methodist Church was created. Bishop Reuben H. Mueller of the Evangelical United Brethren Church joined hands with Bishop Lloyd C. Wicke of the Methodist Church at the Constitution General Conference in Dallas, Texas, to unify the churches.

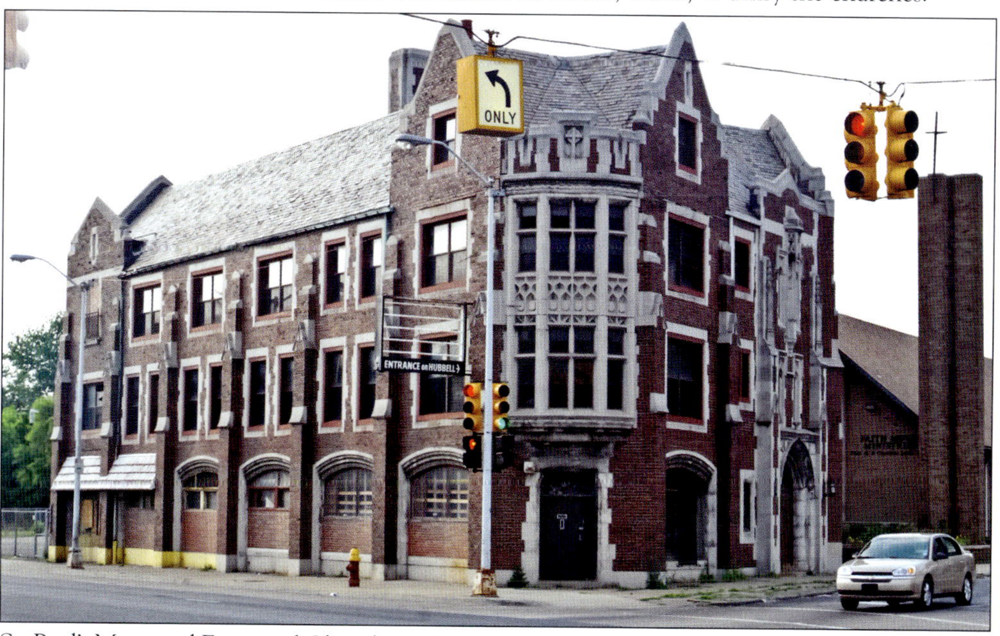

St. Paul's Memorial Episcopal Church was built at Grand River Avenue and 14025 Hubbell Street in 1928 in a Gothic style for $100,000. The first-floor frontage along Grand River was devoted to stores, and the corner was occupied by a bank. The upper floors contained classrooms, a guild room, a dining room, and a gymnasium with an auditorium. Lancelot Sukert was the architect. (Courtesy of Randy Wilcox, detroitfunk.com.)

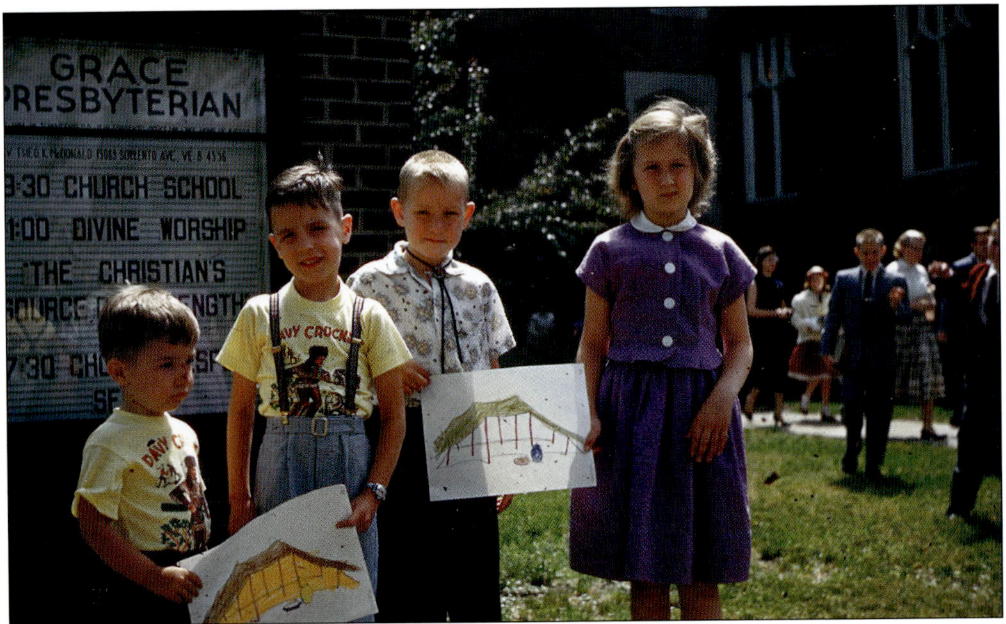

Rev. Paul H. Bucholz, executive secretary of the Detroit Presbytery, and Rev. Arthur W. Ratz, the presbytery's moderator, officiated at the dedication of Grace Presbyterian Church at 15340 Meyers Road in October 1940. The dedication banquet was followed by an organ recital by Irving Dixon, the church's musical director, and a religious service led by Rev. Joseph Vance, pastor emeritus of First Presbyterian Church. Here, children from Sunday school gather on the front lawn of the church in the mid-1950s.

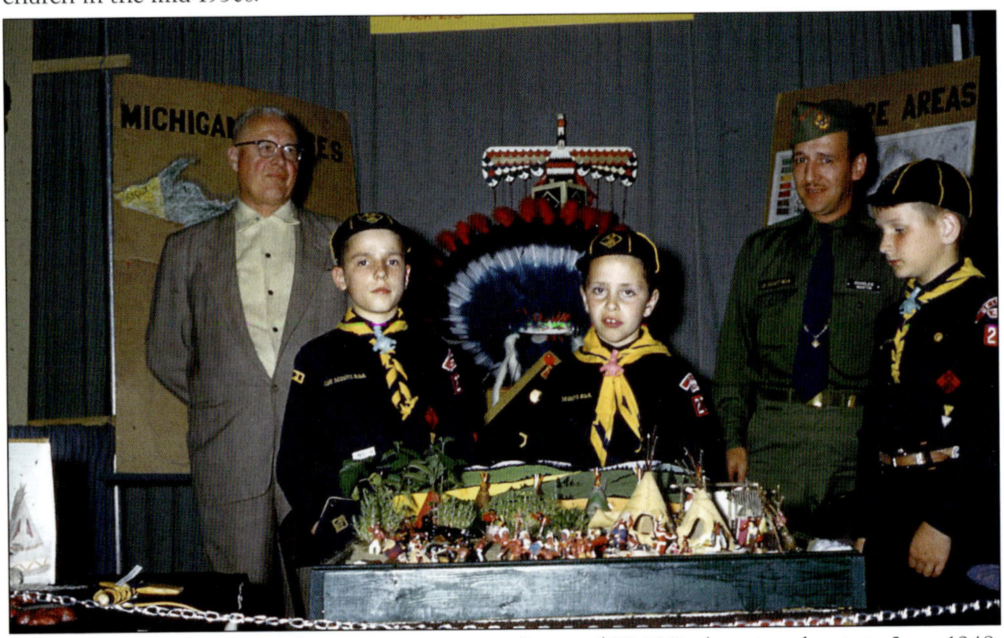

Grace Presbyterian Church began construction of a new $90,000 educational unit in June 1948. The new building was part of a $230,000 building project that would be completed that fall. Many groups, like Cub Scouts, met there. Grace Presbyterian merged with Hope Presbyterian Church in 1971.

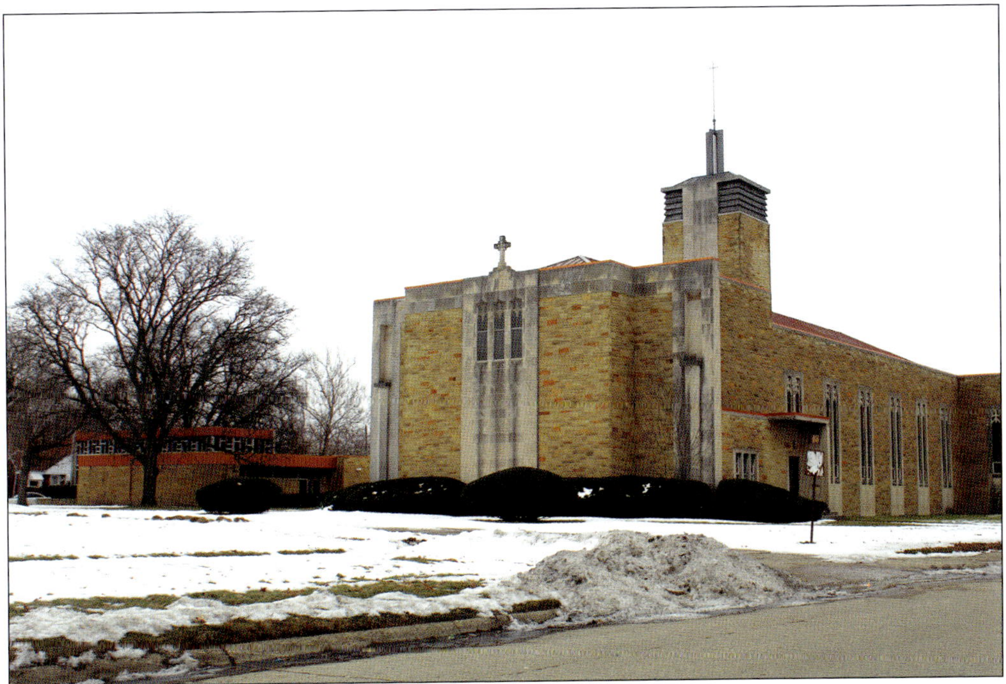

Strathmoor Methodist Church, at 16801 Schoolcraft Road between Memorial Street and Abington Avenue, had moved from Marlowe Street and Schoolcraft Road in May 1954 to a $400,000 complex. The church was designed by Earl L. Confer and made from sandstone and limestone with an aluminum roof. Rev. Luther Butt, pastor, and Rev. Dr. Gordon Phillips, executive secretary of the Methodist Union of Greater Detroit, assisted in the ground-breaking ceremonies.

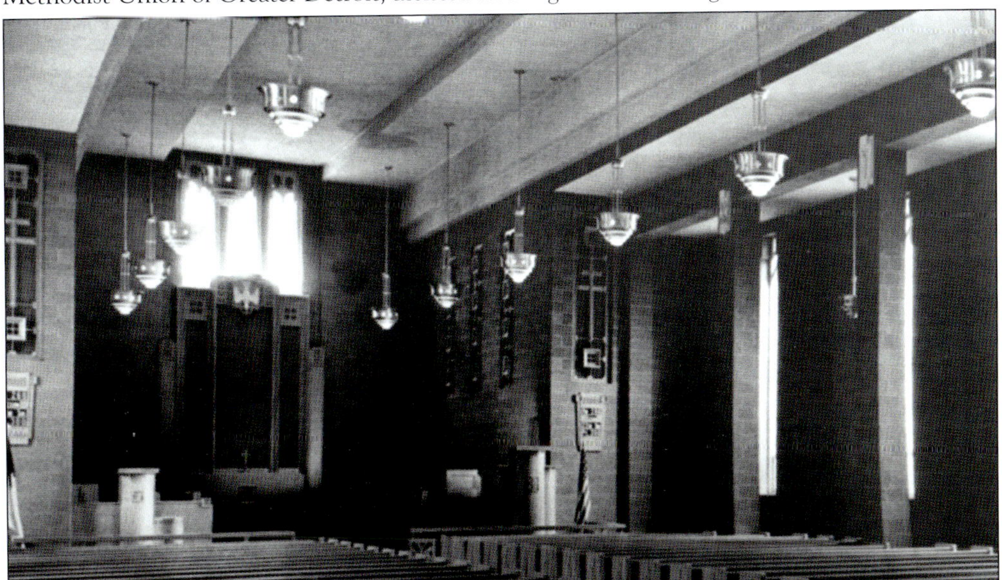

Strathmoor's interior is cinder block painted Caribbean blue. Additions were planned that would nearly triple the size of the church. It now has a seating capacity of 770. There is a nursery and kindergarten for 91 children. The basement dining room can seat 230 people. The building has now become the Greater Burnette Baptist Church.

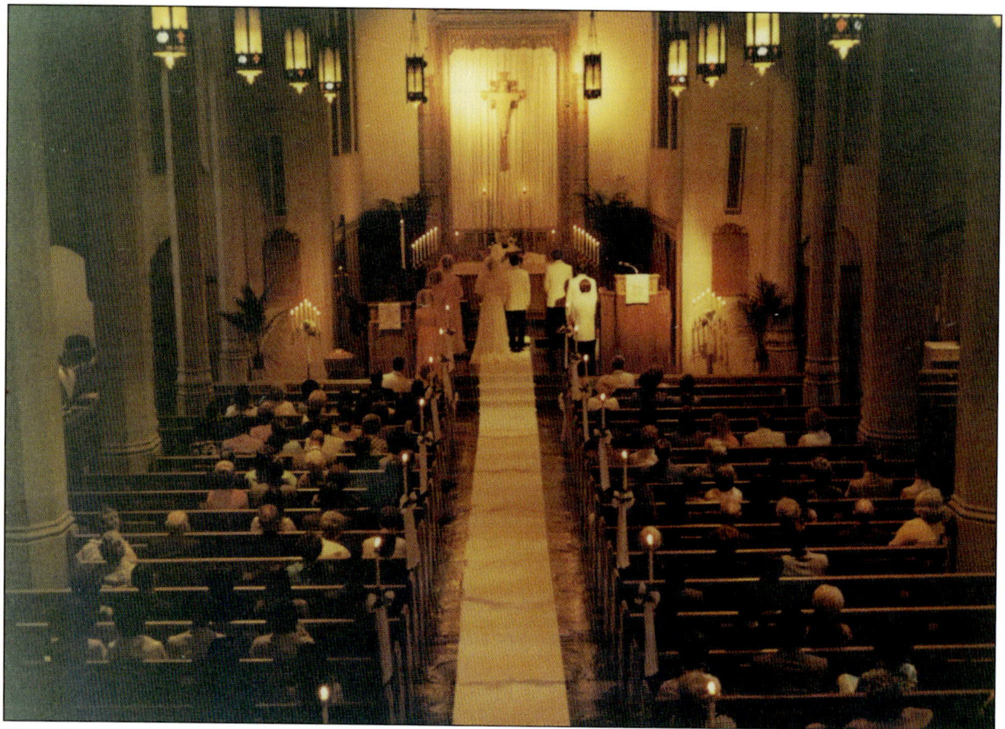

Holy Cross Lutheran Church (Synodical Conference) was founded in 1927. The cornerstone for the $380,000 church was laid at 14213 Whitcomb Avenue in 1950. The building is still located on the corner of Whitcomb and Grand River Avenues. It seated 450 people with a choir and balcony and had a fellowship hall. The Grand River and Greenfield shopping district is just around the corner from the church.

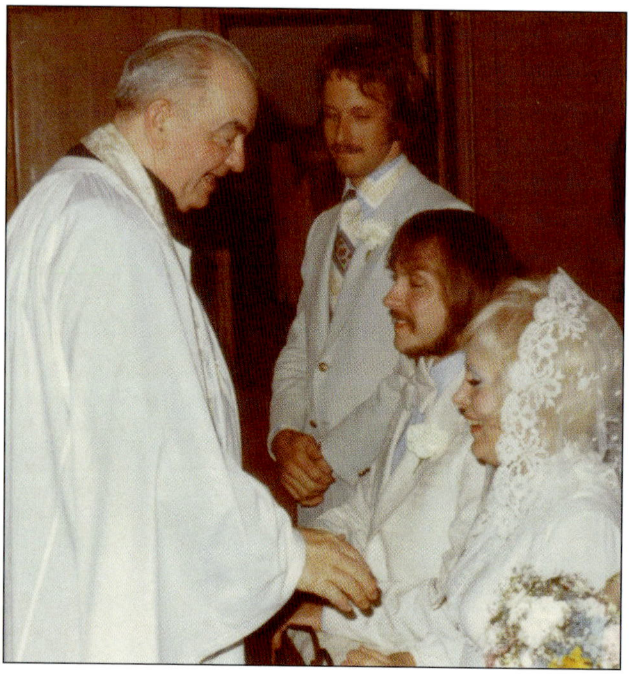

Pastor Armin V. Born came to Holy Cross in 1940 after serving as field secretary for Valparaiso University and serving congregations in Woodburn, Indiana, and Reed City, Michigan. He was a Lincoln scholar and often lectured on the subject in the Detroit area. Reverend Born died in October 1980 while on vacation in California. (Courtesy of Jayne Marts Schmelzer Chrzan.)

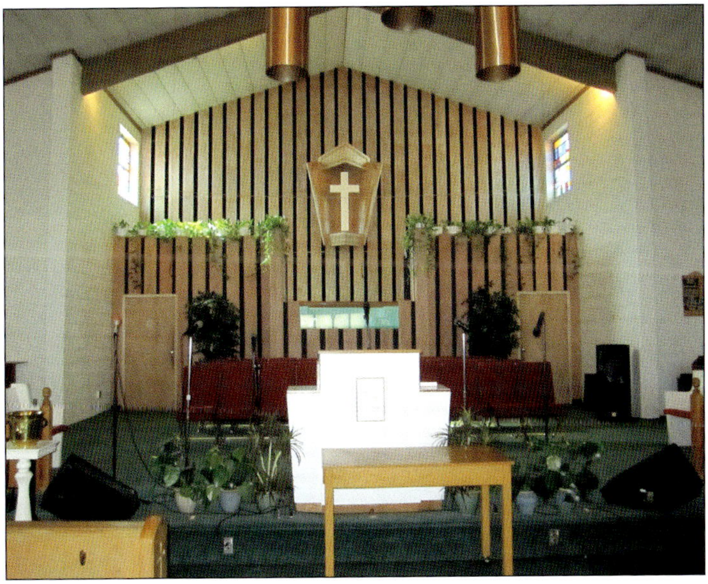

Overcrowding at St. Mary's of Redford Church and grade school and at the new chapel and school at Mother of Our Savior forced Monsignor Edward Hickey to purchase, with the help of the City of Detroit, two blocks east of Southfield Road for the chapel of Our Lady Queen of Hope. Construction started in October 1954 for the chapel and four-room school. The church celebrated its first mass on June 5, 1955. (Courtesy of Hugo Groff.)

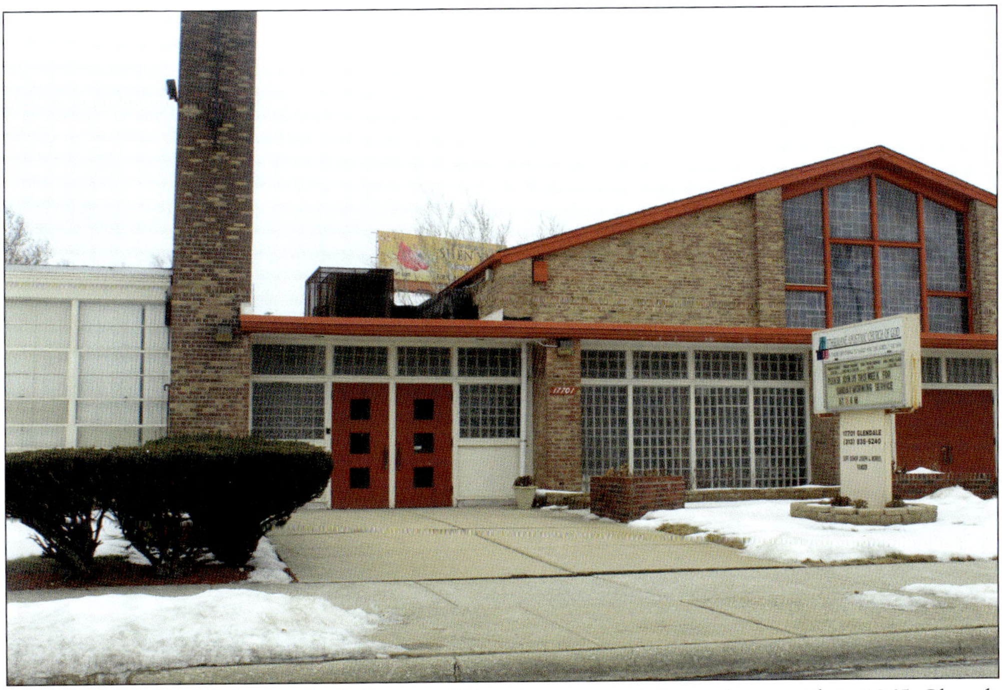

With continued growth, Our Lady Queen of Hope became an independent parish in 1965. Church attendance slowly dropped off in the late 1960s as more families were attracted to bigger homes and lots in the suburbs. The riot in 1967 also contributed to white flight. The church was closed in 1989 by the Detroit Archdiocese in a reorganization plan for the inner city.

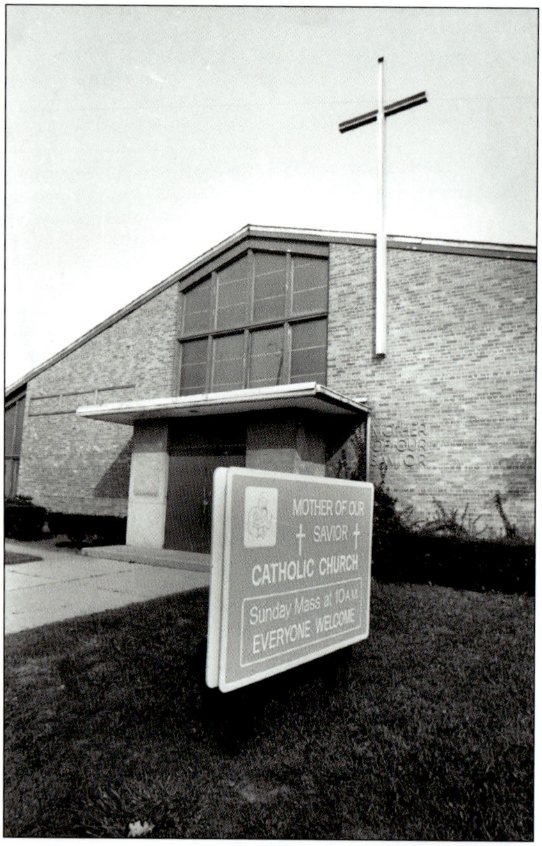

Monsignor Edward Hickey and his five assistant pastors were being overwhelmed by the growth of St. Mary's of Redford when it was decided that an auxiliary chapel should be built nearby. Construction began for the Mother of Our Savior Chapel in January 1953 on property purchased on Greenfield Road. Its first mass was celebrated on August 9, 1953. The firm of Giffels and Rossetti designed the building.

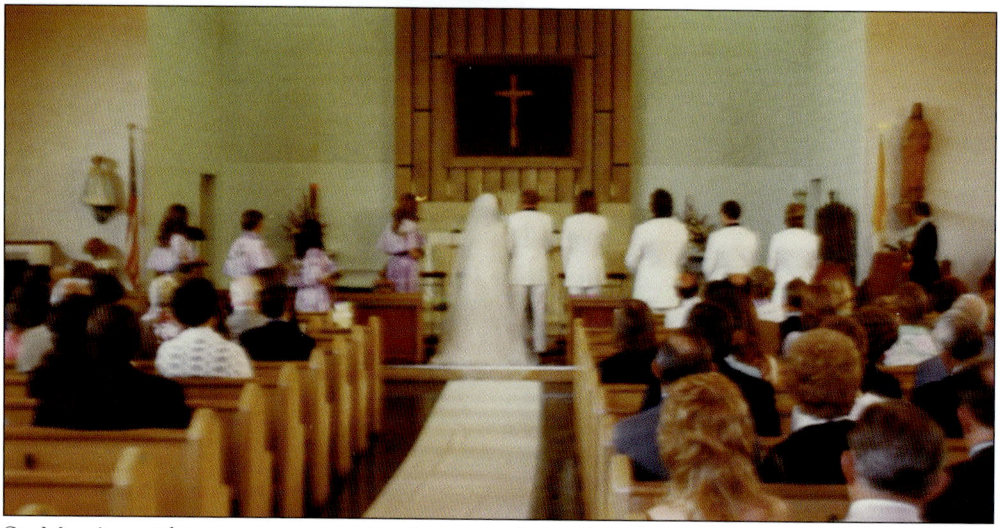

St. Mary's parishioners were permitted to attend the chapel or main church. Steady growth continued through the 1950s and 1960s. Mother of Our Savior became a separate parish in 1959. A convent for nuns teaching the elementary schoolchildren was opened on Prest Street in 1961. The Detroit riot in 1967 marked a turning point in many parishioners' minds. Church attendance declined as more people moved outside the city, and the archdiocese closed the church in 1989. Dunamis Outreach Ministries now operates the building.

In November 1843, Protestant farmer John Blindbury sold a 1.5-acre plot of land south of Grand River Avenue and east of Division Road to Bishop Peter Paul Lefevere for $25. According to Blindbury, the sale was "intended for the use of a church and cemetery for the Roman Catholic Church." In 1856, Fr. Edmund Dumont arrived from Belgium and helped complete a new St. Mary's Church several blocks to the west on Grand River Avenue and Mansfield Street. A model of that church is in the present church by a side altar.

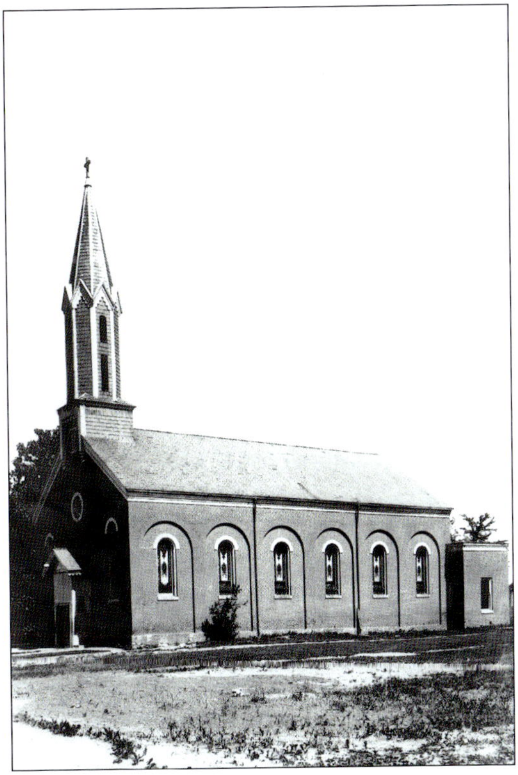

On January 5, 1859, the pastor's residence was burned to the ground, and in April, the church was also torched. Both fires were thought to be deliberate and part of the anti-Catholic sentiment sweeping across America at the time. The church was rebuilt and dedicated on July 14, 1860. At this point, Father Dumont left for Belgium and never came back. (Courtesy of Fr. Charles Morris.)

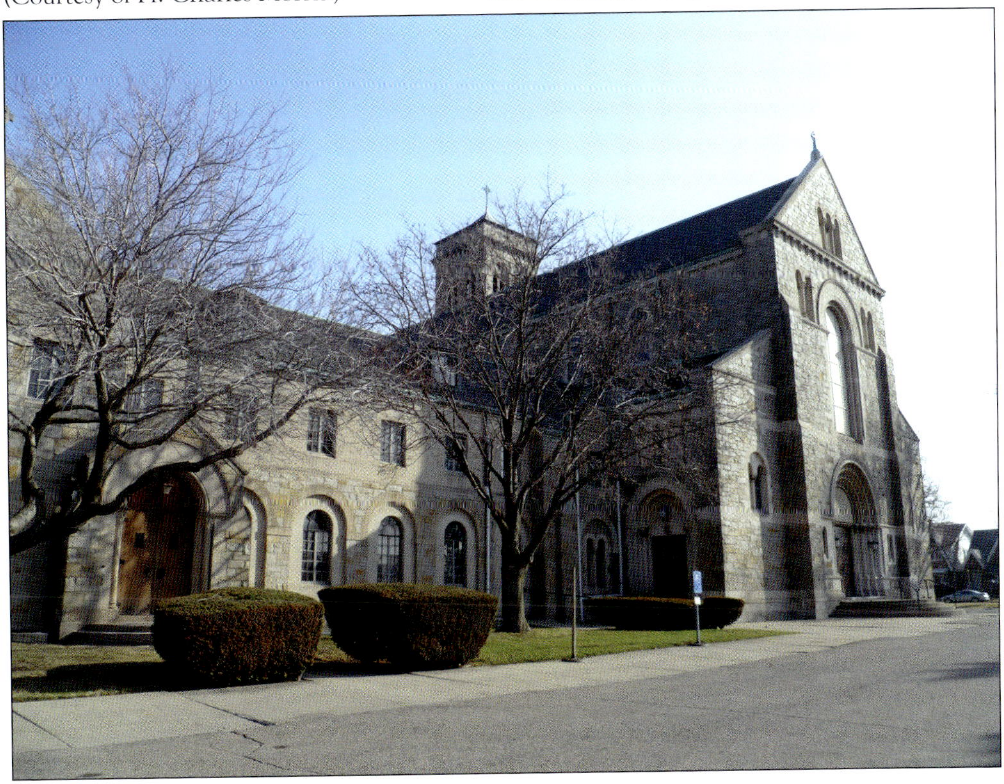

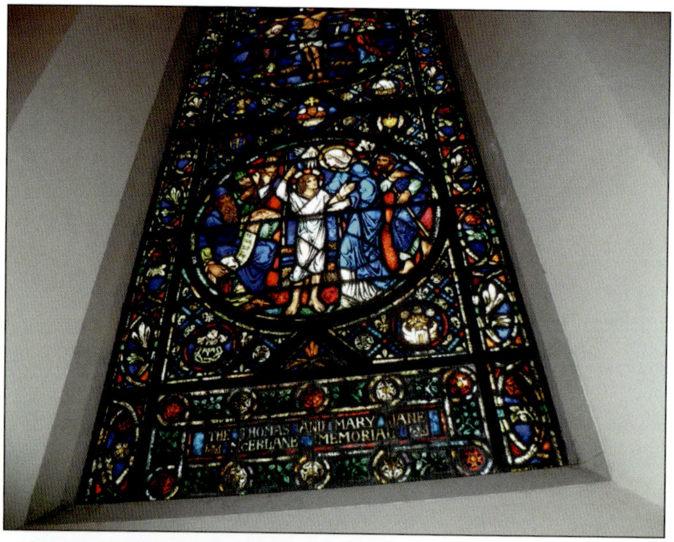

The St. Mary's of Redford Parish was on the verge of collapse when Fr. Andrew Dooling arrived in December 1898. From September 1899 to February 1910, Father Dooling got the church new stained-glass windows, new pews, steam heating, a slate roof, electric lighting, a redecorated interior, and a repainted exterior. Church enrollment was up in 1918, when Father Dooling died during the influenza pandemic that swept the world after World War I.

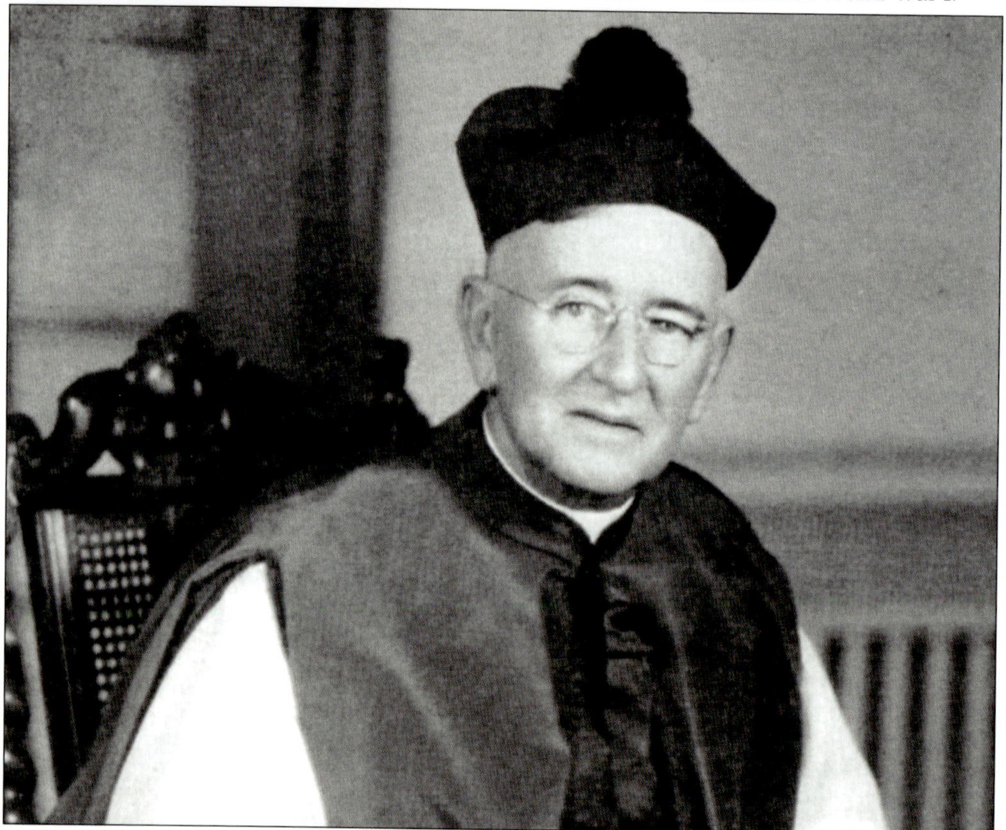

Fr. John Gilmary Cook took over in 1919 and oversaw the opening of the St. Mary's School in April 1920. Residential subdivisions were replacing farmlands, and rising attendance necessitated a new church built by nationally acclaimed architect Ralph Cram in the fall of 1926. Father Cook had three decades of success at St. Mary's of Redford. He guided the church through the Depression and built a convent. There were 4,000 families registered as parishioners when he died on August 10, 1951, from complications of an earlier stroke. (Courtesy of Fr. Charles Morris.)

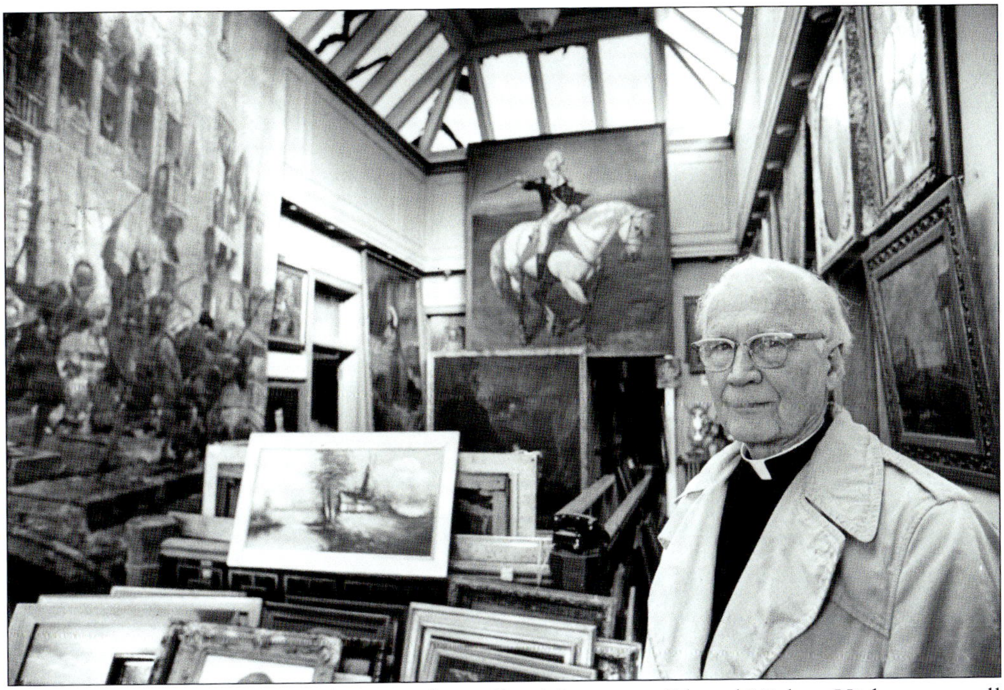

Into the fray stepped the archdiocese's chancellor, Monsignor Edward Hickey. Hickey was well schooled at St. Paul's Seminary, Louvain University, Harvard Business School, and the Catholic University of America. He was also the son of a successful Detroit businessman who was president of J.L. Hudson before opening his own men's store. Hickey was able to collect art his whole life and later sold it off to pay for various church bills and different charities.

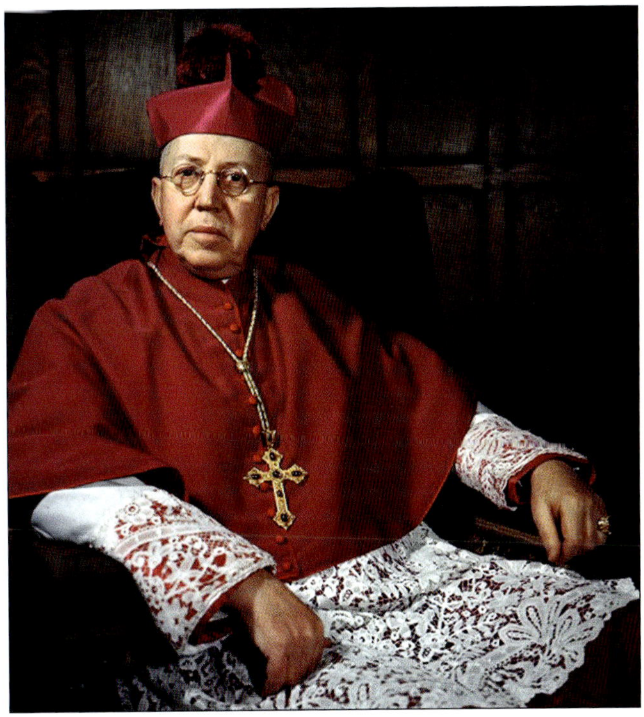

The church enrollment grew to 4,500, and Monsignor Hickey and his five assistant pastors were overwhelmed. Hickey convinced Cardinal Edward Mooney to let him build two chapels with schools in the 1950s to relieve the pressure. Both Mother of Our Savior and Our Lady Queen of Hope doubled their original class size and became separate parishes. (Courtesy of Fr. Charles Morris.)

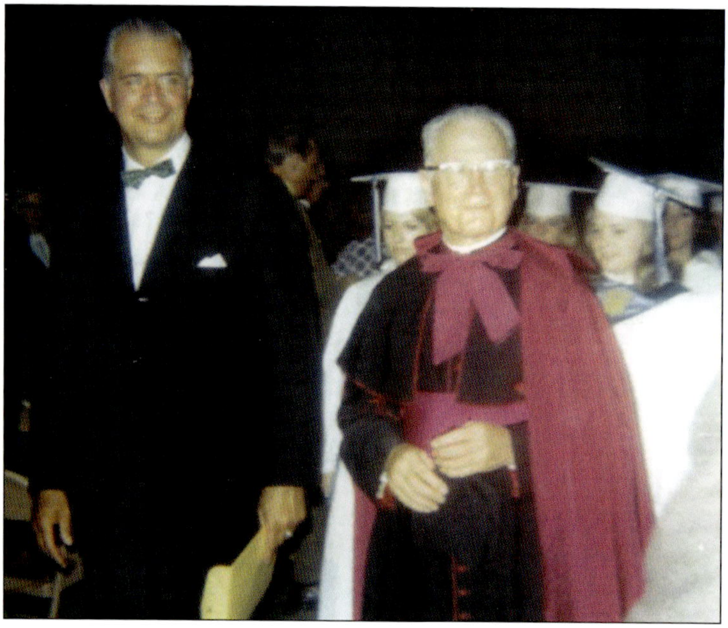

St. Mary's of Redford was now the largest parish in the Detroit Archdiocese. The football program flourished in the 1950s. A new high school was built in 1962 and opened for the 1963 school year. A state-of-the-art gymnasium was built in 1969. Former Michigan governor G. Mennen Williams was the commencement speaker for the class of 1969's graduating ceremonies. (Courtesy of Ralph Altwies.)

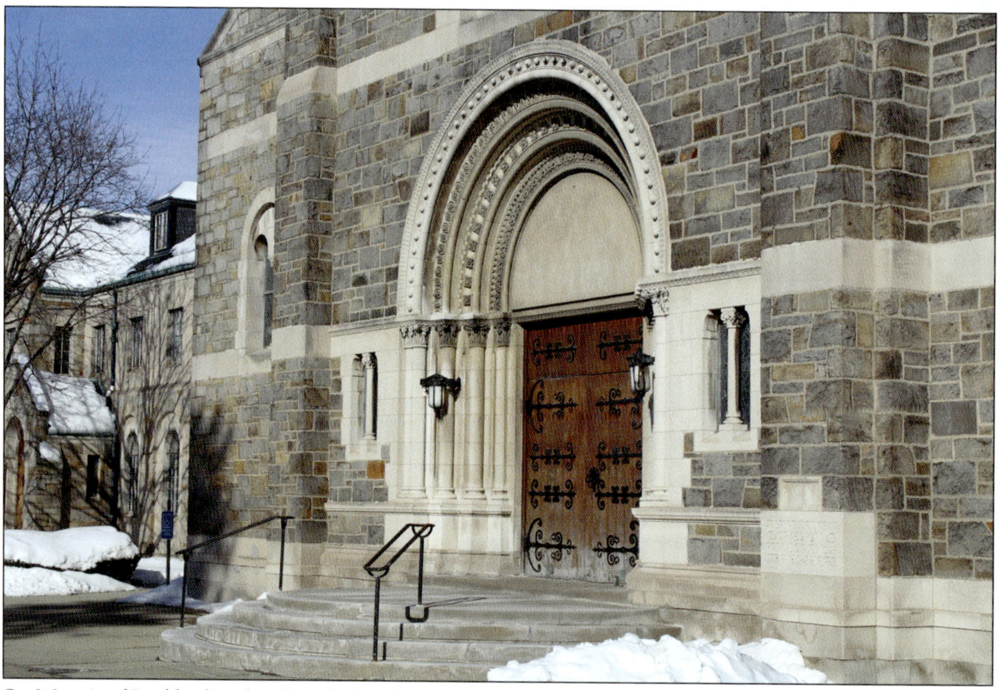

St. Mary's of Redford's school and church were gradually integrated throughout the 1970s. However, declining enrollment forced the closing of the high school and grade school. The church is trying to stay relevant in a mostly non-Catholic neighborhood. A strong alumni body holds fund raisers and reunions to keep the parish alive. The former convent is rented out to businesses. Fr. Charles Morris is the administrator in 2018. (Courtesy of Fr. Charles Morris.)

Four

FUN AND GAMES

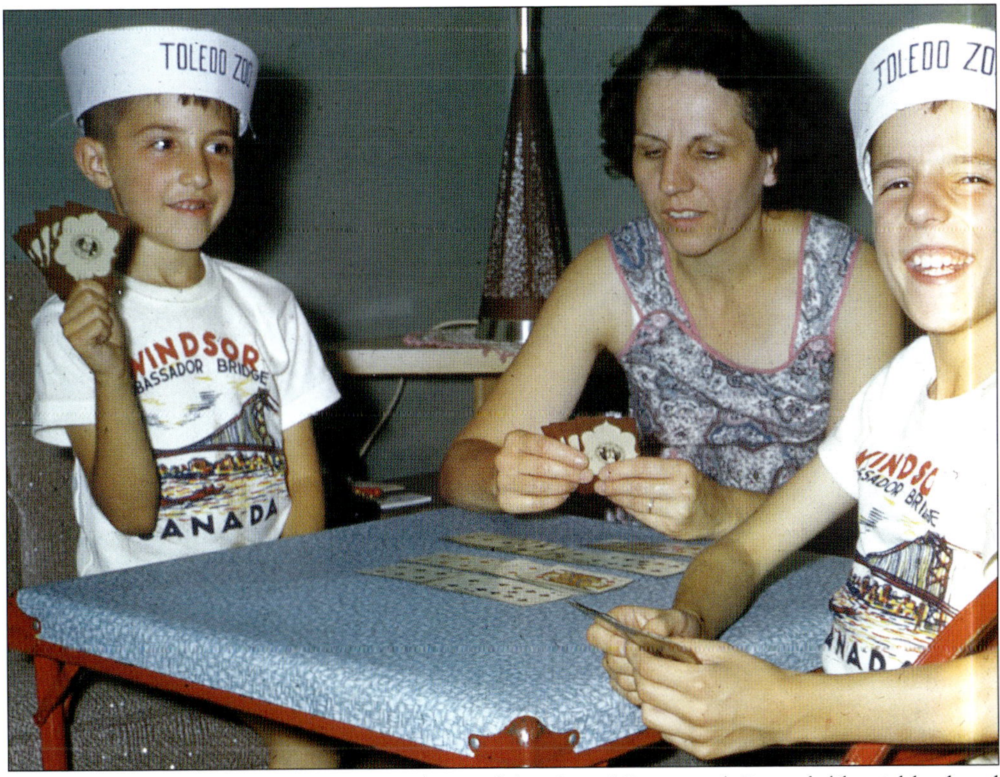

Two public recreation centers kept residents of the Grand River and Greenfield neighborhood refreshed and out of trouble. In addition to patronizing the many bars and bowling alleys along Grand River Avenue, locals also participated in organized sports, pick-up games at the sandlot, swimming in community pools, and skating at local rinks. Closer to home, children could often be found playing on the trampoline or participating in a game of tag or Ping Pong.

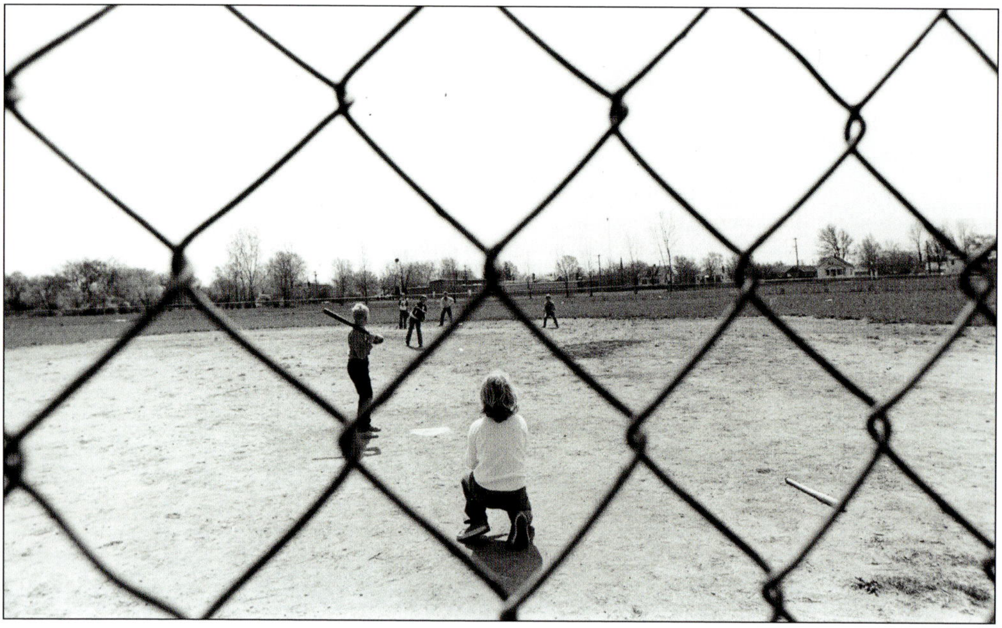

Children played pickup baseball and softball games at different sandlots throughout the area. Burns, Cadillac, Cook Field, Mother of Our Savior, Our Lady Queen of Hope, and Holy Cross Schools were among the local playgrounds. O'Shea and Butzel Recreation Centers provided more organized team sports. (Courtesy of the *Detroit Free Press*/Zuma Press.)

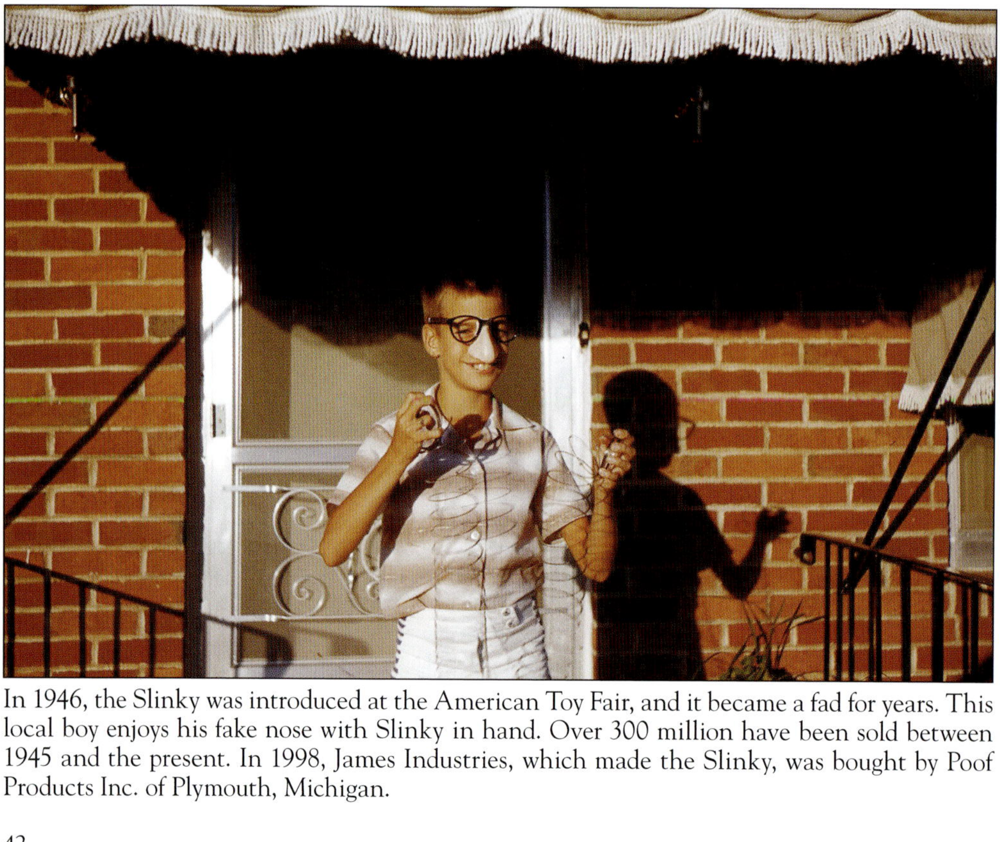

In 1946, the Slinky was introduced at the American Toy Fair, and it became a fad for years. This local boy enjoys his fake nose with Slinky in hand. Over 300 million have been sold between 1945 and the present. In 1998, James Industries, which made the Slinky, was bought by Poof Products Inc. of Plymouth, Michigan.

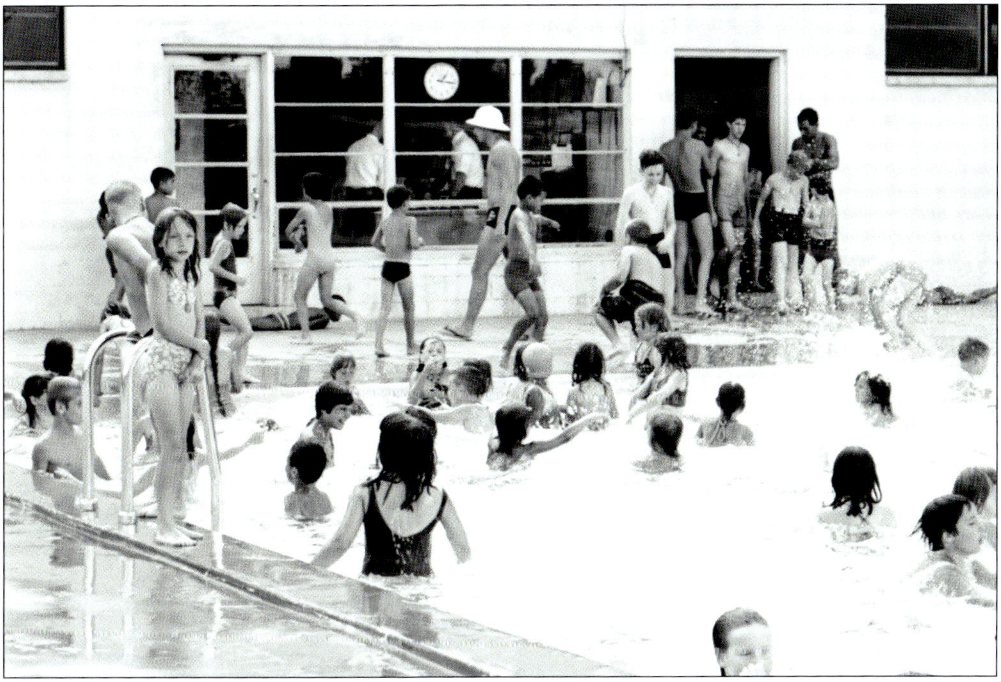

Butzel Memorial Playfield's swimming pool, at 10500 Lyndon Street, opened in 1954. The swimming program in Detroit added 30,000 new swimmers each year. The Red Cross noted that more people learned to swim through public facilities in Detroit than in any other city. It cost 25¢ to swim at Butzel Pool, which was open from 11:00 a.m. to 7:00 p.m. A $40,000 outdoor ice rink was added in December 1956. The baseball field hosted many tournaments over the years. Future Detroit Tiger Frank Tannana pitched there. (Courtesy of the Detroit Historical Society.)

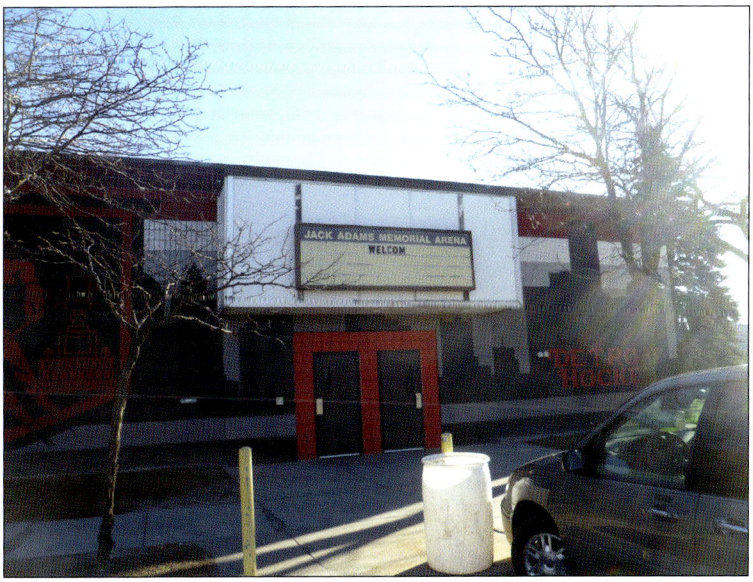

Jack Adams Memorial Arena opened in 1971 with Detroit mayor Roman Gribbs and Jack Adams's widow overseeing the opening ceremonies. Located in the Butzel Recreation Center, the original building has expanded to include an indoor pool and other recreation facilities. Many holiday hockey tournaments are still held there.

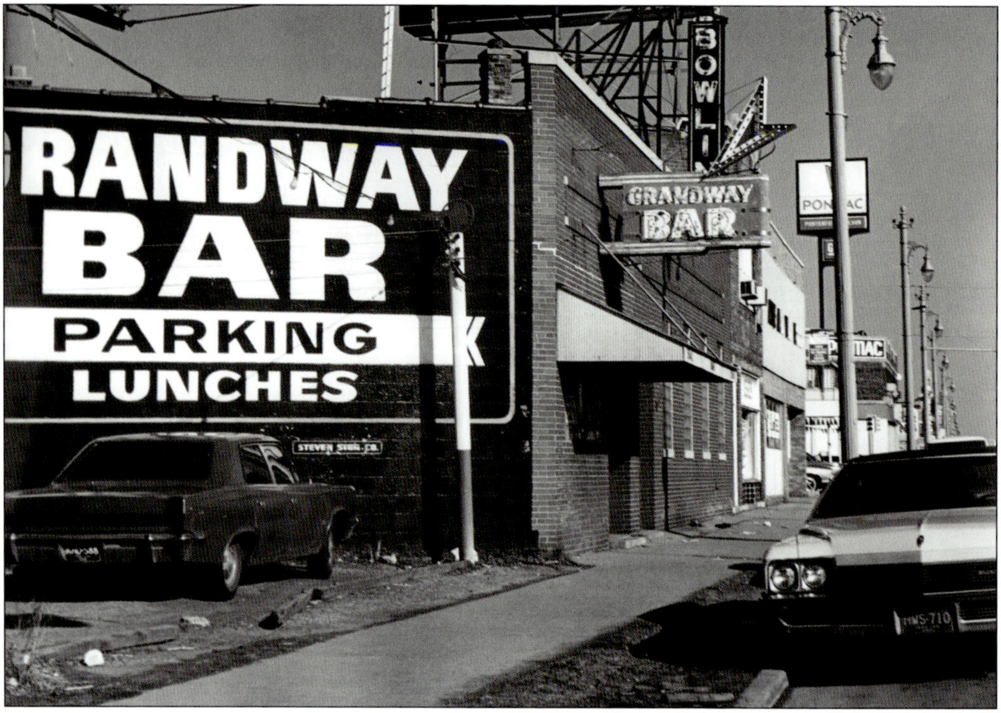

Grandway Bar, at 15942 Grand River Avenue, was owned by John Cronyn from the late 1960s through the mid-1970s. Cronyn would charter a bus to take people to the Thanksgiving parade in downtown Detroit. Afterwards, he would transport everyone back to the bar. Adults would drink on the main floor, while kids stayed in the basement eating donuts and drinking hot cocoa. There was a small bowling alley adjacent to the bar. (Courtesy of Tom Predhomme.)

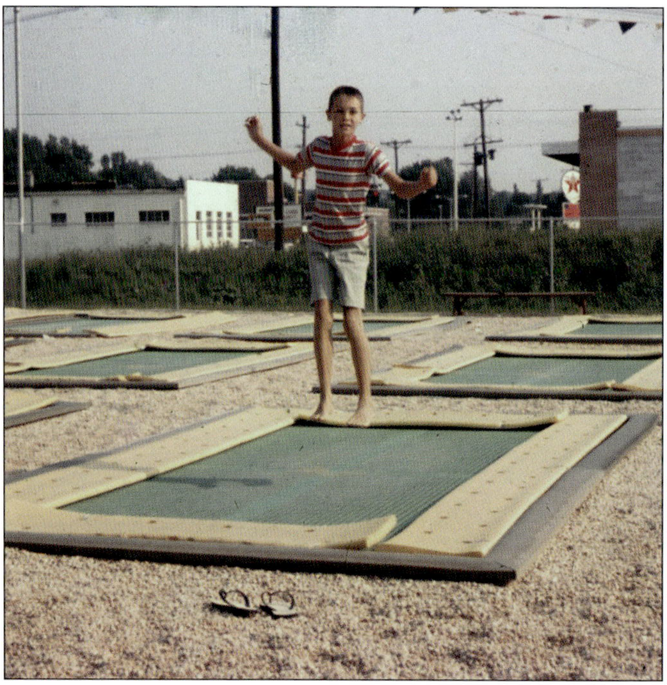

Trampoline centers popped up all over the Detroit area in 1960. Twenty-five trampoline centers in Detroit and the suburbs could handle 500 customers a day. Starting on the West Coast, the fad lasted a few years. David P. Matthews of 13240 Prest Street had a trampoline center on the east side of Greenfield Road between Eaton Avenue and Lyndon Street. Various groups advertised that one could invest as little as $5,000 and earn $1,500 a month. After several deaths, many sprained ankles, and more than a few broken bones, trampoline centers without adequate insurance and safety measures closed down.

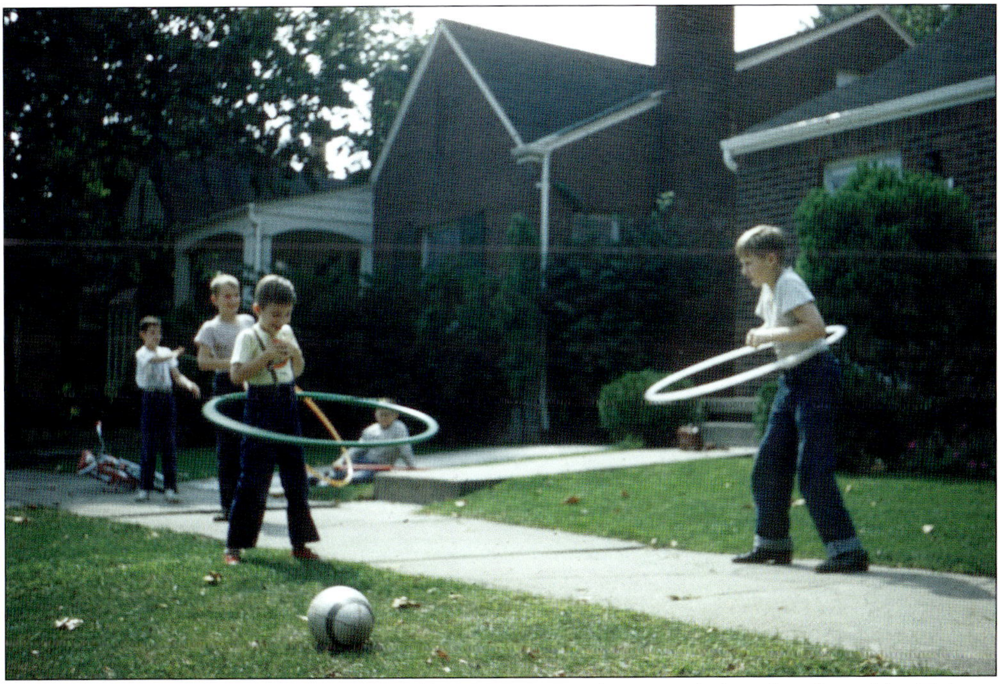

In 1957, a teacher in Australia introduced her students to a hoop made from bamboo. Alex Tolmer, founder of Toltoys, used a new material, polyethylene plastic, and sold 400,000 Hula-Hoops in 1957. The Wham-O toy company bought the design, and after the fad started on the West Coast, 25 million Hula-Hoops were sold in four months. Costing $1.59–$1.98, 100 million were sold in 1958. S.S. Kresge sold one Hula-Hoop per minute. Just about every kid in the Grand River and Greenfield area played with a Hula-Hoop that year.

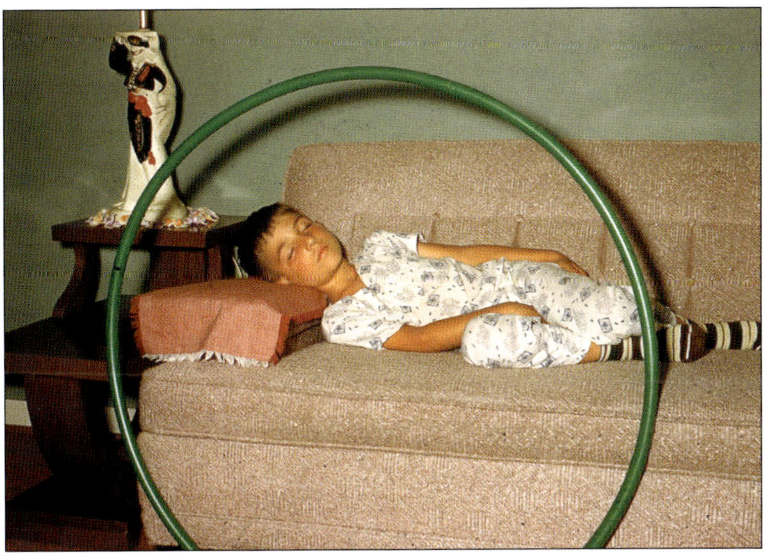

Within a year, the fad had played out. Hula-Hoops were selling for pennies. However, the craze made a comeback in the mid-1960s and again in the 1990s. Hula-Hoop contests and new Guinness world records continue to this day. Here, Nicky Garis of Monte Vista Street is all tired out after Hula-Hooping in the late 1950s.

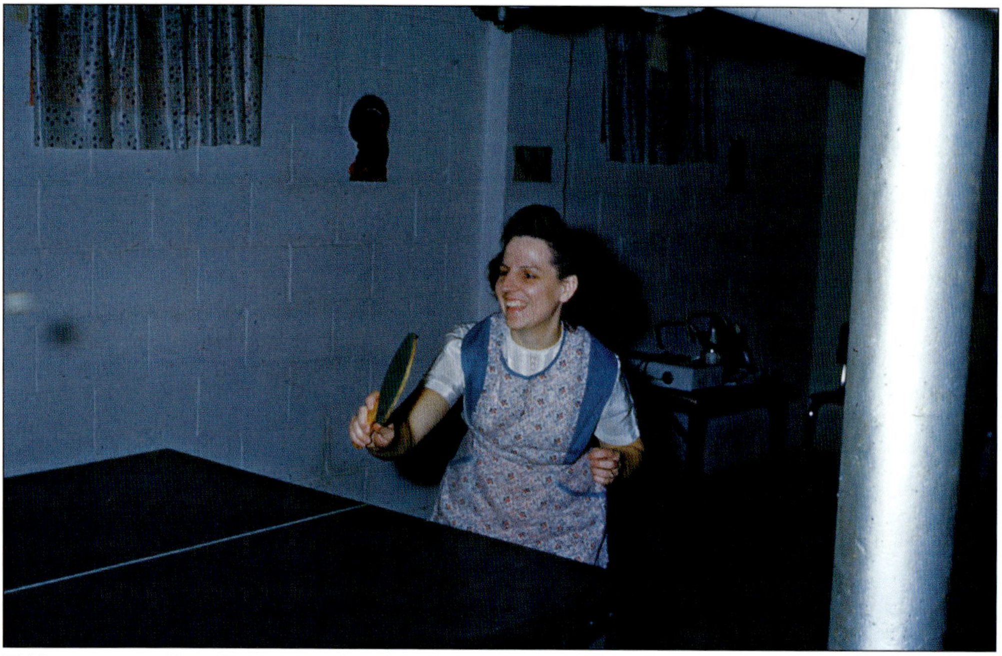

Table tennis, or Ping Pong, was played in countless basements in the Grand River and Greenfield area. Even moms got a few games in when they could push the kids away. Dewey's Lumberville at 15495 Schaefer Road sold table tennis equipment and supplies locally, along with other stores.

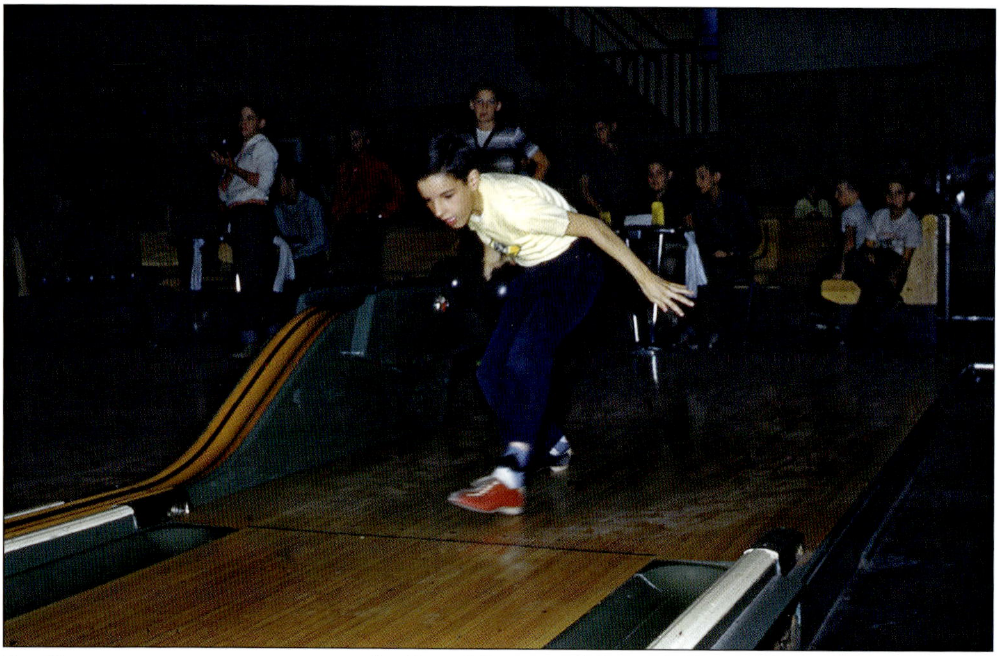

Bowling was a major recreation in the Grand River and Greenfield neighborhood. Grandmont Recreation Inc. and Grand Way Lounge and Bar were less than a mile away from each other on Grand River Avenue. Ambassador Recreation, at 15101 Schaefer Road, and Monte Carlo, at 14923 Plymouth Road, were also popular lanes.

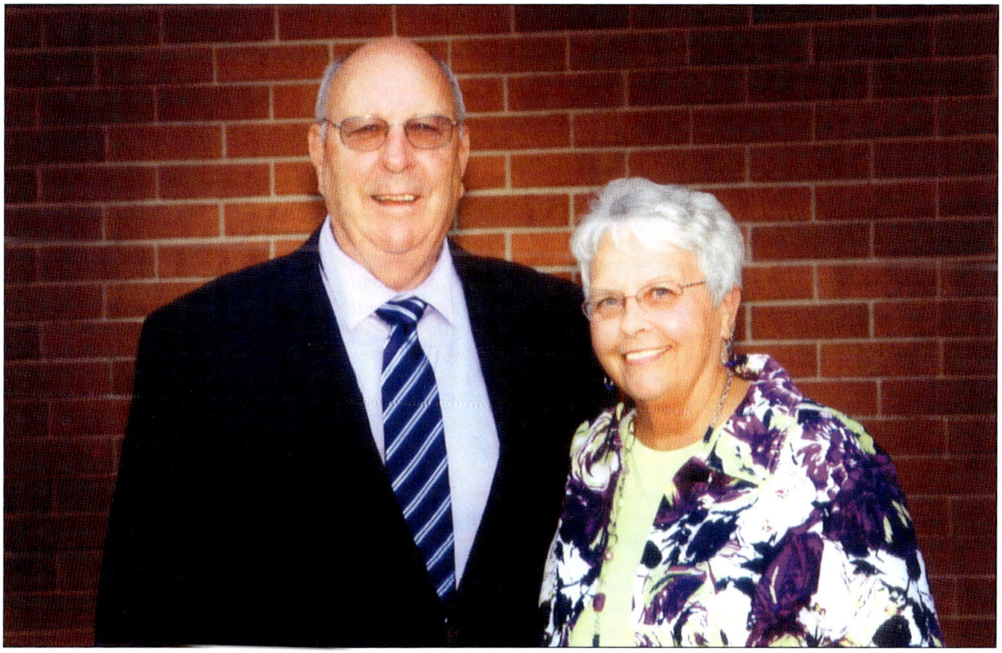

George and Kay Weatherford were volunteer boys' and girls' softball coaches in the early 1960s. George guided his Mother of Our Savior fourth-, fifth-, and sixth-graders to two championships in three years (1961 and 1963). Kay doubled as a front-office volunteer and girls' basketball coach. They have been married for 60-plus years. George has umpired and refereed for almost that long and has been a leading figure for over 50 years in the Northwest Catholic Men's Softball League. Kay worked in the Livonia School District while raising their children.

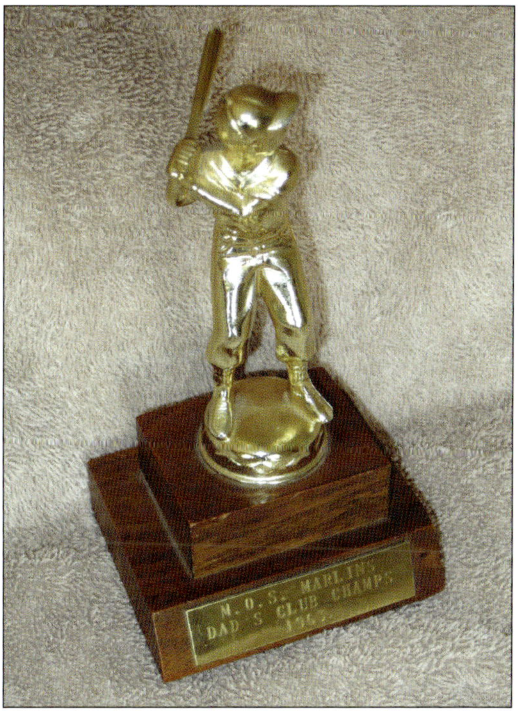

Mother of Our Savior (MOS) playground did not have any swings or slides. It did have a cement parking lot with a backstop and a basketball hoop, plus a dirt playground for softball games. Another field was added after the parish purchased Greencraft Nursery at 13560 Greenfield Road in the early 1960s. The MOS Marlins prospered during that period. The Marlins played in a St. Mary's Dad Club softball league that included a team from Our Lady Queen of Hope and several St. Mary's of Redford teams. Mother of Our Savior won championship trophies in 1961 and 1963 before the league was disbanded.

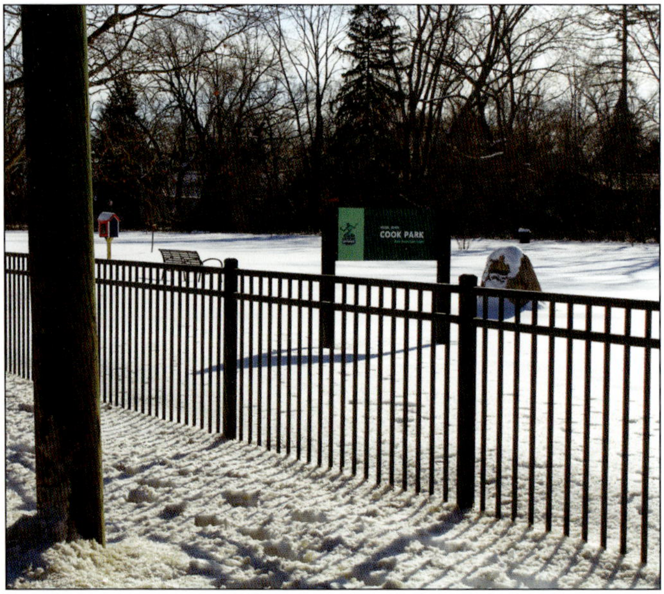

Cook Park, on the south side on Fenkell Avenue near St. Mary's Street, was used as a touch football and softball field for years. There was also a section that had swings, a slide, and a water fountain for neighborhood children. St. Mary's of Redford students often held physical education classes there. Cook Park has undergone a renovation in recent years with a new fence, walkways, new playground equipment, a picnic area, and basketball courts. During the winter, Cook Park was often flooded and turned into an ice rink.

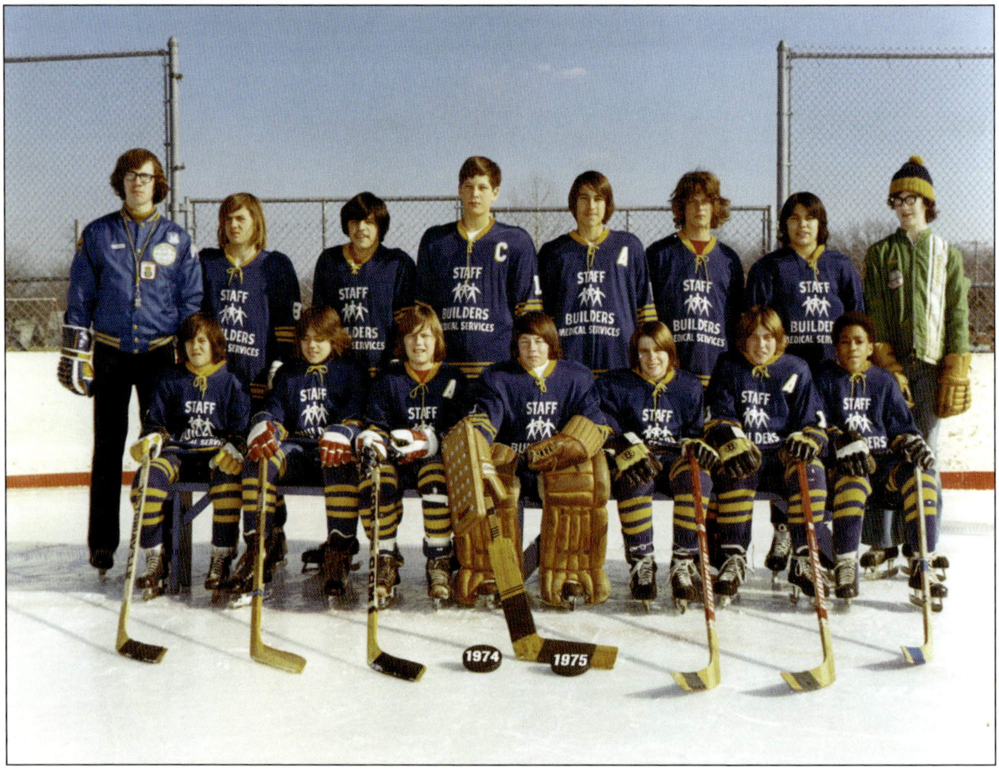

O'Shea Recreation, at 15870 Capitol Street and Greenfield Road, was named after Arthur O'Shea, a *Detroit Free Press* labor writer. The 35-acre playfield was dedicated on August 17, 1951, in front of 1,500 people who saw O'Shea's four-year-old grandson, Arthur O'Shea, unveil a bronze plaque at the base of the playfield's flagpole. Tennis, handball, and shuffleboard courts were part of the center, along with baseball diamonds, a football field, and a community building. Later, an ice rink was added. A proposed swimming pool never materialized.

Jim Burke's varsity Giants beat the Yankees in two straight games to claim the championship series in 1972. There were three divisions of play at O'Shea: junior varsity was for 9–10-year-olds, varsity was for 11–12-year-olds, and senior varsity was for 13–15-year-olds. Pictured from left to right are Richy Jackson, Matt Mallon, and Jim Burke, who all lived on Prevost Street.

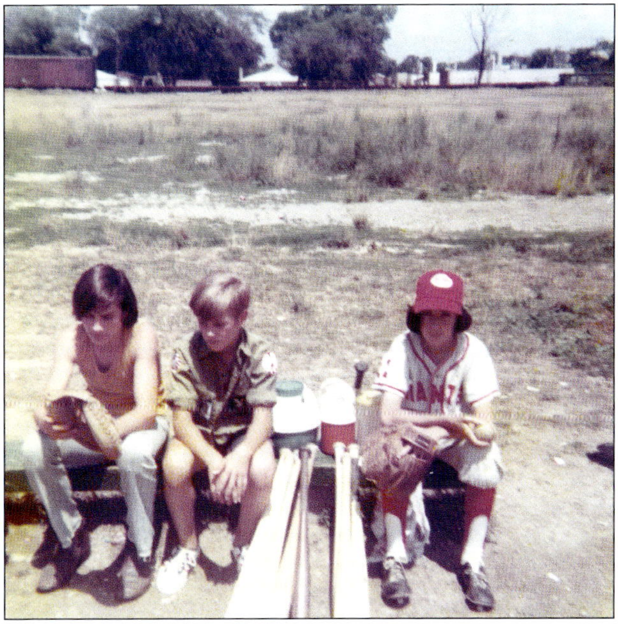

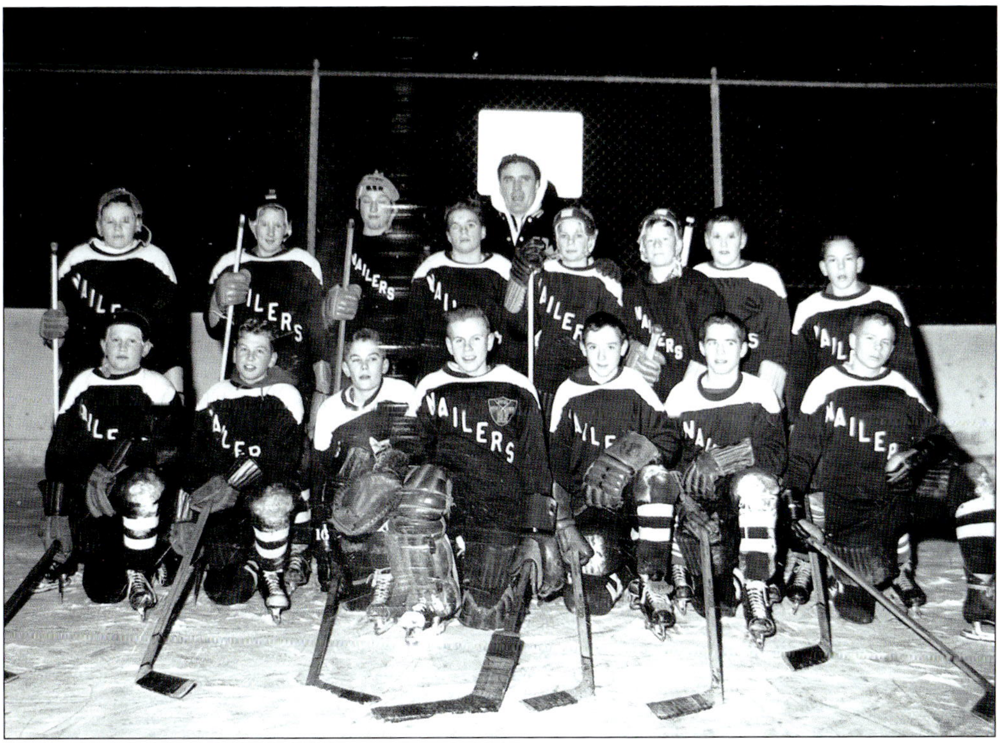

The O'Shea All Stars were a 9–11-year-old boys' football team. The 1958 All Stars had blue-and-white uniforms and were members of an 11-team little league organization from Detroit and adjoining communities. Local sports phenomenon Lennie Maurer was part of the team. Football was still played at O'Shea even as the fields were curtailed by the Jeffries Freeway construction in 1969. Maurer also played on the Nailers hockey team at the O'Shea outdoor ice rink. He is pictured here in the first row, second from right, with the Nailers.

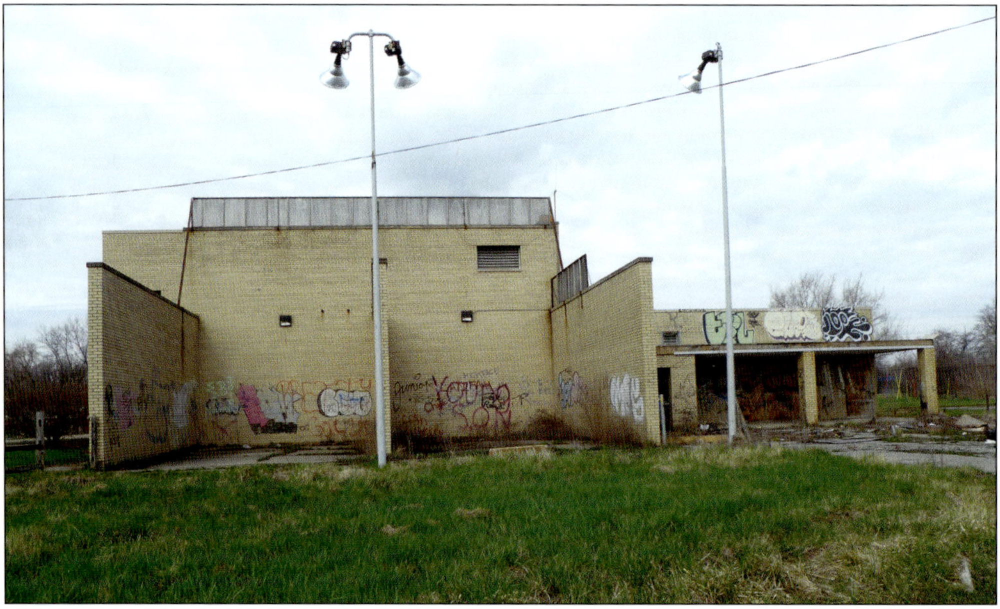

In 1969, one third of O'Shea Park (12 acres) was taken away for construction of the Jeffries Freeway. An ice rink was added, but the park deteriorated, along with the neighborhood, and it was closed in 2006. Much of the area is now used as a solar panel field. The handball courts pictured here are now gone.

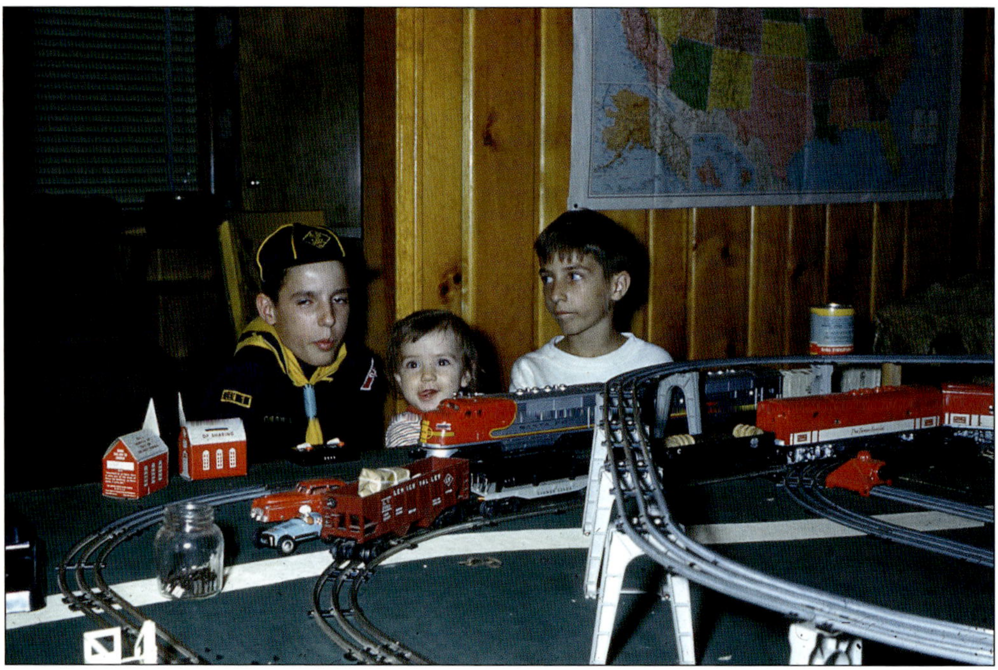

Millions of families had Lionel trains. This Grand River and Greenfield area family had the most popular Santa Fe F3 train. It was manufactured for 19 years (1948–1966). One unique feature of this train was that smoke came out of the smoke stack when a small tablet was dropped into it. The Train Clinic, at 13950 Hubbell Avenue between Grand River Avenue and Schoolcraft Road, was a big seller of these train sets.

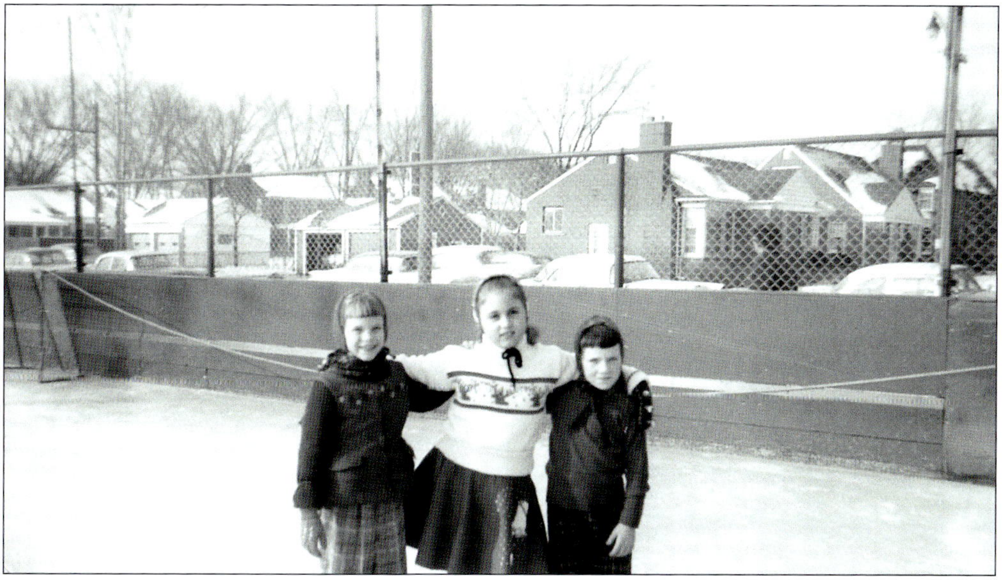

Winter Wonderland Ice Skating Club, at 16611 Schoolcraft Road, opened in November 1955. John and Grace McErlane were owners of a fenced-in outdoor rink that measured 55 feet by 85 feet. It was adjoined by an 84-foot-long heated clubhouse that sold coffee, hot dogs, candy, soft drinks, and hot chocolate. Pictured in 1963 are skaters (from left to right) unidentified, Marilyn Hardy, and Kathy Hafele. Note the hockey goal at left.

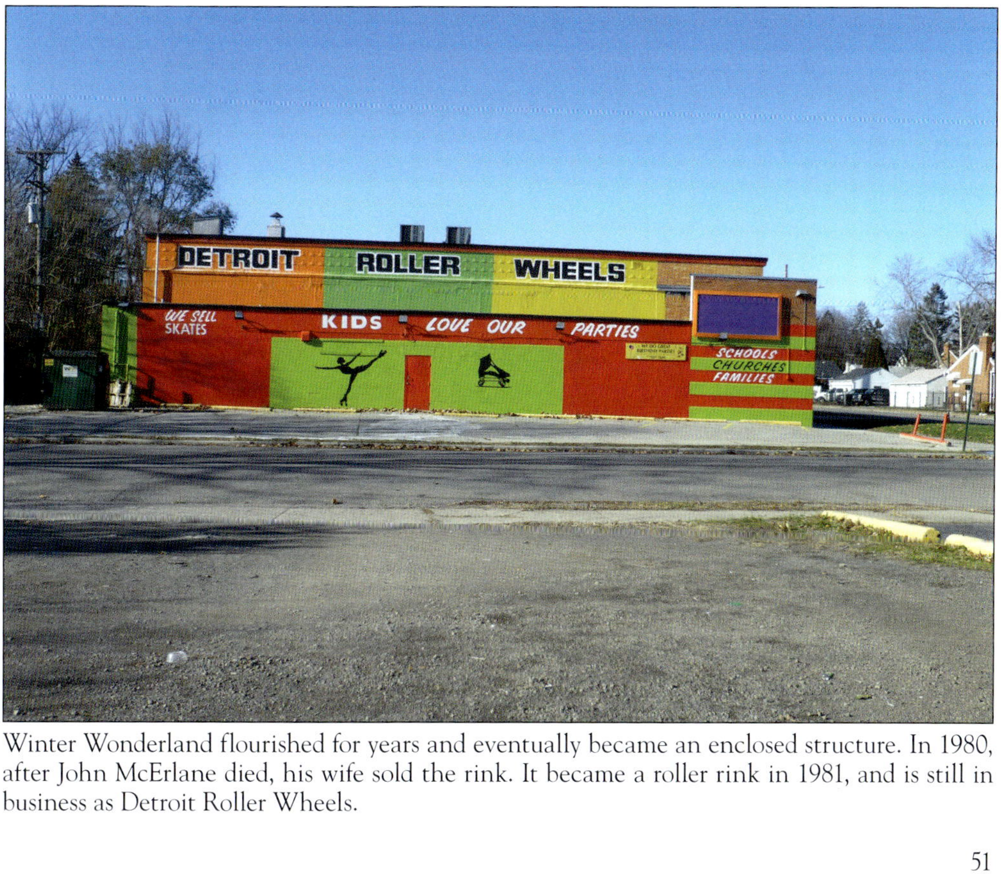

Winter Wonderland flourished for years and eventually became an enclosed structure. In 1980, after John McErlane died, his wife sold the rink. It became a roller rink in 1981, and is still in business as Detroit Roller Wheels.

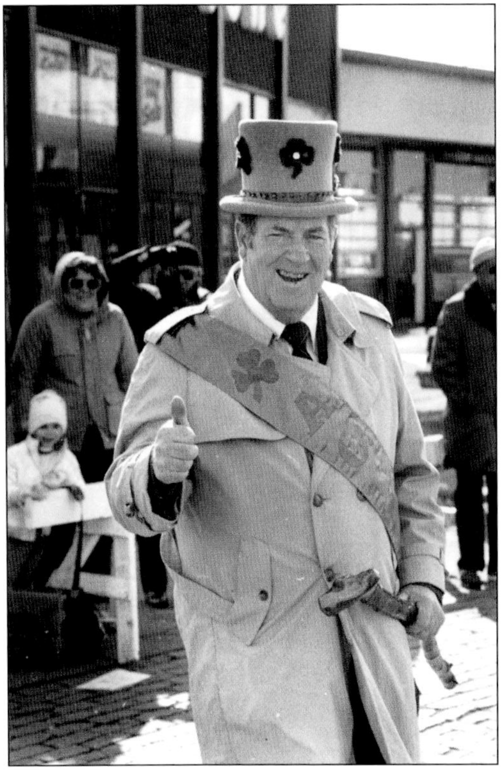

Jack Kelley, a colorful Detroit councilman in the 1970s and 1980s, was proud of his Irish heritage and not shy about telling people so. Although he admitted to having a drinking problem, he still frequented neighborhood bars like Dooley's on Grand River Avenue, where he got in a St. Patrick's Day fight when a patron knocked his hat off his head. On St. Patrick's Day, according to one patron, customers had to go out the front door, walk down the parking lot to the back of the building, and use the back door to have any hope of getting to the restrooms. (Courtesy of the *Detroit Free Press*/Zuma Press.)

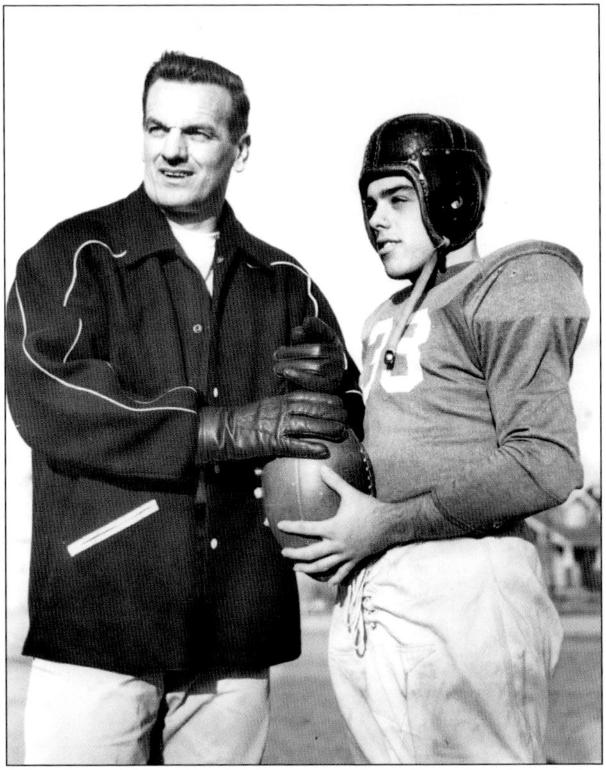

St. Mary's of Redford coach Alex Chesney and football team captain Chuck LaFave ponder the next strategy for the Catholic League high school powerhouse. The Rustics won the most Soup Bowl games (seven) between 1948 and 1967. The Soup Bowl was played between the two top Catholic League teams at the end of the year. St. Mary's of Redford also played in the most Goodfellow games (seven) as the Catholic League representative against the top Detroit Public School team for the city championship. (Courtesy of the *Detroit News*/Zuma Press.)

Five

NEIGHBORHOOD

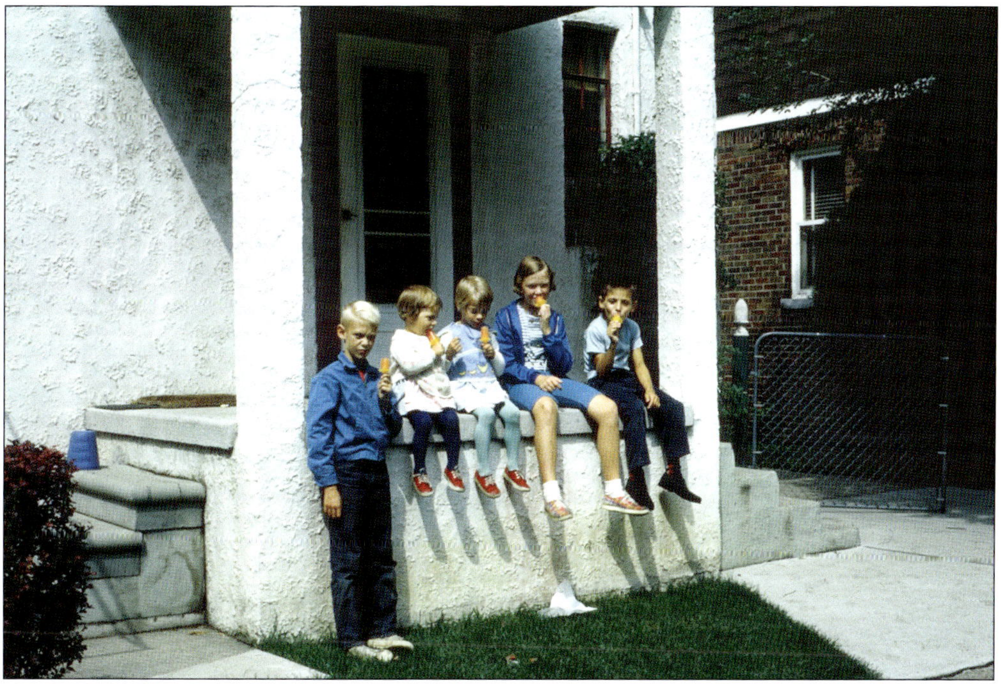

The Grand River and Greenfield neighborhood had families representing a wide array of ethnicities, and almost everyone got along. Many of the kids became very successful adults, and more than a few outdid their parents. Jews, Protestants, and Catholics lived side by side and would watch out for each other's kids. Common family names included Sloan, Bishop, Togasaki, Stoll, Sauve, Szymanski, Soderstrom, Coujoumjian, Murray, and Hoban.

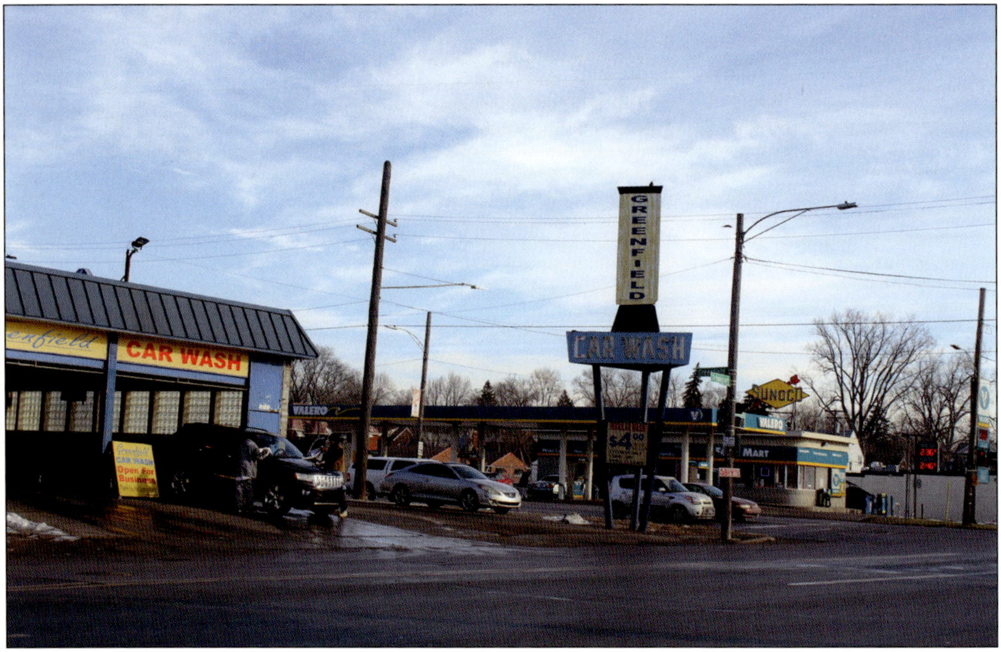

This neighborhood car wash at 15500 Schoolcraft Road has been known as Jax Kar Wash, Mac Car Wash, and now Greenfield Car Wash over the past 57 years. It had a candy machine that a lot of schoolkids used on their way home. A gas station that was introduced next to the car wash in the 1970s is now gone. A used car lot once filled this space in the 1950s.

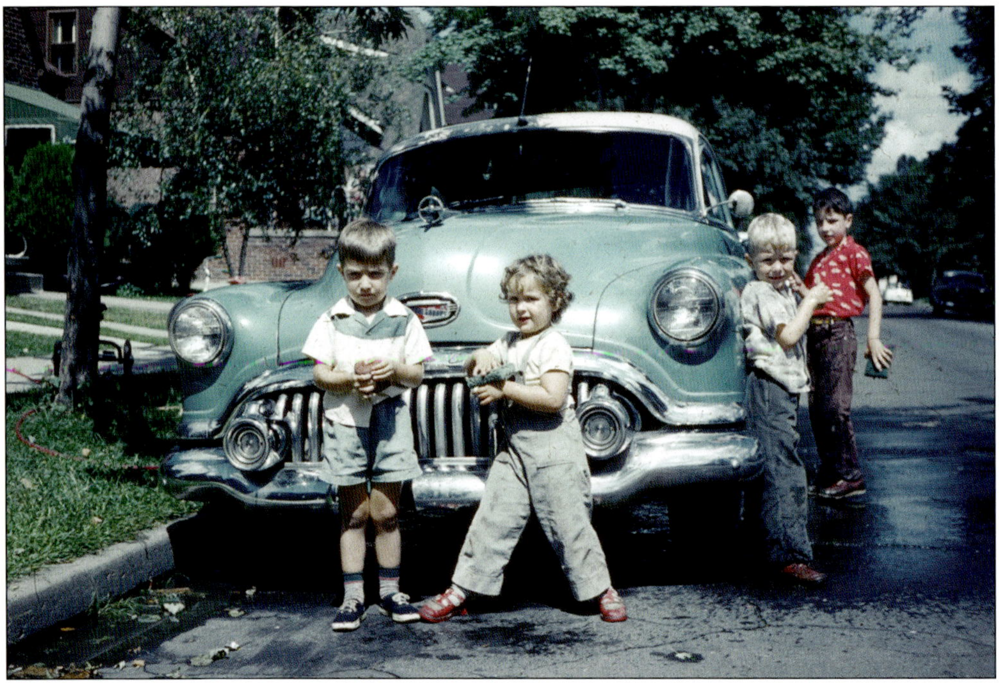

A less professional car wash is provided by these kids on Monte Vista Street. Armed with a bucket of suds and sponges, they tackle dad's car parked in the street. Parents took pride in keeping their cars clean, and kids often wanted to help.

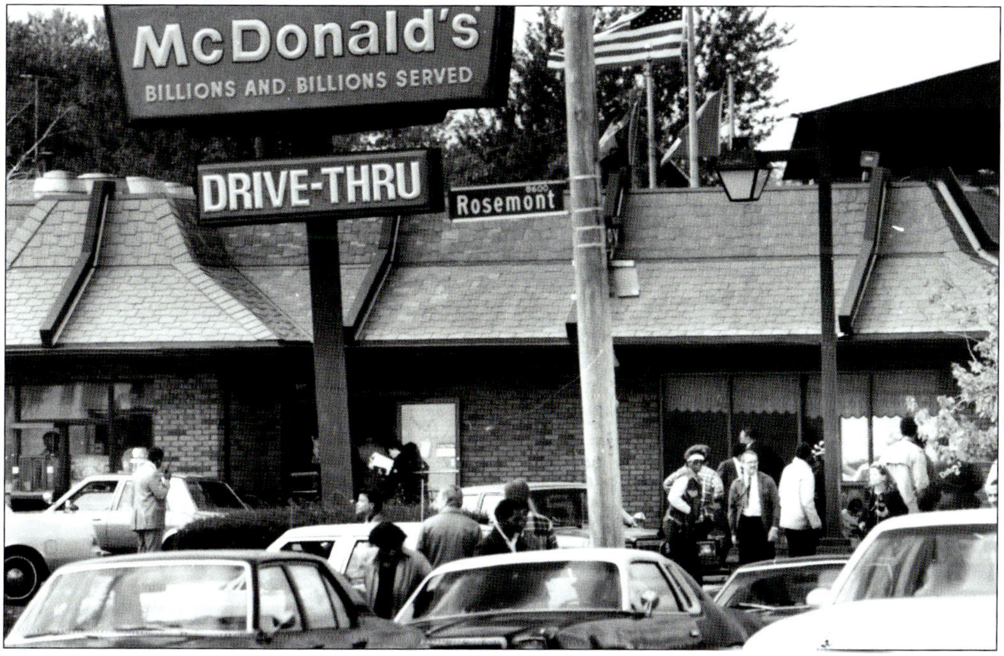

The McDonald's drive-through at Rosemont and Grand River Avenues, near the Rosedale neighborhood, was a teen hangout from the moment it opened in the early 1960s. Occasionally fights would break out, and the sound of squealing tires was not unheard of. Surrounded by Grand Land Shopping Center, this McDonald's always had a lot of customers. (Courtesy of the *Detroit News*/Zuma Press.)

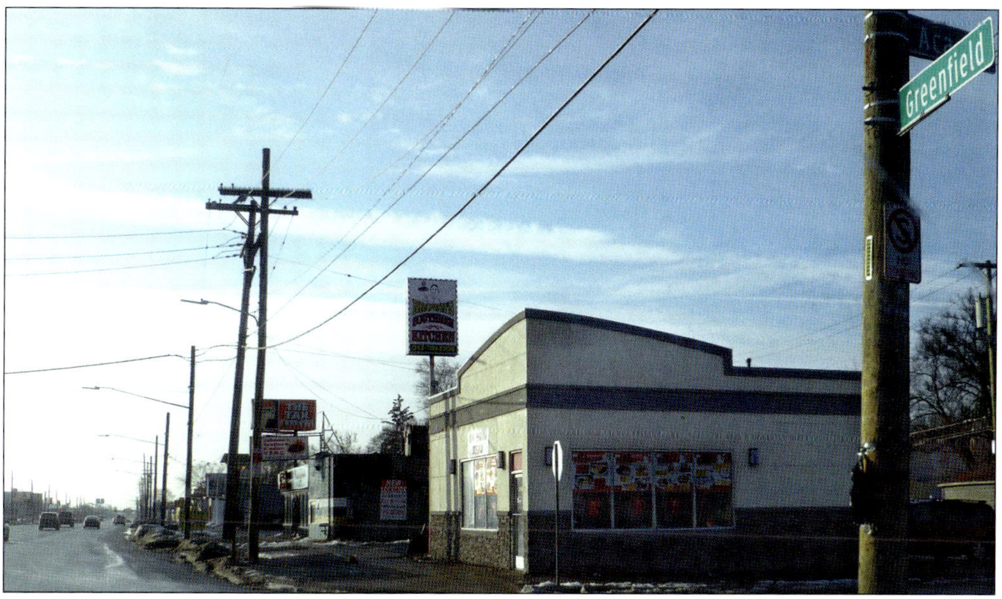

Likers Crystal Tower at 14253 Greenfield Road was run by Helen and Ed Liker. For many years, it was open 24 hours a day, 365 days a year. It was a true neighborhood mainstay through the 1950s, 1960s, and 1970s. The building is still on the corner of Acacia Avenue and Greenfield Road and has been a Mexican restaurant, Coney Island Restaurant, and now Brown's Southern Kitchen.

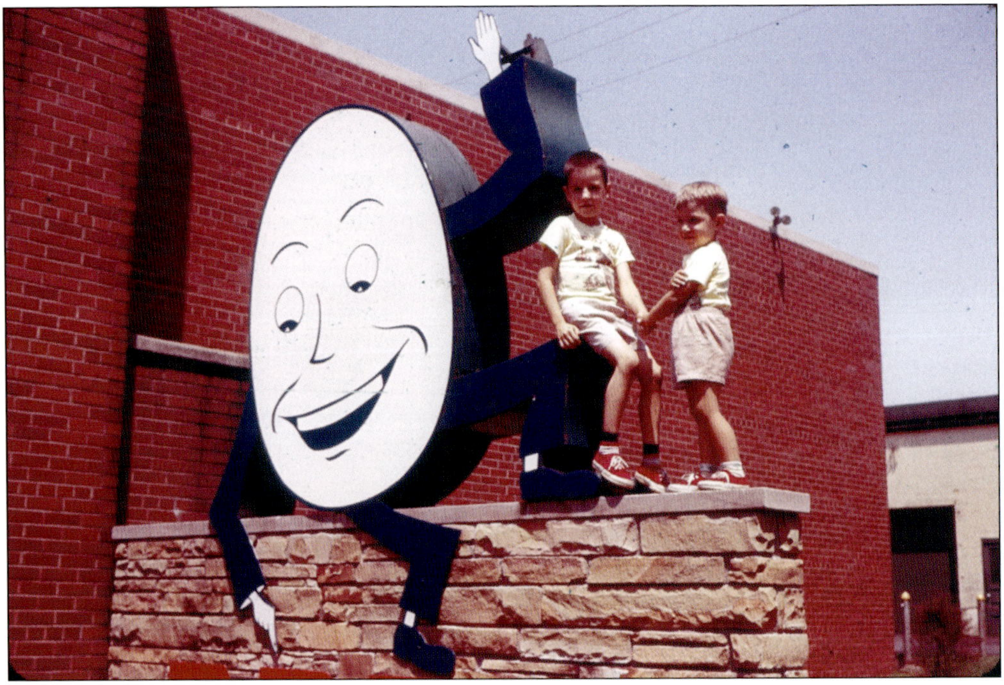

Page and Cox Egg Company at 12150 Greenfield Road processed a million eggs a day at its plant during its heyday in the 1950s and 1960s. It supplied eggs to a variety of local supermarkets and other stores. It had a Humpty Dumpty sign that was familiar to everyone for miles around. This proved to be a popular photo opportunity for many families.

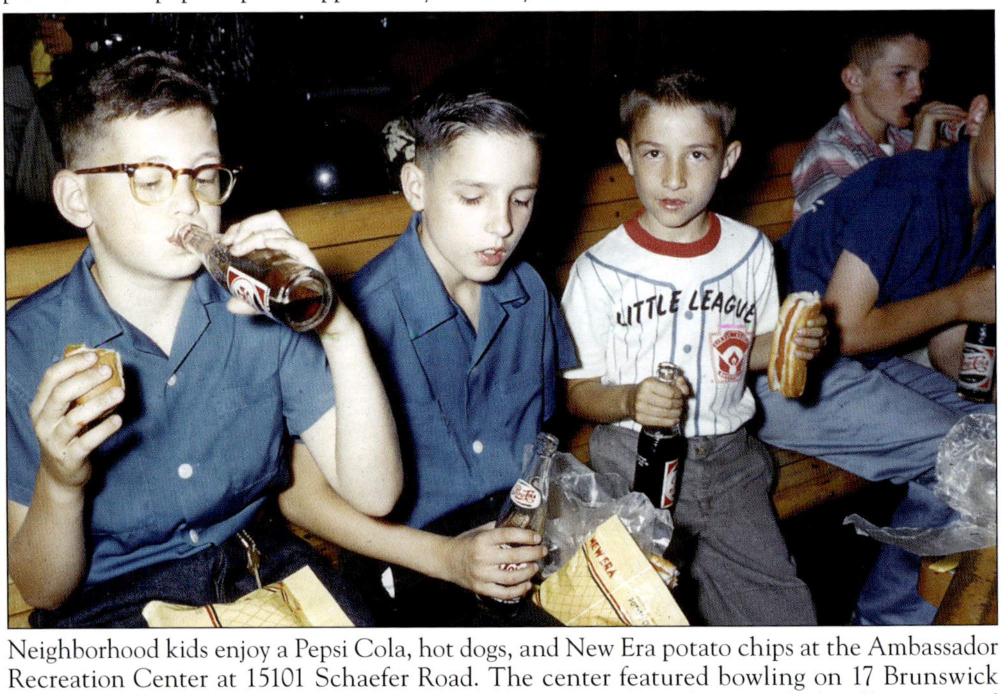

Neighborhood kids enjoy a Pepsi Cola, hot dogs, and New Era potato chips at the Ambassador Recreation Center at 15101 Schaefer Road. The center featured bowling on 17 Brunswick alleys, a cocktail lounge, and a billiards room. This was a favorite hangout for locally sponsored bowling leagues.

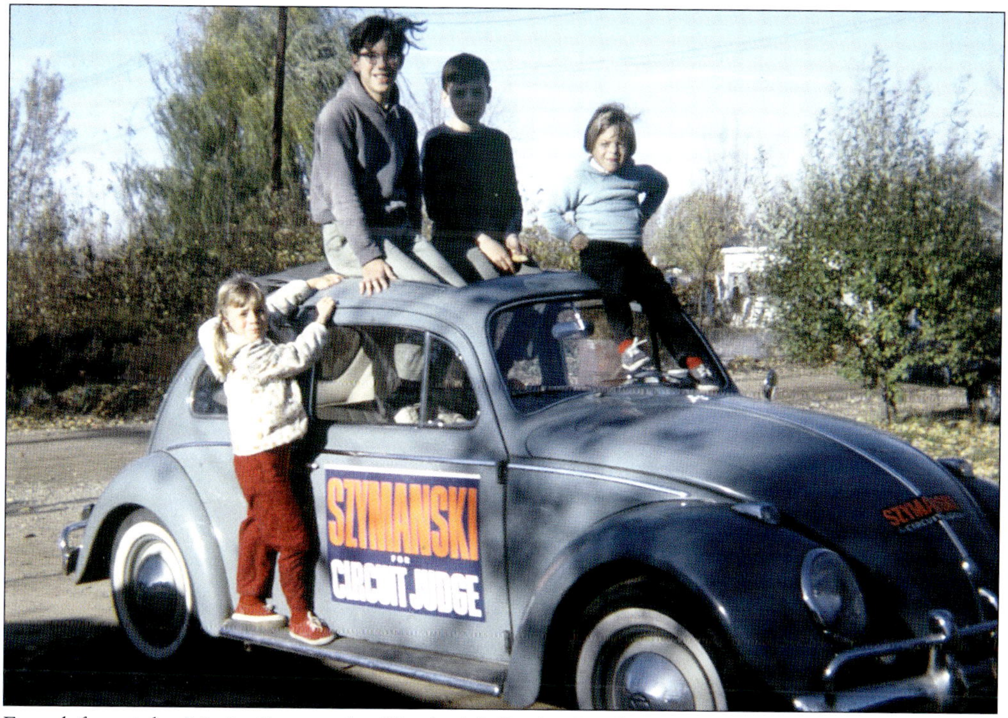

From left to right, Marisa Szymanski, Charles McCauley, Mark Szymanski, and Annette Szymanski are all onboard for their dad and friend Anthony Szymanski becoming a judge. These volunteers joined many other neighbors in Szymanski's run for judge in the early 1970s. (Courtesy of Marianne Szymanski.)

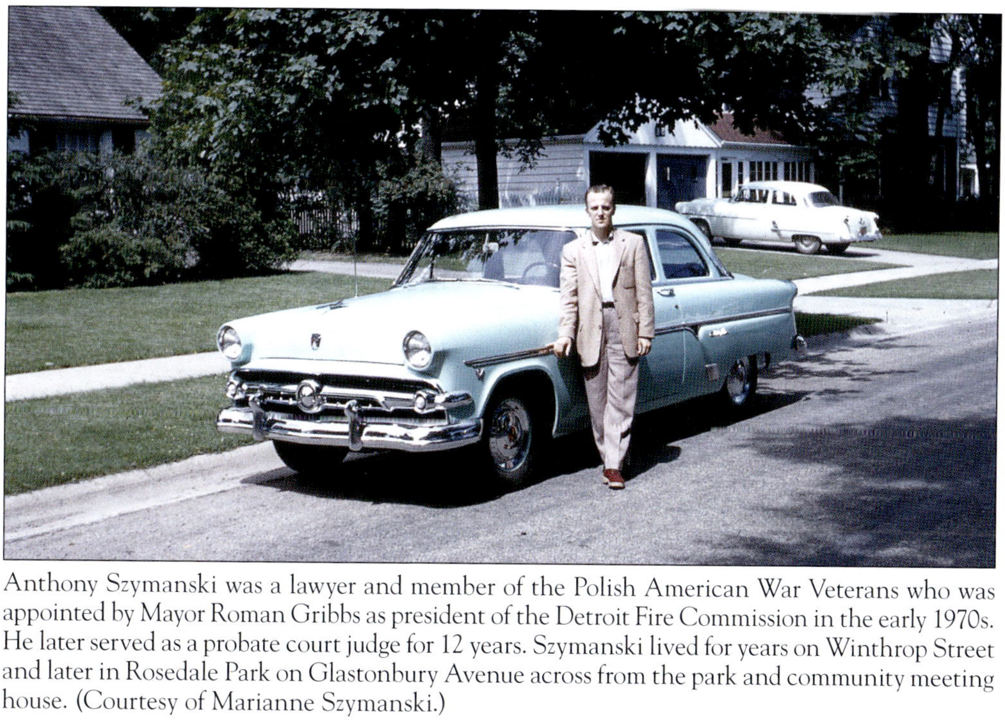

Anthony Szymanski was a lawyer and member of the Polish American War Veterans who was appointed by Mayor Roman Gribbs as president of the Detroit Fire Commission in the early 1970s. He later served as a probate court judge for 12 years. Szymanski lived for years on Winthrop Street and later in Rosedale Park on Glastonbury Avenue across from the park and community meeting house. (Courtesy of Marianne Szymanski.)

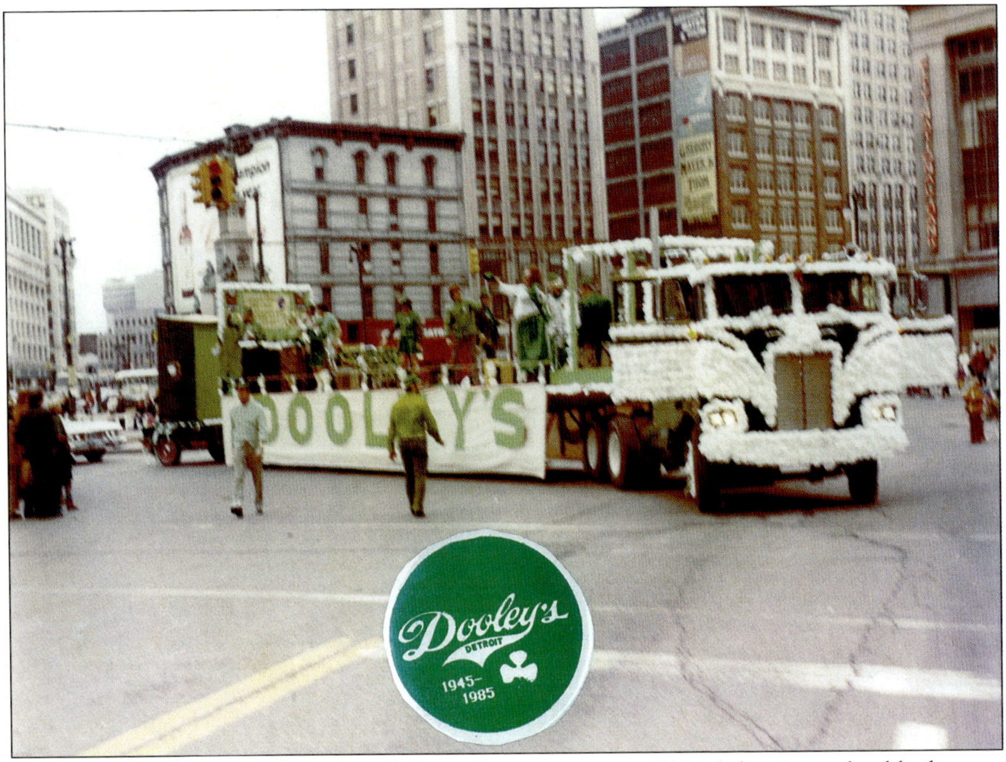

Dooley's Bar, located at 16334 Grand River Avenue, was an old Irish bar just a few blocks west of St. Mary's of Redford Church and School. St. Patrick's Day celebrations were legendary in the neighborhood. Dooley's Bar sponsored many sports teams and cultivated a diehard clientele. Detroit councilman Jack Kelley was a frequent patron. This float was used every year at the St. Patrick's Day parade in Corktown on Michigan Avenue by old Tiger Stadium. (Courtesy of Tom Predhomme.)

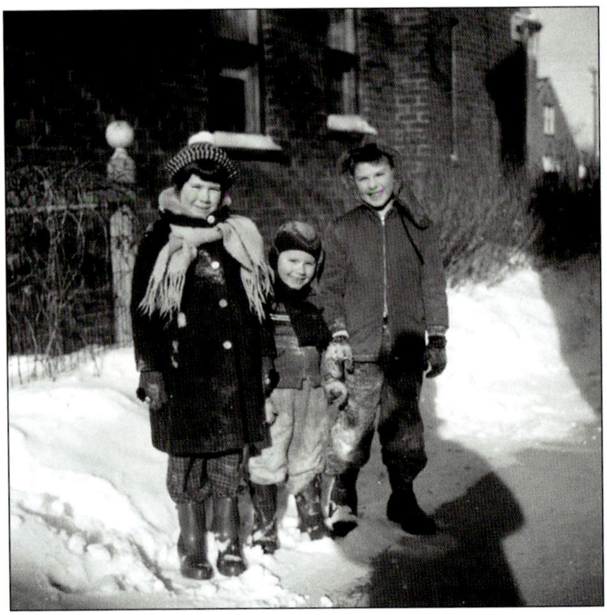

The Stoll children, pictured from left to right in the late 1950s, Barbara, Donald, and David (oldest John is not shown), lived at 14035 Winthrop Street. Their mother, Dorothy, raised her children after their father, Kenneth, died in the early 1960s. All of the boys worked for Dean Sellers Ford at 16700 Grand River Avenue for many years. The family had a log cabin playhouse in their backyard with shingles on the roof. (Courtesy of Ruth Murray.)

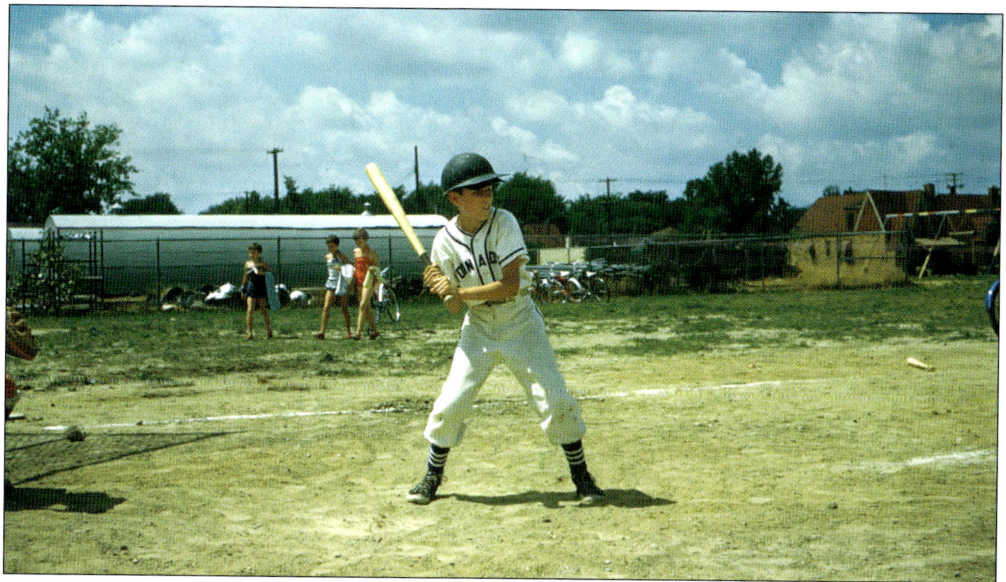

George Garis gets ready to hit on the Butzel baseball field while girls with their towels are leaving the outdoor swimming pool behind him. The Butzel Recreation Center was shaped like an L around the cemetery on the northwest corner of Meyers Road and Lyndon Street. The center is named after Fred Butzel, a lawyer who practiced mainly for philanthropy. Butzel sat on the board of directors for many Detroit foundations, banks, African American hospitals, and automobile businesses.

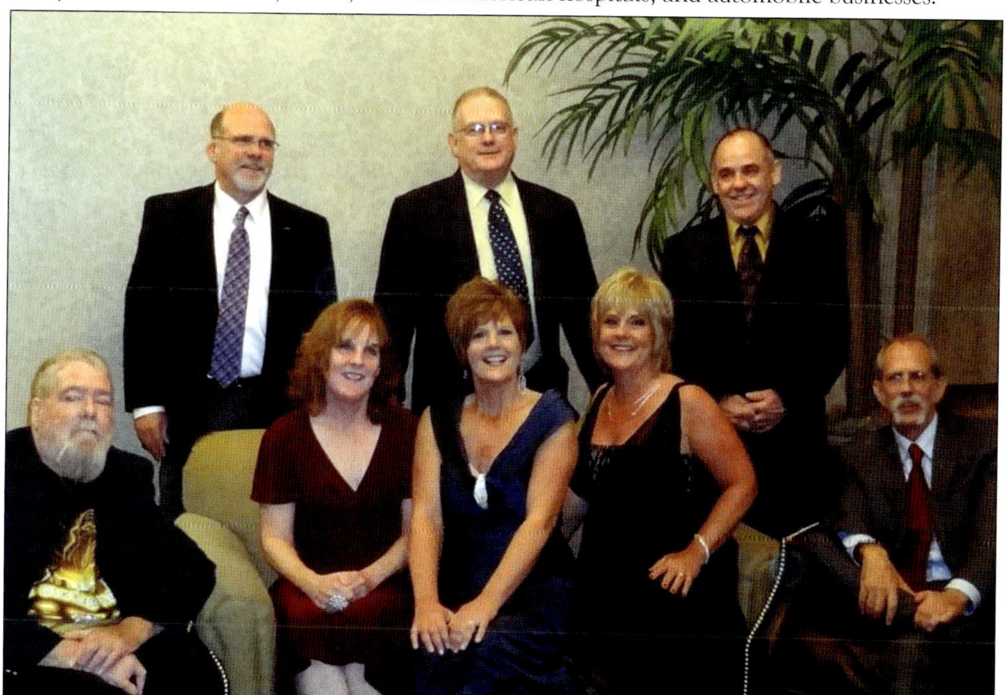

The Haas family lived at the dead end of Forrer Street, just south of Davison Street. From left to right are (first row) George, Mary, K.C., Ann, and Charles; (second row) Andy, Mike, and Fred Haas. Beyond the fence at the end of Forrer Street was a field that included a pollywog pond and an old abandoned school bus. (Courtesy of the Haas family.)

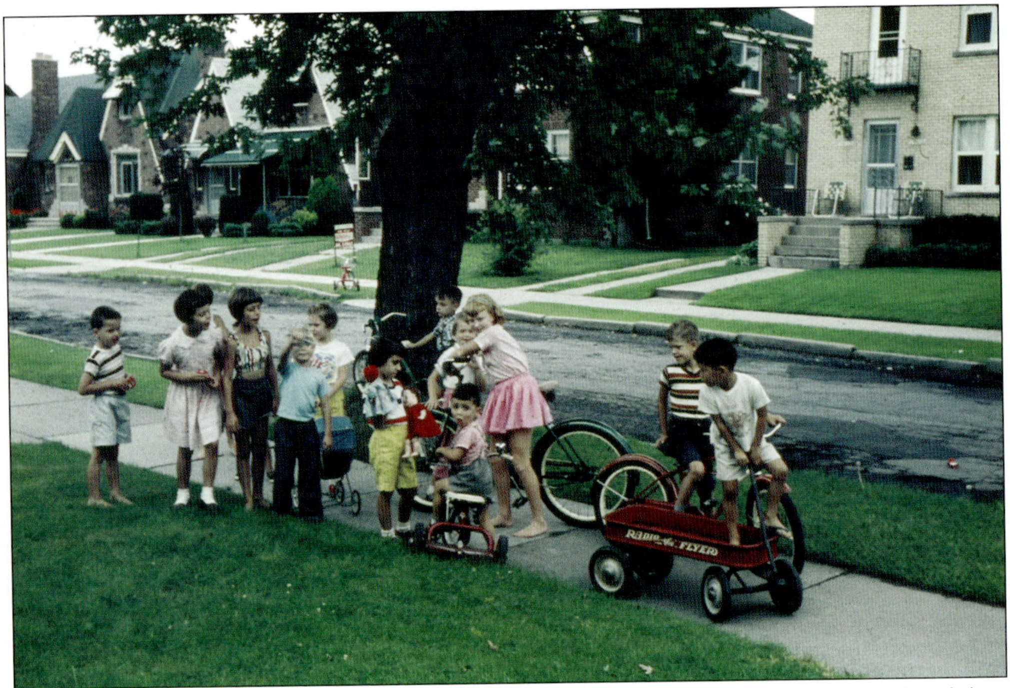

Children gather on Winthrop Street between Acacia Avenue and Kendall Street with their bikes, trikes, baby carriages, and wagon. Mark and Dana Pearson are on the far left, followed by, from left to right, Denise Clayton, Tom Schmittdiel, Suzann Fitzer, Mark Szymanski by the tree, Sue Schmittdiel, Beverly Hurd in pink, Charles Szymanski on a tricycle, dark-haired Theresa Fitzer, Bill Fitzer on a bike, and Kenton Matsumoto with his wagon. (Courtesy of Marianne Szymanski.)

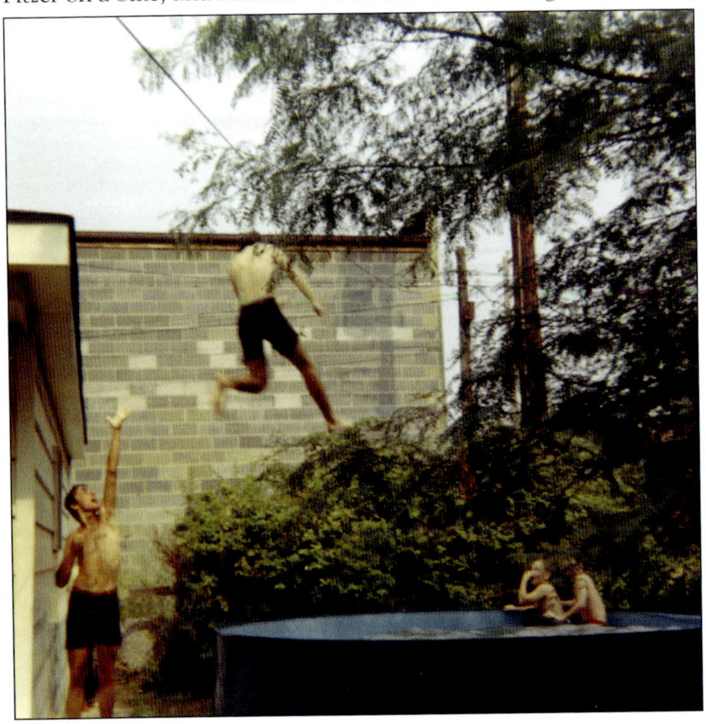

Kids are jumping off a garage roof into a small pool at 14034 Winthrop Street. This scene was repeated throughout the neighborhood whenever a garage was close to a pool because lots were so small. Parents were often working or busy making dinner when this occurred. Fortunately, no one was ever seriously hurt.

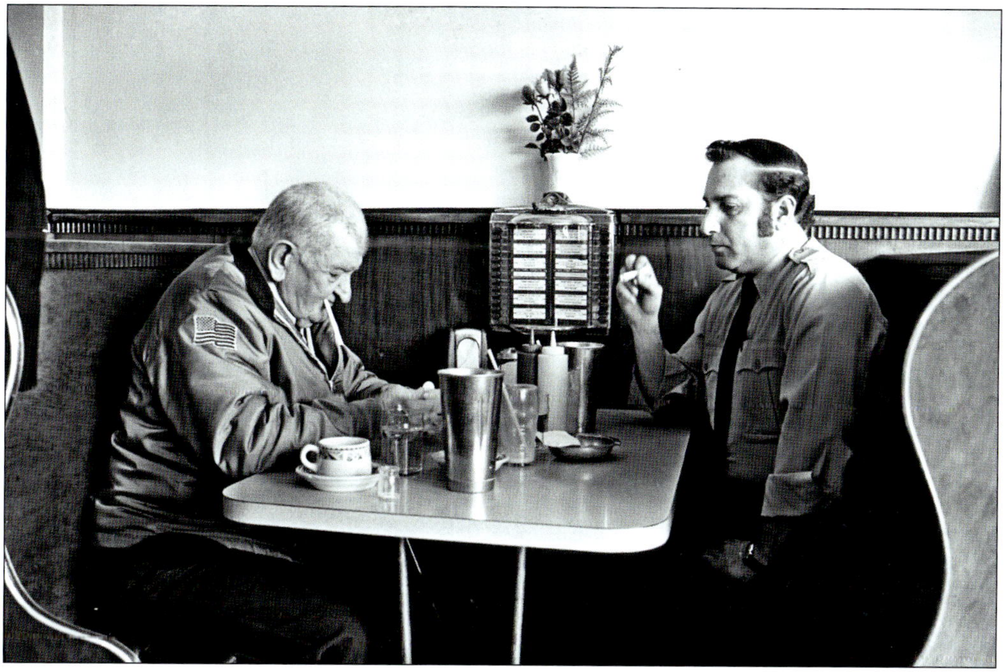

Men share a shake, a coffee, and a smoke in a booth with a jukebox. The jukebox gave six plays for a quarter. This scenario was prevalent at Lefty's Hamburgers and the Palace Restaurant, situated along Greenfield Road, and other eateries nearby. (Courtesy of the *Detroit Free Press*/ Zuma Press.)

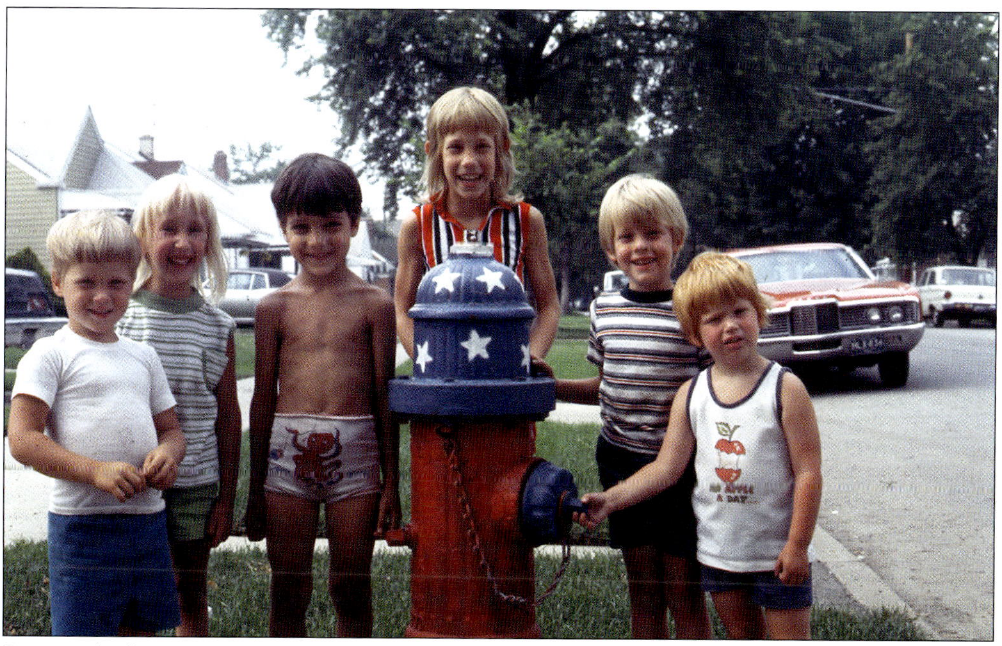

During the bicentennial year of 1976, cities in the Detroit area had fire hydrants painted red, white, and blue. There was a wave of patriotism and nostalgia that came over the nation following the end of the Vietnam War and Watergate. These children gathered around a colorful hydrant on their block.

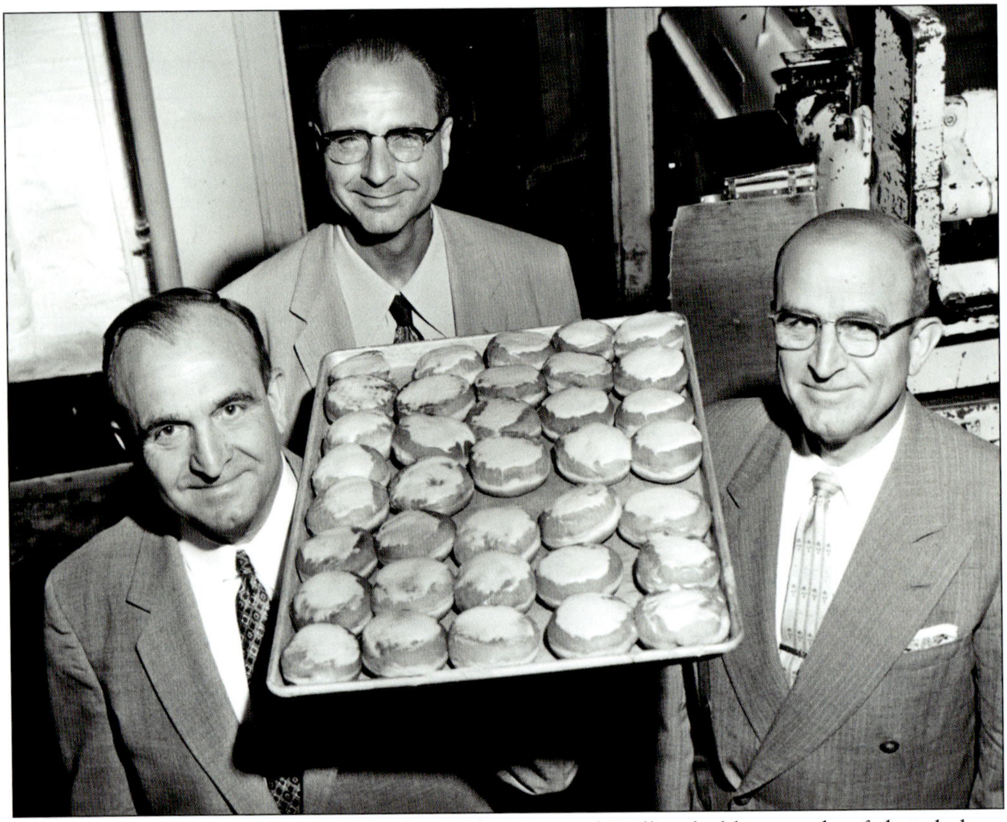

Awrey brothers (from left to right) Elton, Thomas, and Wilbur hold a sample of their bakery products in 1956. They were respectively the company's treasurer, president, and vice president. Awrey's had 120 Detroit supermarket service counters in the 1950s. When the company celebrated its 50th anniversary in 1960, it had 160 locations. (Courtesy of the *Detroit News*/Zuma Press.)

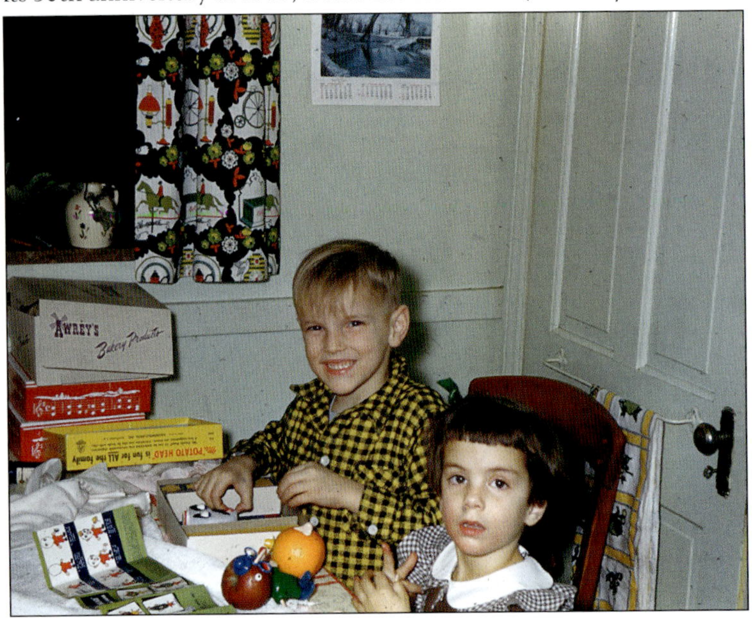

More than a few homes had Awrey bakery products in them. These children play with their Mr. Potato Heads with an Awrey's box nearby. The company also had a home delivery fleet of 110 independently owned and operated trucks. In 2018, it has an outlet store on Farmington Road in Livonia, Michigan.

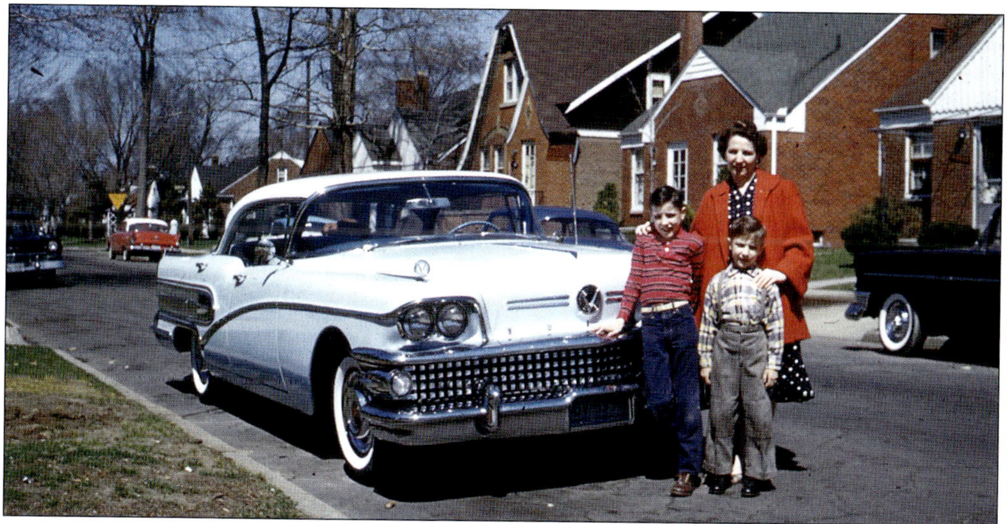

George (left) and Nicky Garis pose with their mom in front of the new family Buick. The family, with their father and sister, lived on Monte Vista Street for over 20 years. The surrounding homes and automobiles were typical of the Grand River and Greenfield neighborhood. Getting a new automobile every three years was typical for many families.

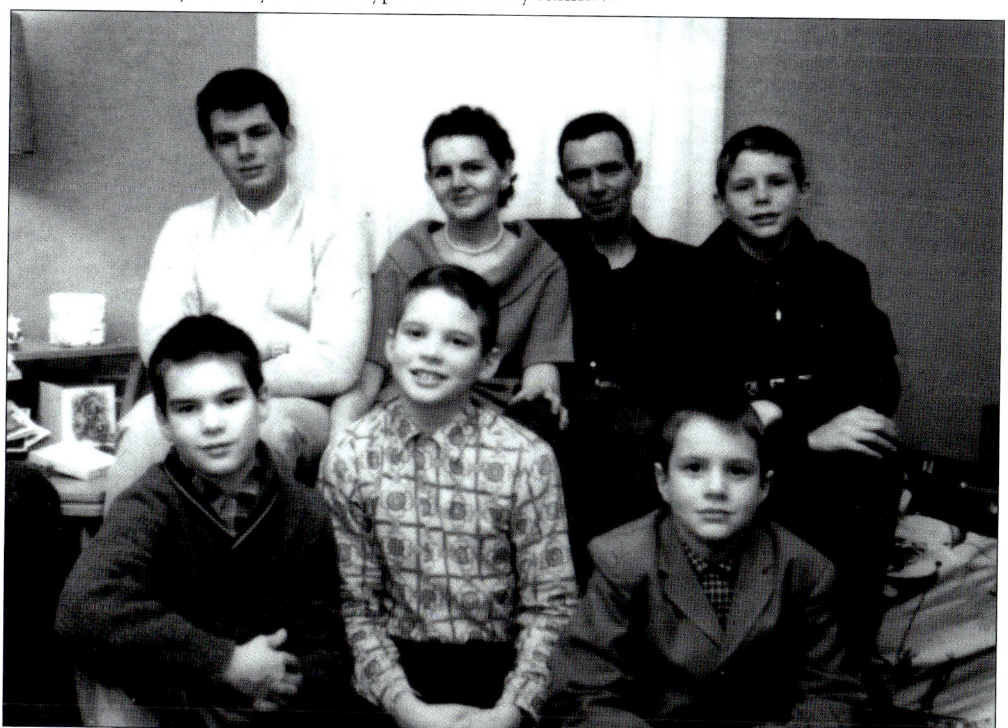

The Sloan family lived at 13526 Winthrop Street. From left to right are (first row) James, John, and Joseph; (second row) George, mother Shirley, Gerard Sr., and Gerard Jr. After Gerard Sr. died in 1964, Shirley went back to school and became a teacher to support the family. The Sloan household hosted many sporting events in the backyard (hockey, basketball, and swimming) as well as indoor activities like billiards, slot car racing, and pinochle games with a visiting priest from India, Father Richard Fernandez. (Courtesy of the Sloan family.)

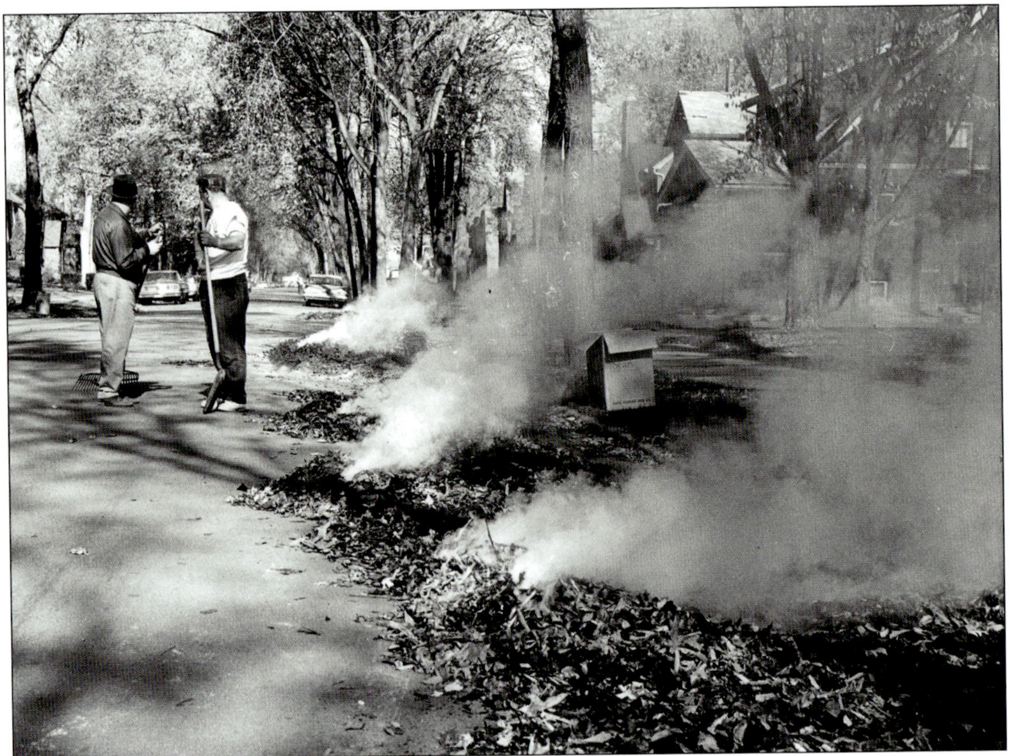

Burning leaves was an annual fall event in the Grand River and Greenfield neighborhood. Although the dangers of the practice (smelly clothes, lack of visibility for drivers, and air pollution) were known, a lack of funds prevented the Detroit Department of Public Works from collecting the leaves until 1969. Residents were then required to package their leaves in boxes or plastic bags. (Courtesy of the *Detroit Free Press*/Zuma Press.)

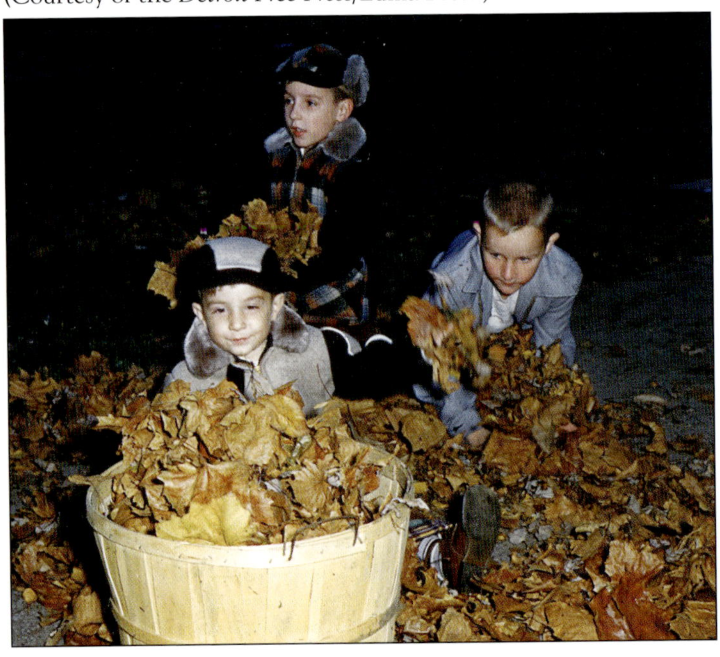

Kids on Monte Vista Street collect leaves to be burned curbside. Leaf burning had to be attended by an adult and was restricted from 11:00 a.m. to 6:00 p.m. by city ordinance. Because collecting leaves was estimated to cost an extra $600,000 a year, it was considered cost prohibitive. Proposals to collect leaves failed in 1952 and 1955; cancer and other health hazards finally forced the city to collect bundled leaves in 1969.

The Wrigley's supermarket at 14040 Greenfield Road was one of the main grocery stops in the neighborhood for years. It was later a Packers grocery store and Great Scott supermarket as the grocery wars heated up and mergers gobbled up competing stores. It is now a Food Giant. This photograph was taken from the McCauley backyard on Winthrop Street in 1963. (Courtesy of the McCauley family.)

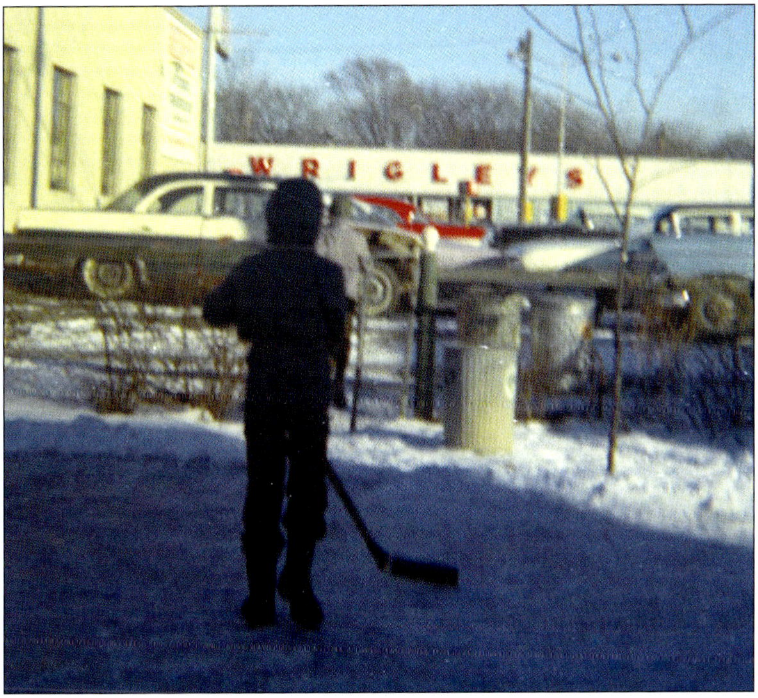

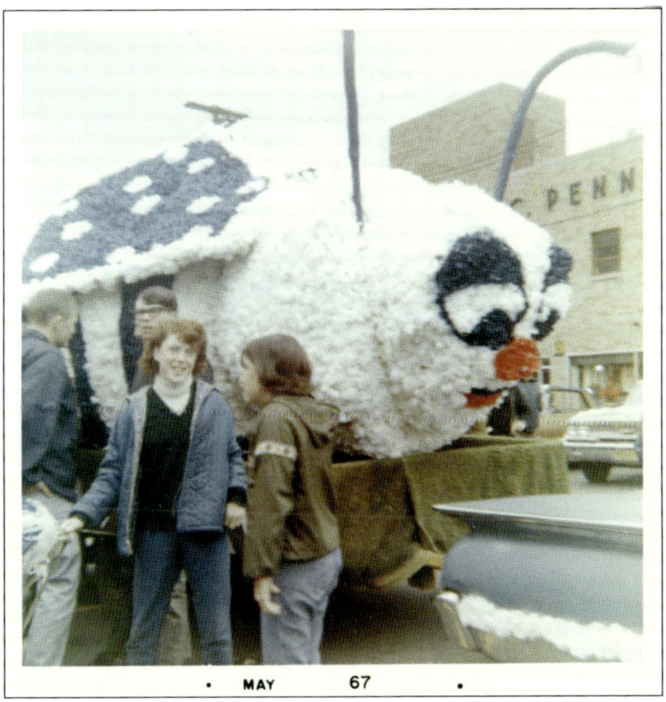

St. Mary's of Redford High School students gather around one of many floats being staged in the J.C. Penney parking lot behind 15240 Grand River Avenue. The store was one of four buildings erected in 1949 by architect Theodore Rogvoy. There were many J.C. Penney back-to-school parades along Grand River Avenue that culminated with a movie at the Great Lakes Theater nearby. (Courtesy of Marilyn Hardy Schewe.)

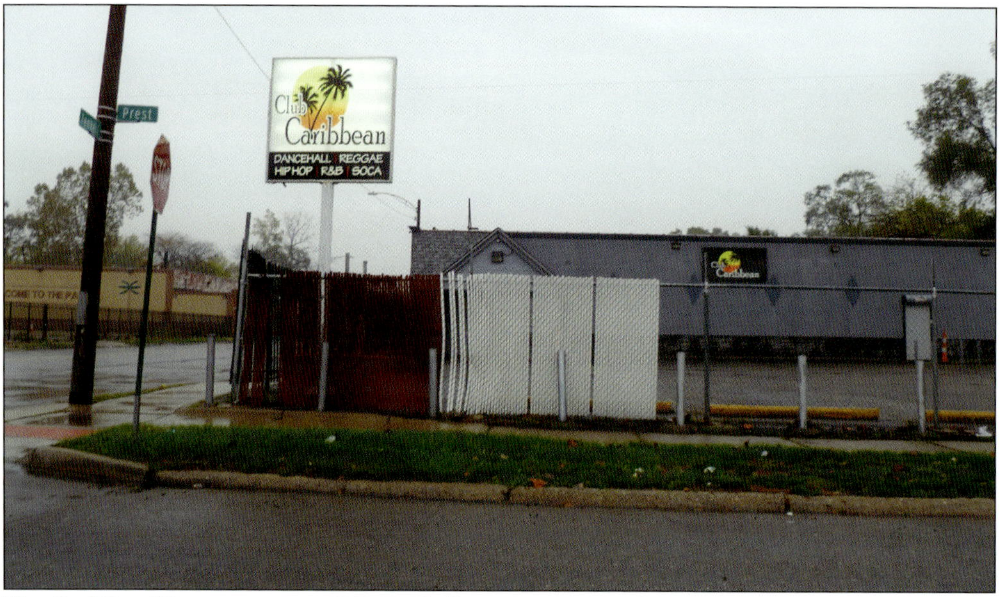

The Red Devil Restaurant, at 15337 Fenkell Avenue, was perhaps the most beloved dining spot in the Grand River and Greenfield neighborhood. The Red Devil (also known as La Diavola Roso) featured 20 kinds of pizza along with 20 kinds of spaghetti, 10 kinds of homemade ravioli, and 11 other Italian dishes. It also featured a full menu of American dishes. Families, groups, paperboys, and neighborhood takeout made this a go-to sensation. The old location is now Club Caribbean.

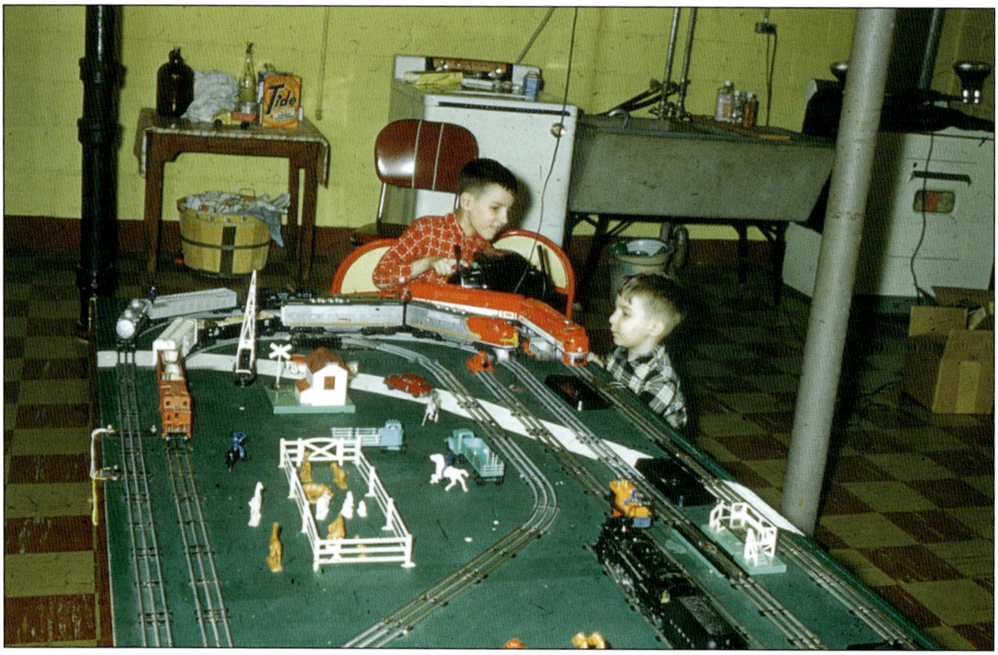

Brothers George (left) and Nicky Garis play with their model train set in their partially finished basement, typical in the 1950s and 1960s. Cement industrial tubs were quite common, along with washers and dryers plus the popular Tide nearby. The basement also functioned as an overflow dining area during large family holiday gatherings like Thanksgiving.

Six

Our Downtown and All Around

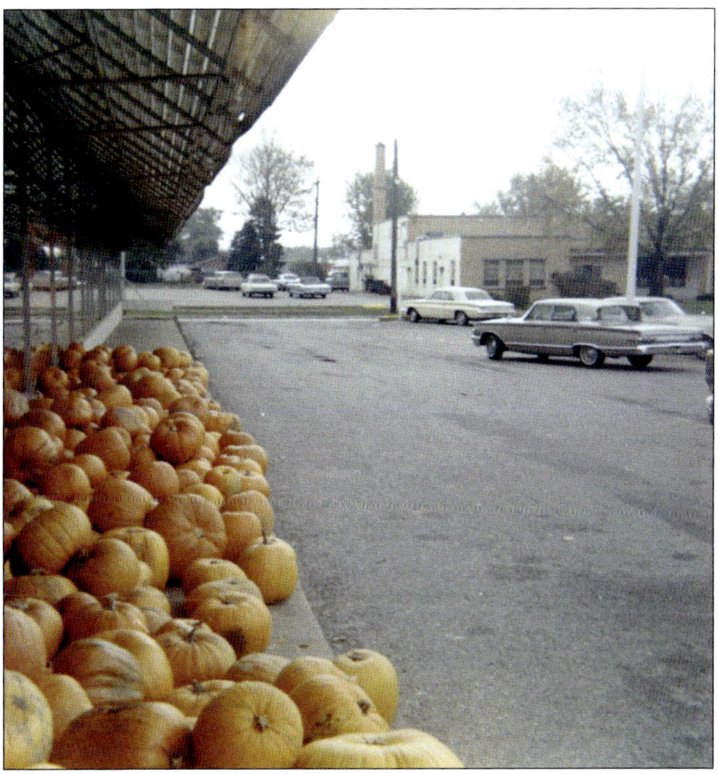

There were so many stores and businesses along both Grand River Avenue and Greenfield Road that it was almost impossible to keep track of them. Whatever services or household goods one needed, they were only a few blocks away. Parents often sent their kids out for smokes or maybe with a note to the meat market without any reservations. These stores were a favorite shopping destination for kids and adults. Wrigley's parking lot, at 14040 Greenfield Road facing the American Legion building, is shown here with Halloween pumpkins on sale.

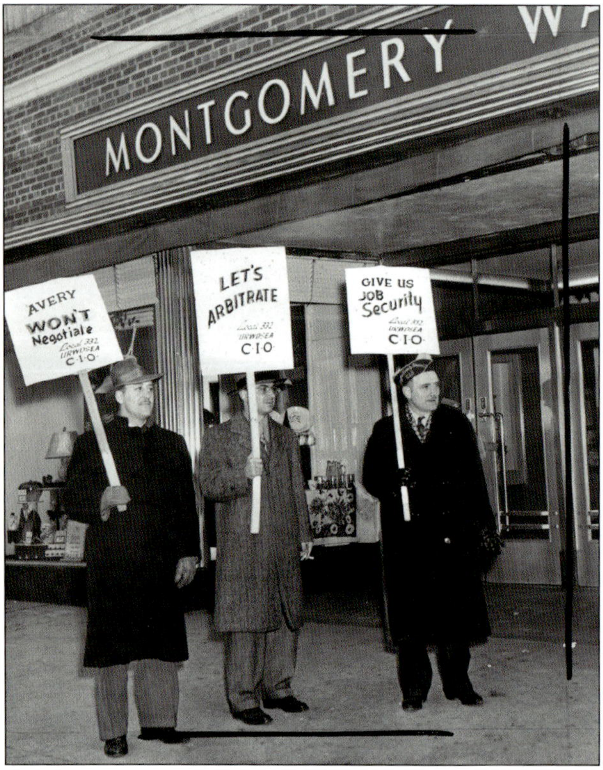

From left to right, union officials E.J. Bouche, David Chaney, and Sam Sage picket outside the Grand River and Greenfield Montgomery Ward store in a 1945 nationwide strike. Company president Sewell Avery refused to recognize the union in spite of an order by the War Labor Board. Pres. Franklin Roosevelt seized all of Montgomery Ward's property nationwide, citing his wartime powers under the Constitution as commander-in-chief. (Courtesy of the *Detroit Free Press*/Zuma Press.)

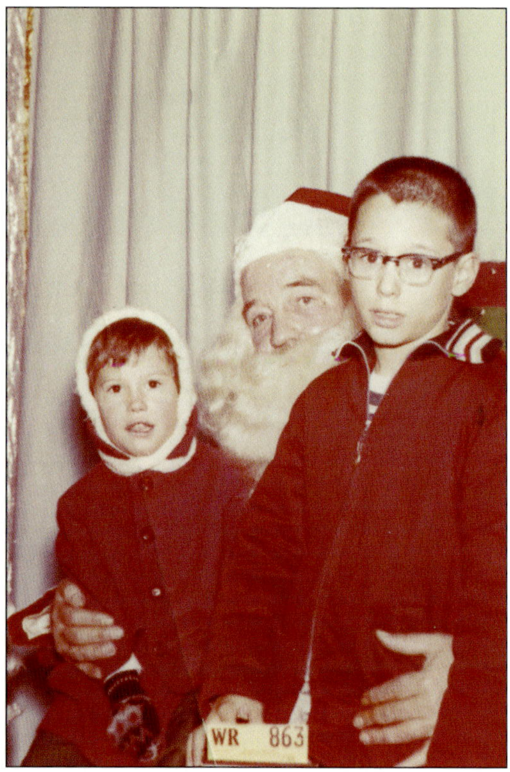

Montgomery Ward was a full-service department store. Besides a shoe repair store, there were also an eyeglass department, candy counter, men's and women's clothing, appliance department, and Santa Claus at Christmas time. Cooking classes and a Wendy Ward's Charm School also made it a special destination. Mary McCauley and her brother Joe get ready to give Santa their lists in 1959.

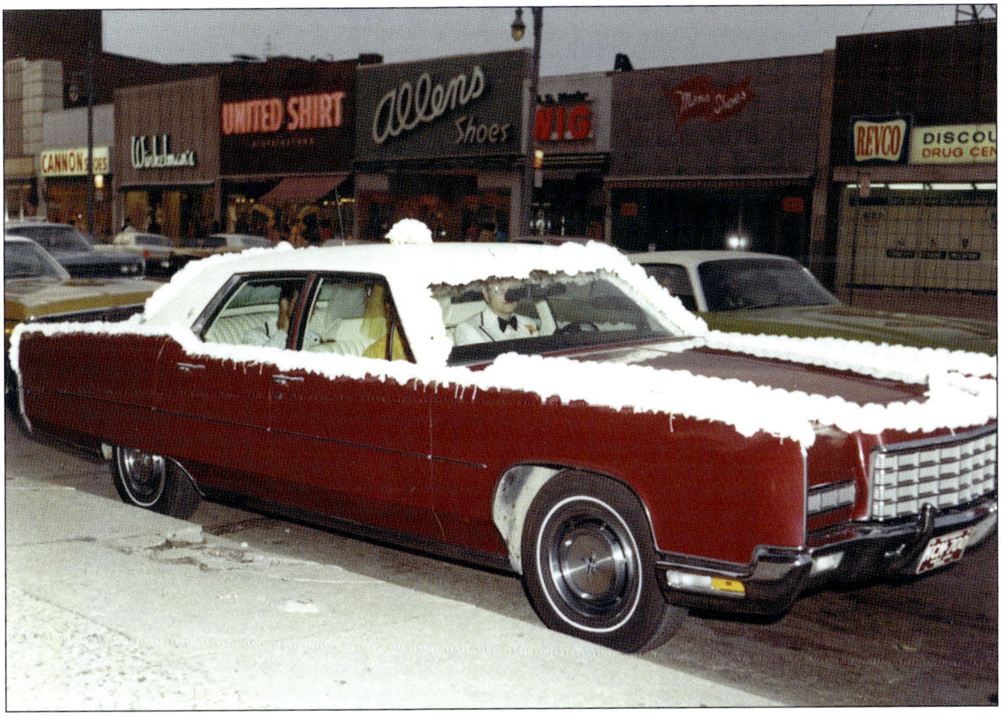

The red car is part of the Christine Tishler Davis wedding party and is parked in front of Holy Cross Lutheran Church on Grand River Avenue south of Greenfield Road in 1972. Across the street are Cannon Shoes, Winkelman's, United Shirt Distributors, Allen's Shoes, a wig store, a shoe store, and Revco drugstore. Just west of these were the Kresge and Ward's stores. (Courtesy of Christine Tishler Davis.)

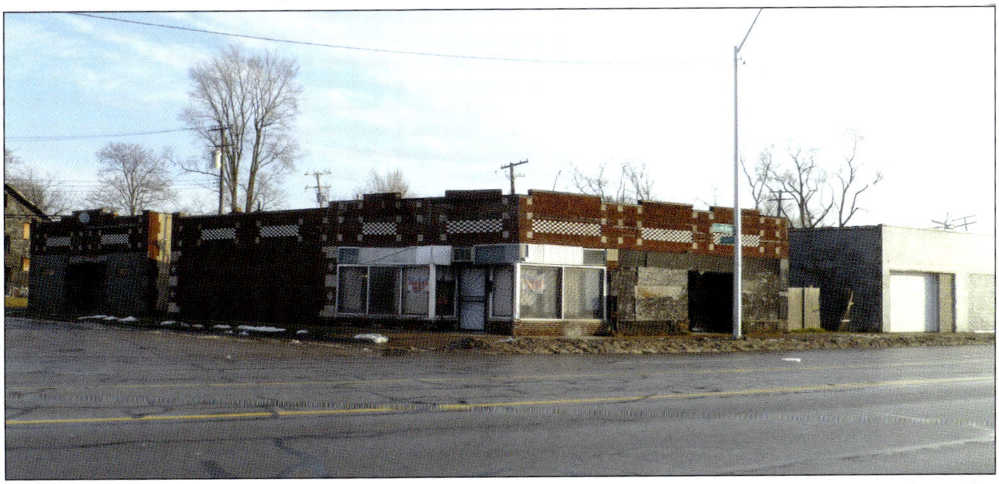

The Blue Dot Barber Shop, at 15040 Grand River Avenue, was owned by Mike Licata's father, who learned to barber in Sicily and went to school to learn English so he could get his barber license in Detroit after he moved here in the late 1930s. After getting married and moving into a house on Marlowe Street, Mike's dad bought the Blue Dot Barber Shop plus the remaining buildings on the block in the early 1940s. He walked about three miles to work each day because he did not own an automobile. He sold the barbershop a few years after the 1967 riots and worked at two other shops until he retired. The barbershop is still in operation.

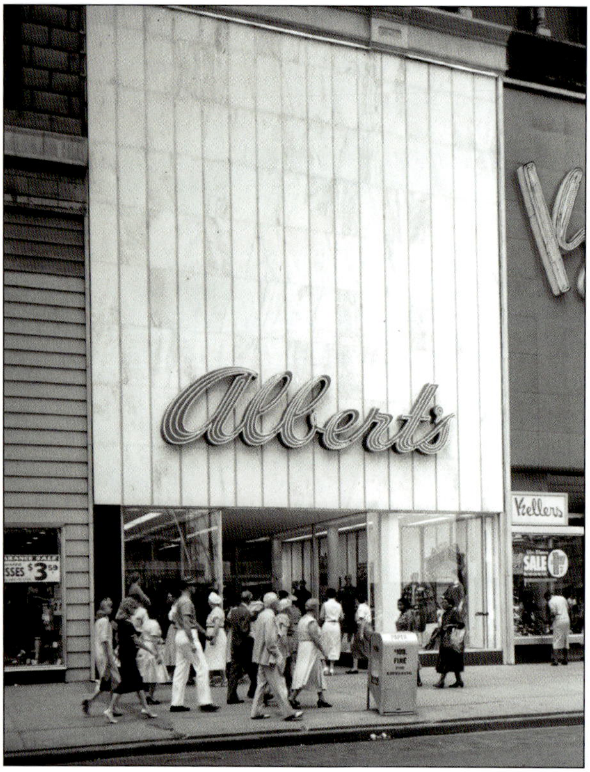

Albert's, a fast-growing women's specialty dress store, opened its 11th store at 15550 Grand River Avenue on Thursday, March 3, 1960, next to the F.W. Woolworth store on the northwest corner of Grand River Avenue and Greenfield Road. The store featured striped marble outside and pink and gold inside. The Albert's tower above the store replaced the Howard's Clothing sign. (Courtesy of the *Detroit Free Press*/Zuma Press.)

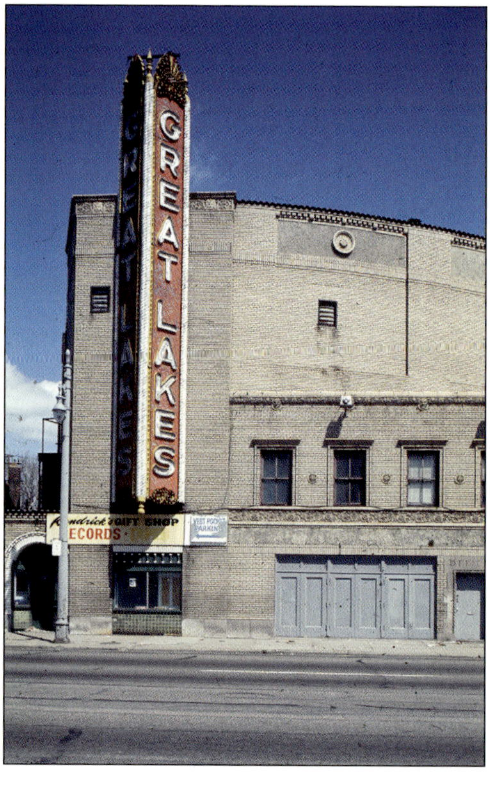

Great Lakes Theater and Vest Pocket Theater were located at 14830 Grand River Avenue. The Great Lakes Theater was designed by George Mason, opened in 1927, and seated over 1,795. It hosted live stage shows and movies for the first few years and then movies until 1969, when it became the Vest Pocket Theater. The plays *The Boys in the Band* and *Hair* were the most successful runs at the Vest Pocket from 1969 to 1972, when it closed. A church occupied the building for a number of years before it was vacated and fell into disrepair. It was torn down in 1999.

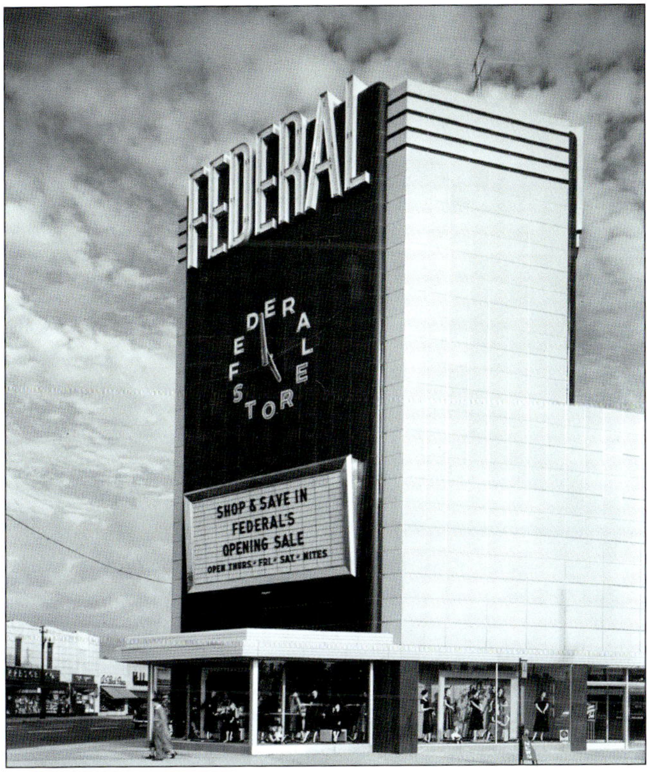

Charles Agree was the architect for the Federal department store that opened in 1949 at 15401 Grand River Avenue. The Detroit-based store was built over the former St. Mary's Cemetery, which was closed in 1926. Federal served a blue-collar segment of the population as a kind of down-scale Sears. In 1961, Federal bought out Sam's Cut Rate stores and began expanding into other Michigan cities. (Courtesy of the Detroit Public Library, Burton Collection.)

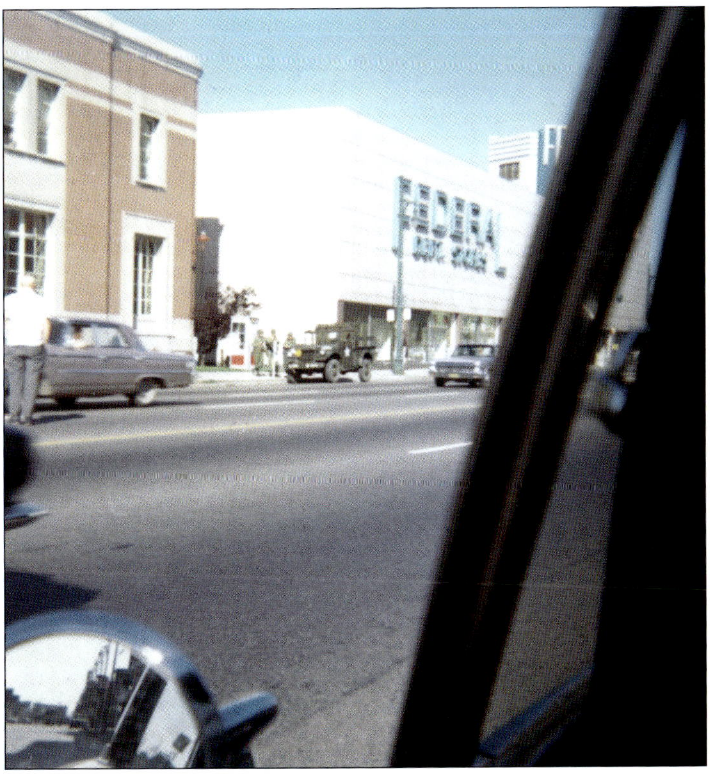

Pictured in 1967 as the Detroit riots were subsiding, this Federal store was part of a reorganization plan while the company closed other stores. A National Guard jeep is stationed by the store a few days after the worst of the riot. By 1977, Federal was a takeover target of Steven West, who had purchased the Robert Hall clothing stores. Several fires broke out at various stores, and West was a suspect. In 1980, after the chain of 54 stores was reduced to two, Federal was sold to Kingsway Stores.

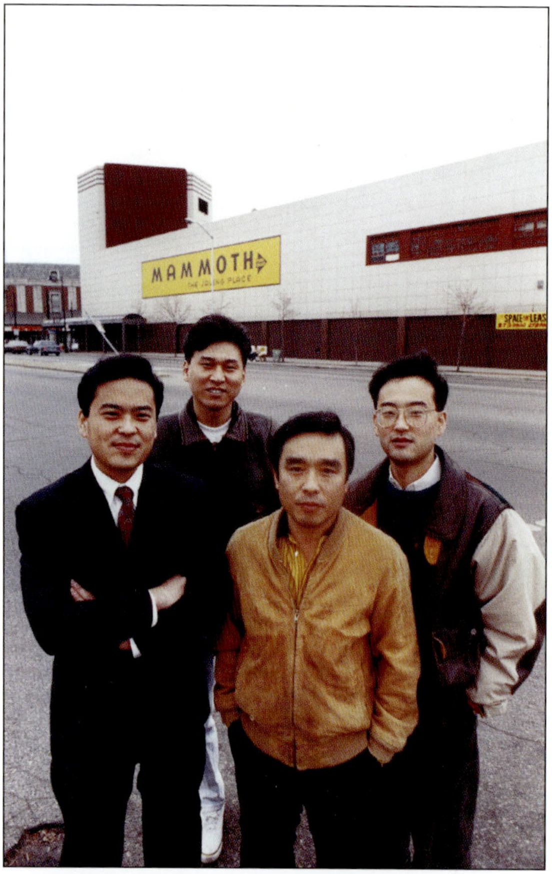

From left to right, partners Daniel Rim, Young Kim, Tong Yoo, and Ray Rim stand beside their Mammoth shopping center on the southeast corner of Grand River Avenue and Greenfield Road. Mammoth sat on the former site of the Kingsway and Federal department stores. In November 1990, it showcased goods from 100 merchants. (Courtesy of the *Detroit News*/Zuma Press.)

This building, at 15270 Grand River Avenue, originally housed the H.L. Green variety store in 1949. Three other stores along this block were built and designed by Theodore Rogvoy: Mary Jane Shoe Company, York Stores Inc., and J.C. Penney filled in the block between Whitcomb and Sussex Streets along Grand River Avenue. Crowley, Milner, and Company bought out H.L. Green in March 1959. This was Crowley's second store outside of downtown Detroit, and it had 45,000 square feet of shopping space on two floors. Despite good sales, this store closed in 1987 after a dispute with the landlord. Foot Locker now occupies the building.

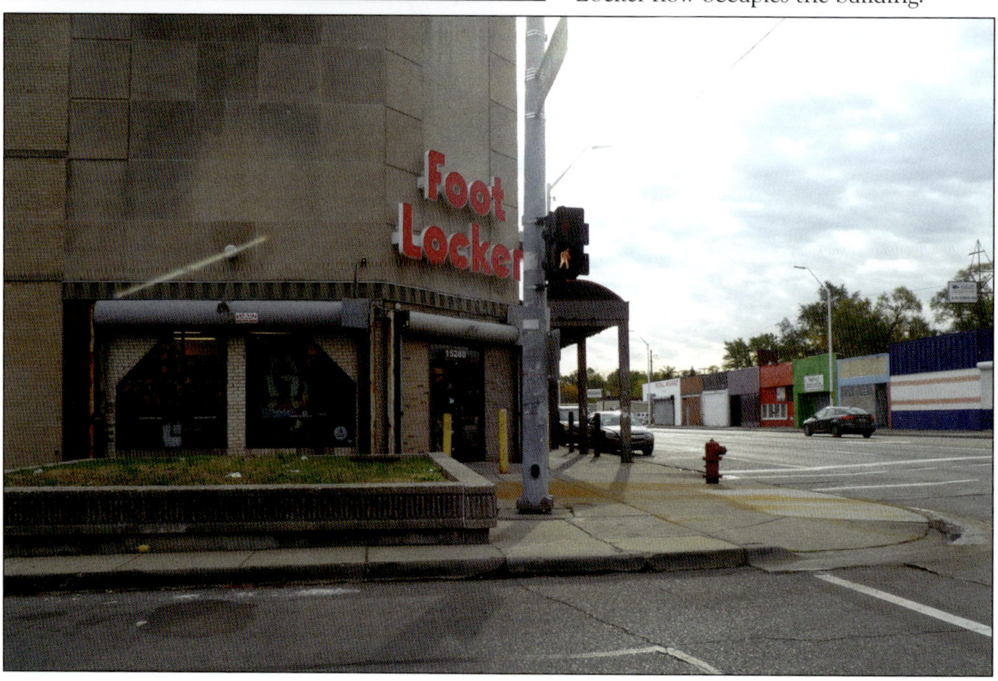

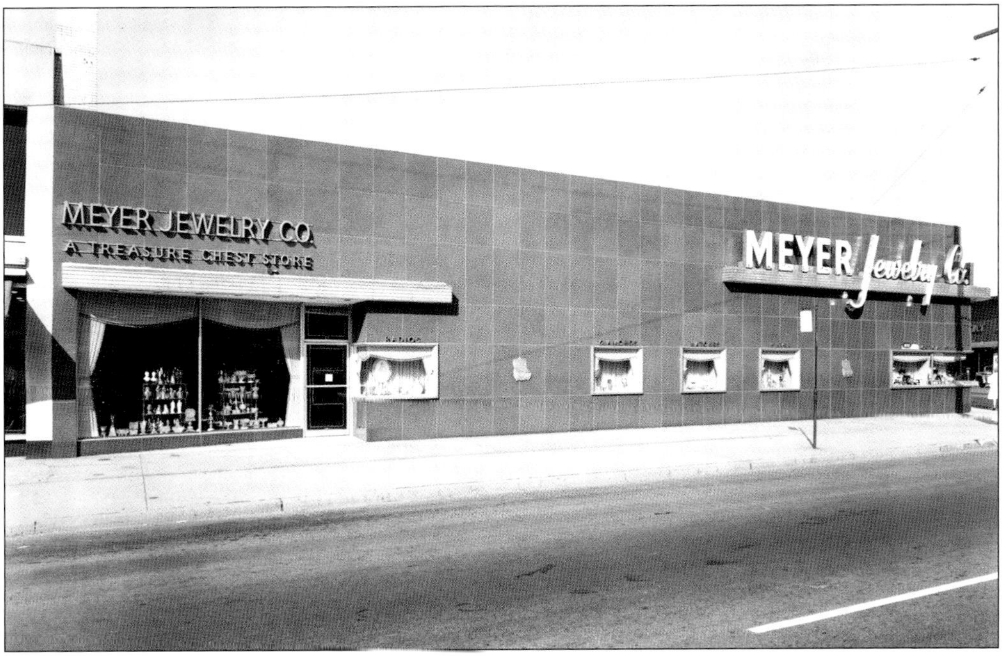

Meyer Jewelry Company opened its fifth store at 15501 Grand River Avenue on Thursday, October 11, 1951. The building was designed by Detroit architect Charles Agree and was of glass and pearl-like granite, with a large glass entrance. The store opening featured a display of the famous Treasure Chest collection of jeweled museum pieces. (Courtesy of the Detroit Historical Society.)

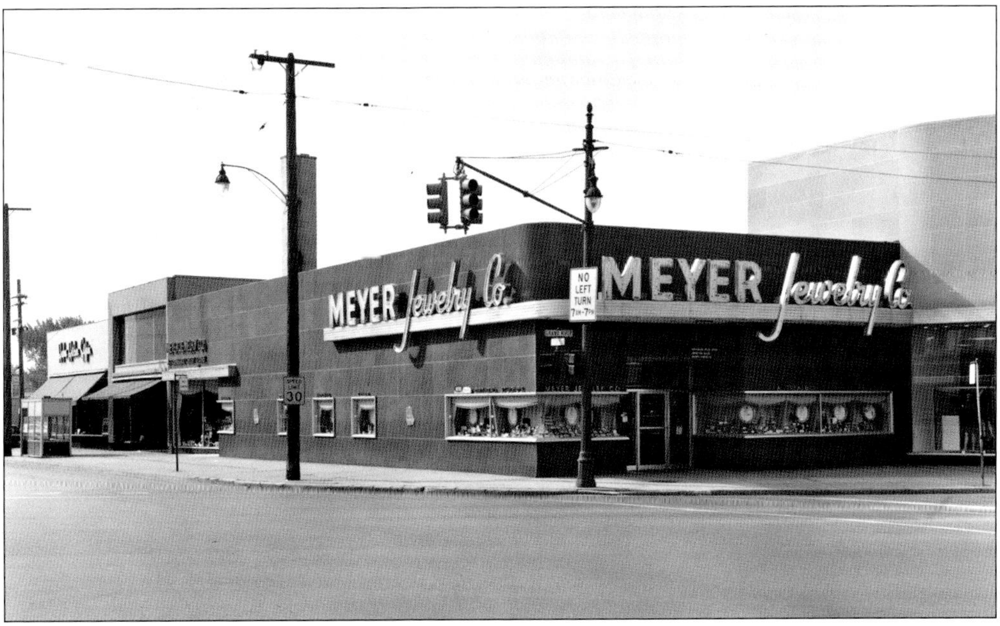

Three Detroit and Michigan beauty queens, Miss Michigan 1951 Delores Berruez, Detroit's 250th Anniversary Empress Pauline Yvonne Gugelky, and a Miss Detroit Street and Railways October helped open one of the nation's largest neighborhood jewelry stores. This 1961 photograph shows the L-shaped Hughes Hatcher Suffrin men's clothing store at the right and left; it surrounded the Meyer jewelry store on the corner. (Courtesy of the Detroit Historical Society.)

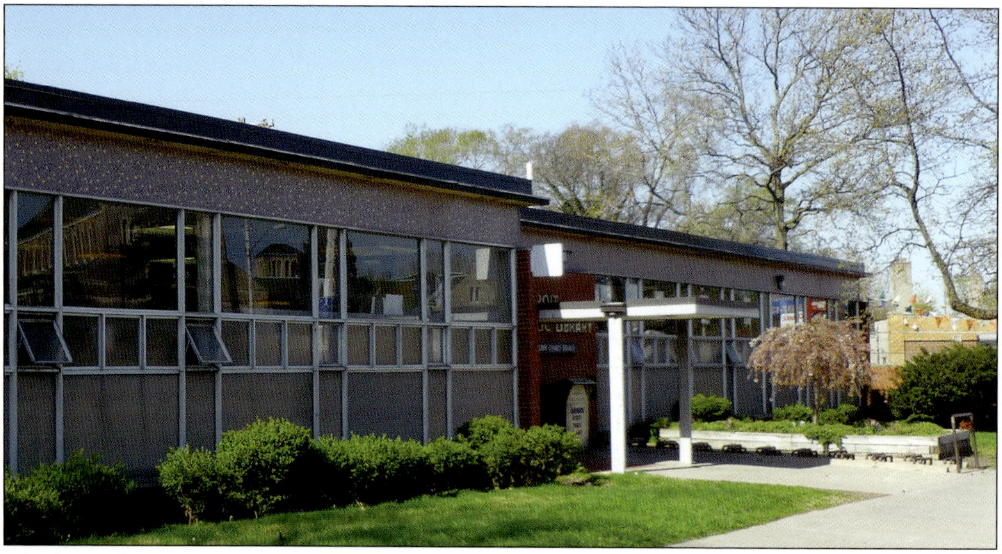

The Henry Chaney branch of the Detroit Public Library at 16101 Grand River Avenue opened in 1955 and was designed by Louis Redstone with McKinstrie Construction Company as the general contractor. The library served 50,000 people and had 30,000 adult and juvenile books. The building is set back 10 feet from the street for noise protection and landscaping. The acoustical tile and sound-absorbing ceiling serves as a sound buffer between the children and adult sections.

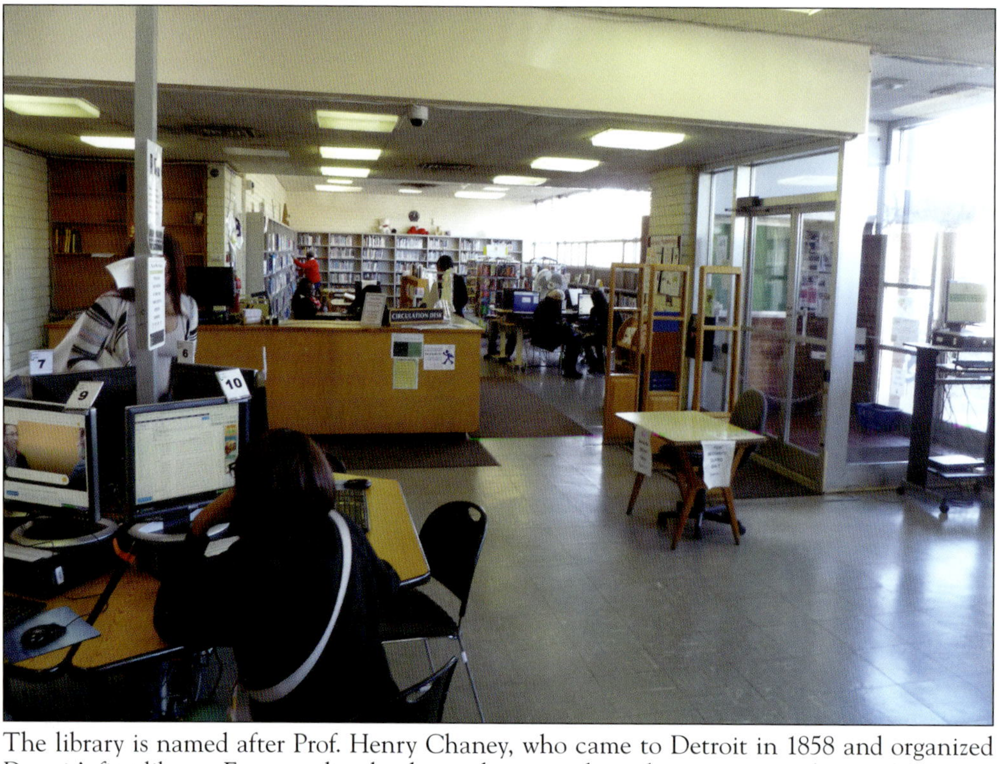

The library is named after Prof. Henry Chaney, who came to Detroit in 1858 and organized Detroit's first library. Free-standing bookcases have see-through sections to enhance the feeling of openness. The juvenile section still looks much like it did in the 1950s. The water fountain was famous for having the coldest water in the neighborhood during the summer.

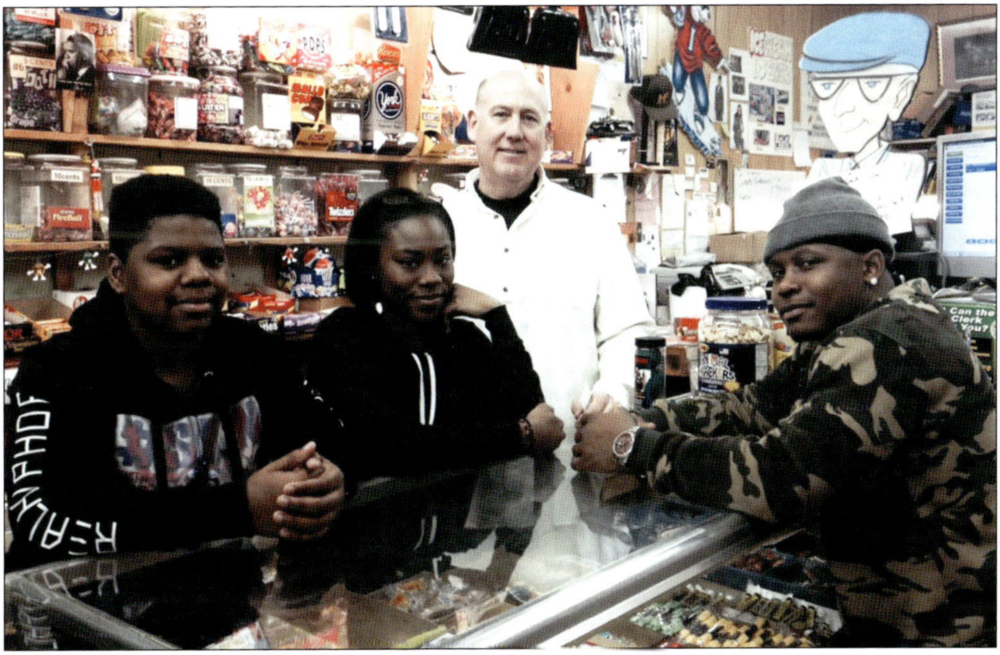

Starting in 1928, Leddy Brothers made and sold chocolates out of their store on West Grand Boulevard. By 1945, Leo Leddy had done well, gotten married, and had nine children. He moved his store to 15928 Grand River Avenue, near the Grand Way Lounge and Bowling Alley, and the business is still distributing candy, snacks, and beverages over 89 years later. Current owner James Nall (rear) poses with employees (from left to right) Camreon, Rhondee, and Jasper.

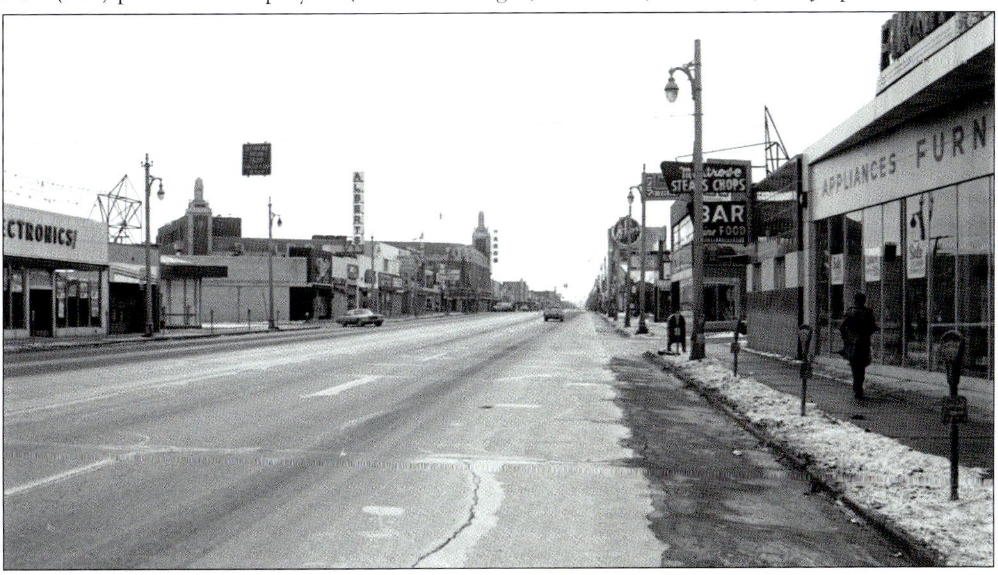

Looking east on Grand River Avenue by Montrose Street, Raimi Furniture and Appliance is on the right at 15725 Grand River Avenue. The owner was the father of Sam Raimi, Hollywood director. The Raimi store was built in 1949 with Louis Redstone as the architect. Olson Electronics is to the left, with the tower of Albert's women's clothing store on the left near the Sander's candy store, on the corner of Winthrop Street. Montrose bar is seen to the right, with the Elias Big Boy restaurant just beyond, close to Greenfield Road. (Courtesy of Wayne State University, Reuther Library.)

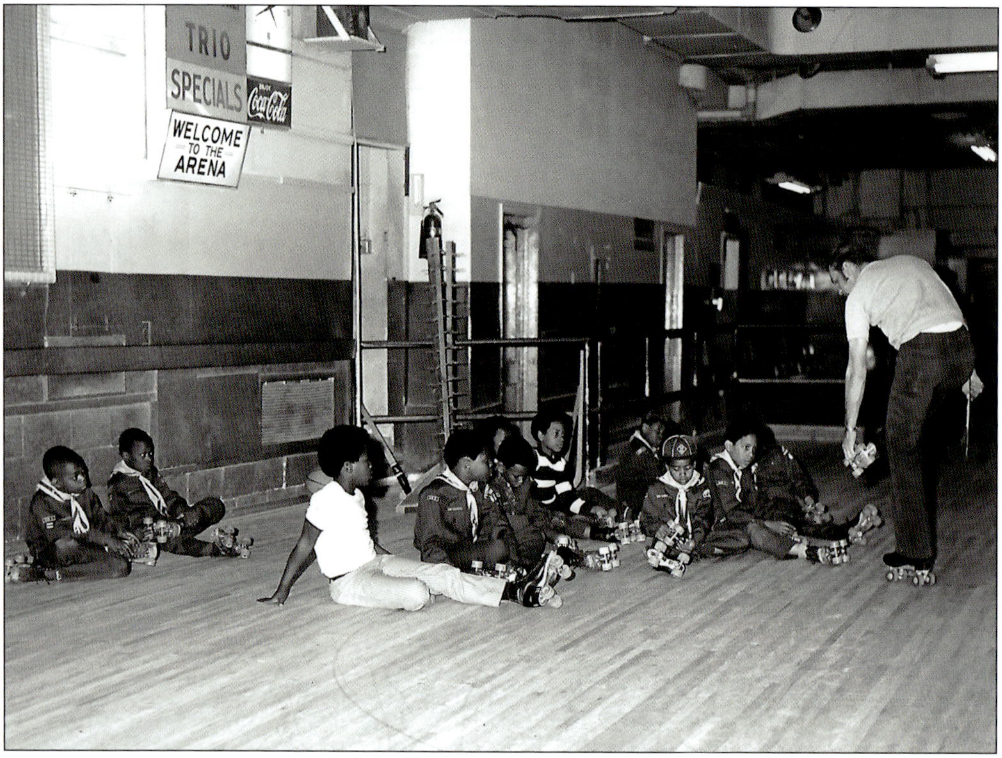

Arena Skate Club was a converted Big Bear grocery store at 14527 Greenfield Road when it first opened in 1961. All seven James children worked at the rink as teachers, coaches, and ticket takers, behind the soda fountain, in the coat room, and in the skate rental room. The club burned to the ground on July 16, 1971. The Arena hosted dances and was home to Explorer Post 650. Stanley Wallace "Wally" James was about to get full ownership of the club on its 10th anniversary when it burned down. An arson investigation was inconclusive. Lou Parker is seen here teaching a Cub Scout class. (Courtesy of Kathlyn Snow.)

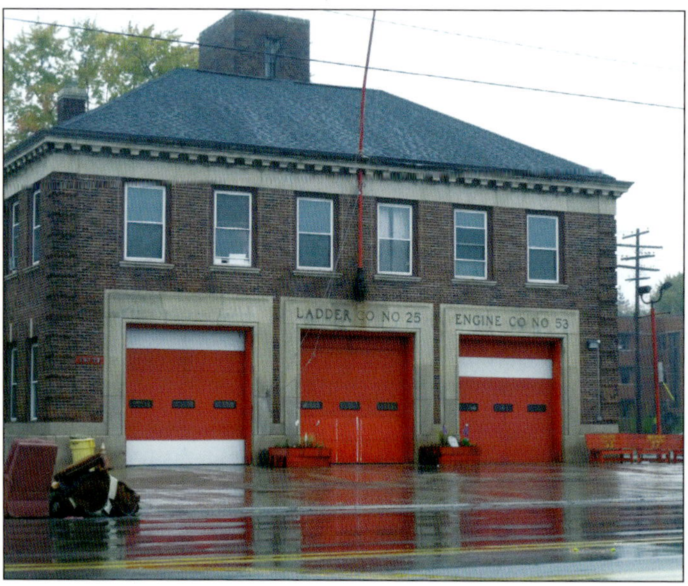

Ladder Company No. 25–Engine Company No. 53, at 15121 Greenfield Road, was opened on September 25, 1926, at a cost of $68,272.05. Hans Gehrke was the architect, and the contractor was Max Bartholomaie and Sons. Besides fighting fires during the 1967 riot, one of its biggest fires was the Banner Lumberyard fire at 12844 Greenfield Road in 1955, which drew over 10,000 spectators. Howard Hoban Sr. was a neighborhood fireman at the station.

Seven

Cause for Celebration

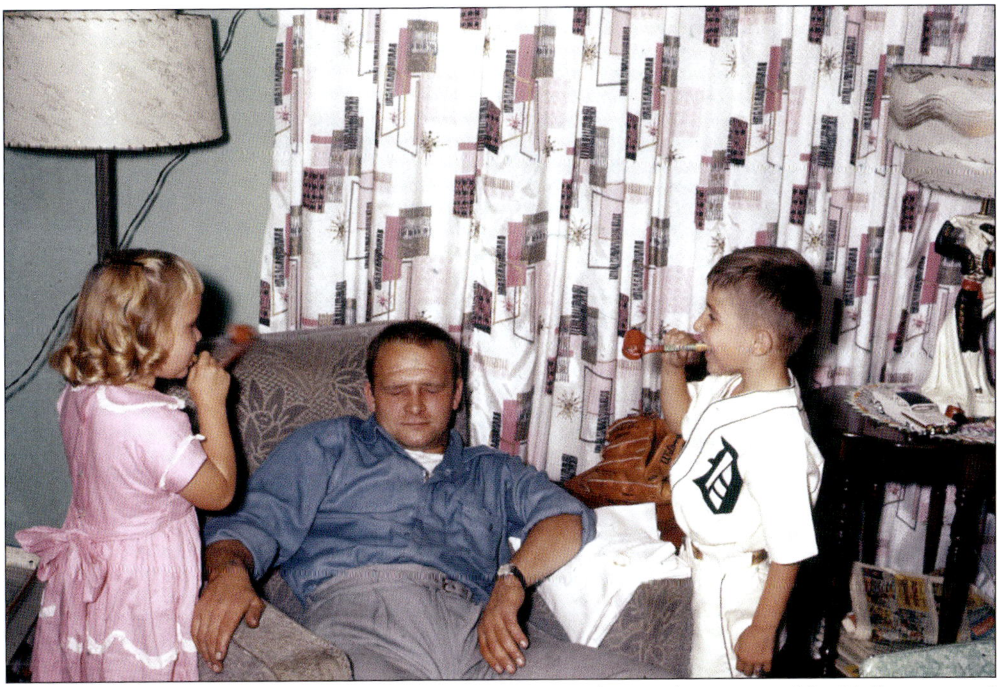

Religious holidays, government holidays, New Year's, and special occasions like Halloween and Thanksgiving brought out the best in most families. Parades, like the J.C. Penney back-to-school parade along Grand River Avenue, were very popular. The American Legion Hall on Greenfield Road always seemed to have something going on, from bingo to wedding receptions to dances. These children apparently do not appreciate that loud noises are not always welcome on New Year's Day.

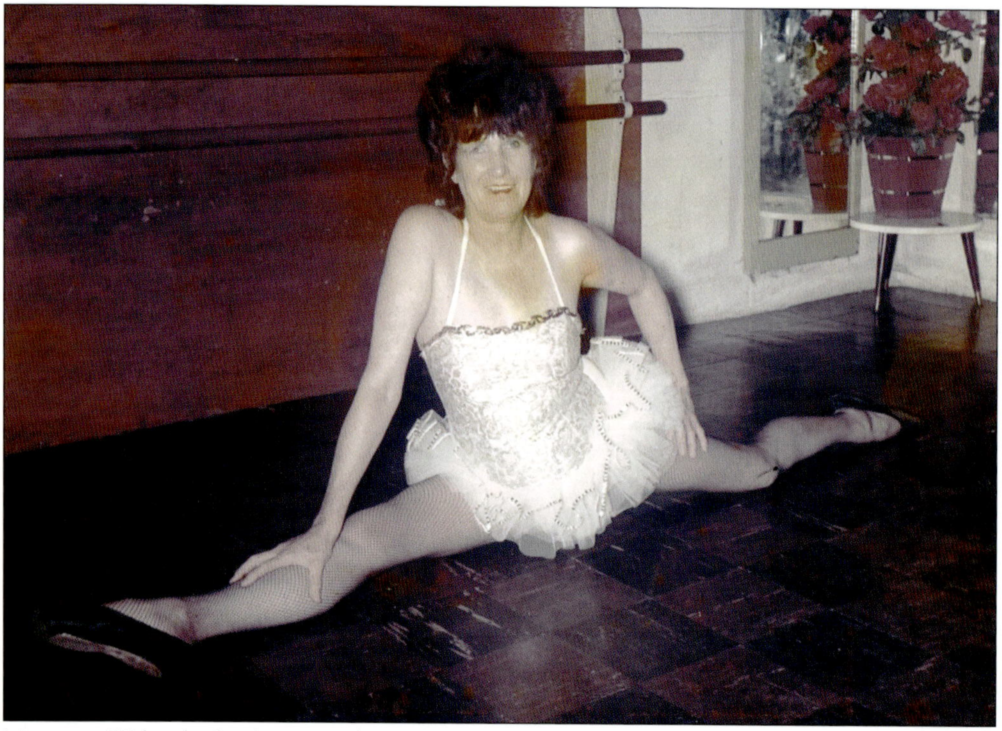

Margaret Weber had a dance studio in her basement at 13954 Forrer Street. This well-known local dance teacher taught ballet, toe, tap, and acrobatics classes from 1946 through the 1970s. Weber is shown practicing what she preached by doing the splits. (Courtesy of Kathrine Weber Wolfe Videcoq.)

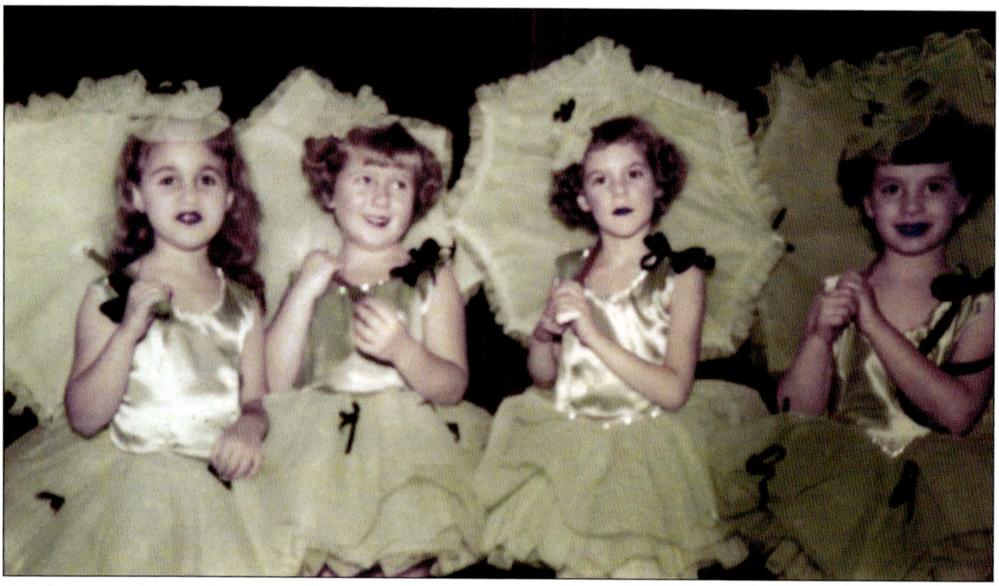

Students at the Weber Dance Studio pose during a recital. There were often dance recitals at the Monaghan Knights of Columbus on Leisure Road. Marilyn Hardy Schewe, far left, is shown with three of her ballerina friends. Many women still talk online about their experiences as girls at Weber's dance classes. (Courtesy of Marilyn Hardy Schewe.)

Homemade backyard ice rinks in the Grand River and Greenfield area were the craze in the 1960s. Long periods of cold weather made them easy to maintain. Girls practiced figure skating, and boys played hockey when they could get enough players with sticks and skates. This was before local communities started building rinks. Michael Koch practices his slap shot in the McCauleys' backyard rink.

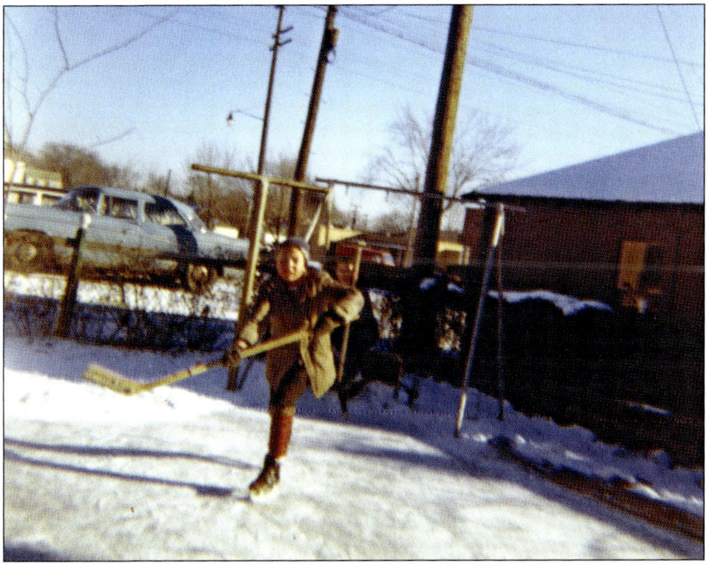

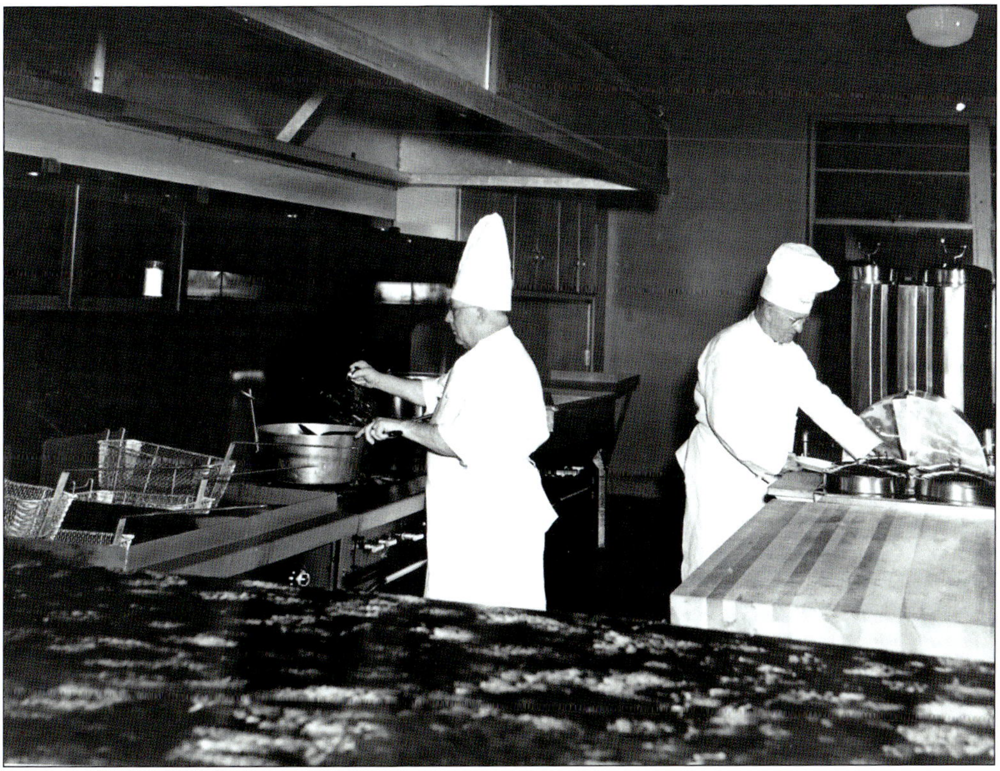

Cooks Louie Dimambro (left) and Herb Mitchell are hard at work in the kitchen of the Monaghan Council of the Knights of Columbus building, at 13530 Leisure Road near Grand River Avenue and Schaefer Road. This Catholic fraternal benefits organization was founded on June 9, 1928. Monaghan served up food for fish fries and wedding receptions, and members could stop in for a game of pool or a cold beverage. Teen dances, dance recitals, and boxing lessons also took place there. The Monaghan Knights of Columbus relocated to Farmington Road in Livonia. (Courtesy of Marianne Dimambro Mitchell.)

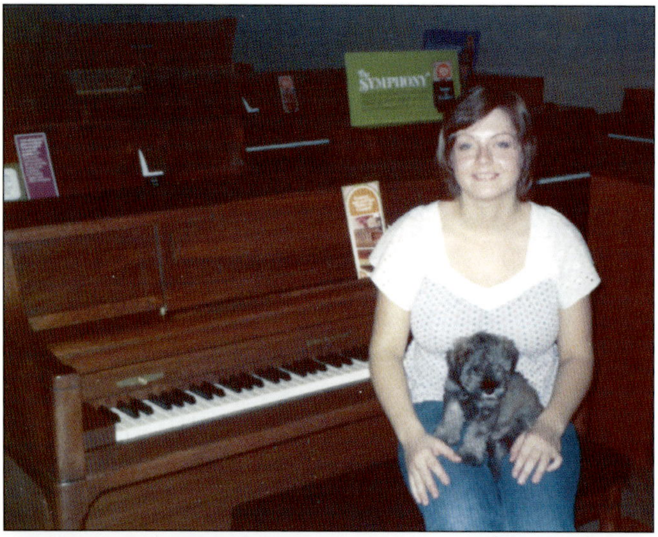

Joanne Marie Rumford took piano lessons at Grand River Piano Company at 14820 Grand River Avenue. Pictured with her miniature schnauzer Jason in 1973, she remembers the store owners Stan, Gene, and Ted Starck. She took lessons on the second floor, where a window overlooked the alleyway by the Great Lakes Theater next door. The Junior Achievement building and Ted's Confectionery were just east on Grand River. (Courtesy of Joanne Marie Rumford.)

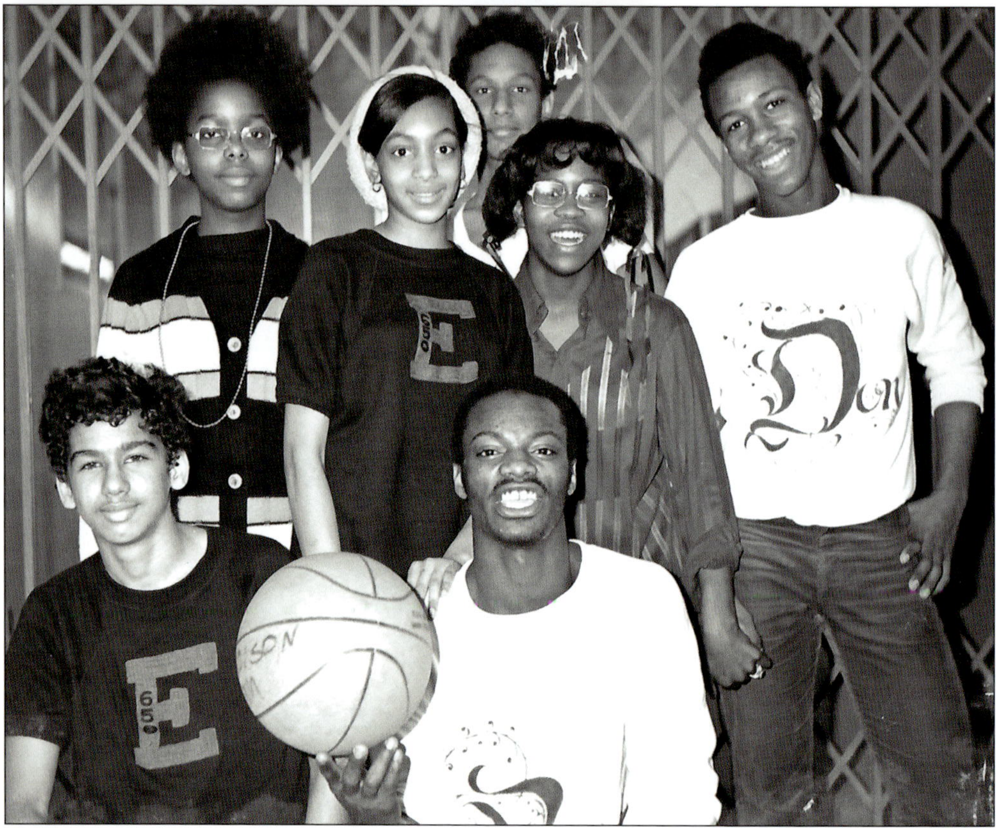

The winning team in the 1970 Greenfield district basketball tournament was from Explorer Post 650, which met in the Arena Skate Club at Greenfield Road and Lyndon Street. From left to right are (first row) Eric Babcock, president of Post 650, and Bishop Lewis, first vice president; (second row) Junetta Wynn, second vice president Joan Lewis, Priscilla Walker, and Explorer Donald Heywood; (third row) Ronald Johnson. The Arena also hosted dances as well as regular roller skating. (Courtesy of Kathryn Snow.)

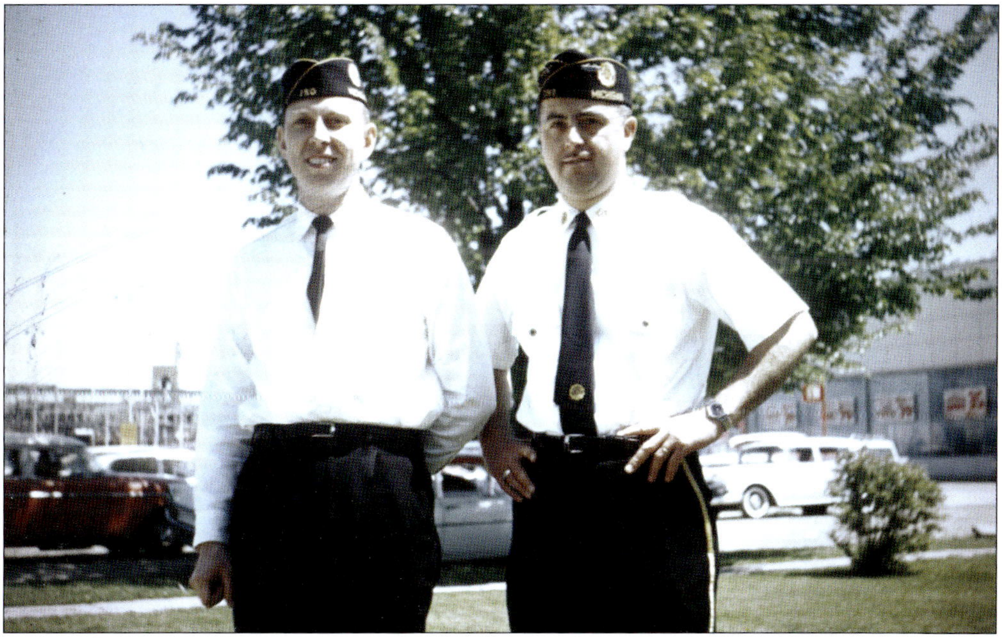

Harry Allen (left) and an unidentified man pose on the American Legion Post 190 front lawn at 13980 Greenfield Road. The Wrigley's supermarket can be seen in the background. The American Legion was a neighborhood hot spot for everything from Memorial Day celebrations to parades, bingo, teen dance parties, political meetings, and wedding receptions. Allen supervised many Legion activities at the hall. Sons of the American Legion meetings were held every Monday night. (Courtesy of Sam Allen.)

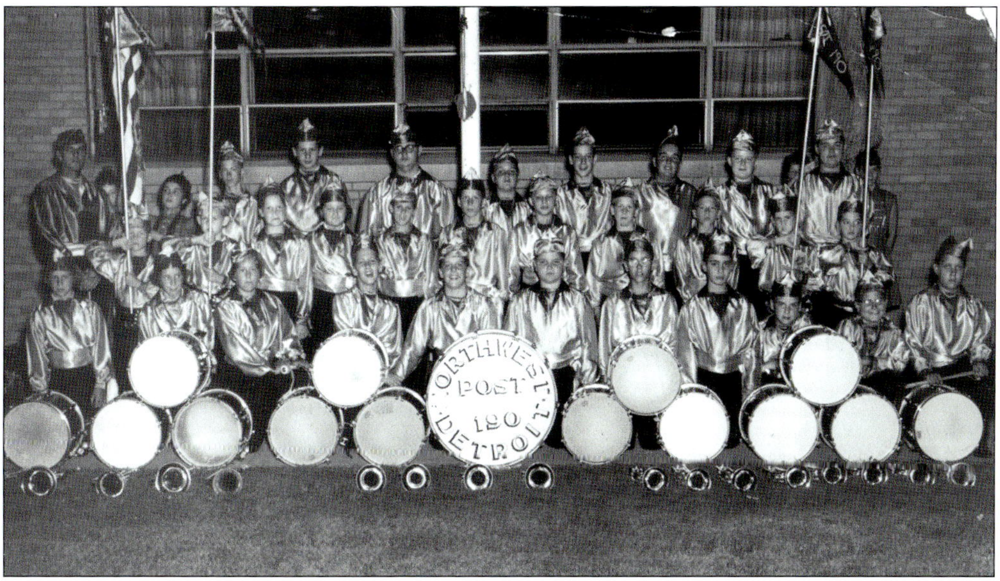

Harry Allen's children (not pictured), Claudia, Jim, Nancy, Sue, and Sam, were part of the American Legion Post 190 band and helped out at a variety of Legion functions. The band played at many Legion activities and at various parades over the years. The post held an annual Christmas party with a movie and a visit from Santa. Hot dogs and soda pop were shared during summer events there. (Courtesy of Sam Allen.)

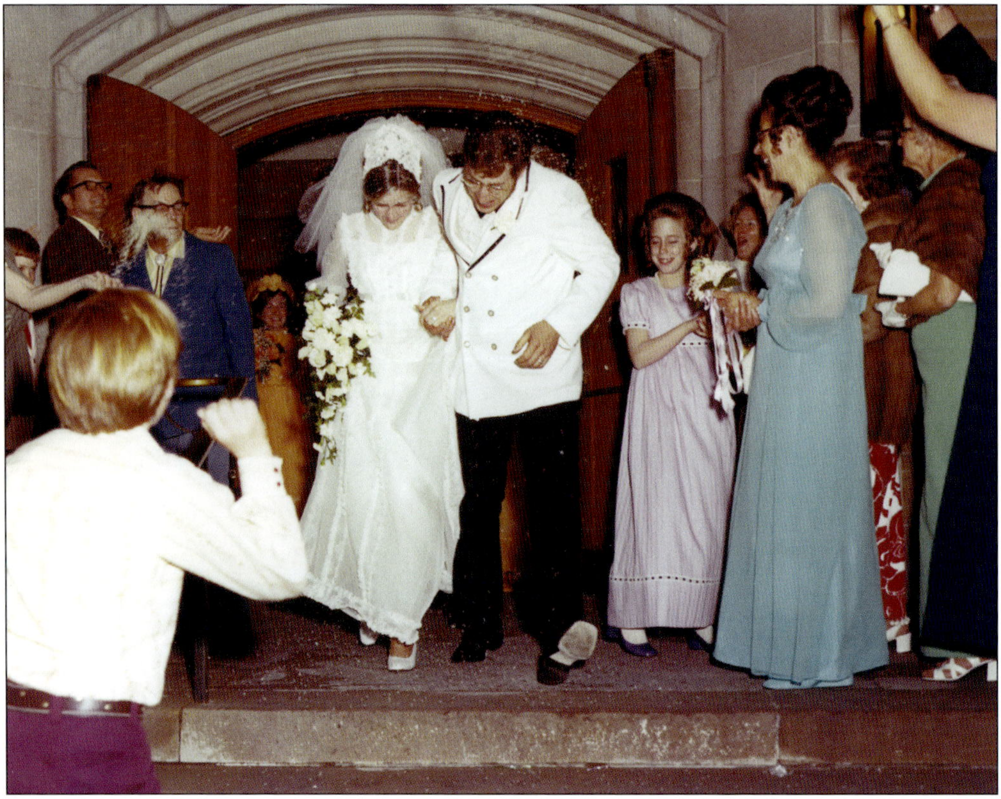

Former student at the Holy Cross grade school and new bride Christine Tishler Davis is showered with rice as she leaves the Holy Cross Lutheran Church at Grand River Avenue and Whitcomb Street on May 6, 1972. Christine and her husband, Larry, live in Grosse Ile, Michigan, and have been married for 46 years. (Courtesy of Christine Tishler Davis.)

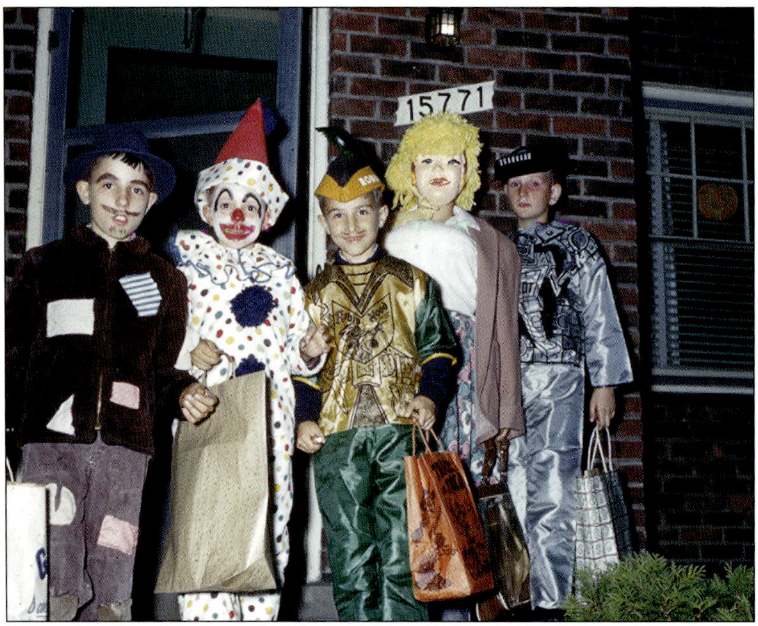

"Help the Poor" was a unique local saying as popular as "trick or treat" on Monte Vista Street in the Grand River and Greenfield neighborhood. Kids often crossed smog-filled streets because of leaf burning still going on in the late 1950s and 1960s. More children were unattended and on their own on Halloween night than now.

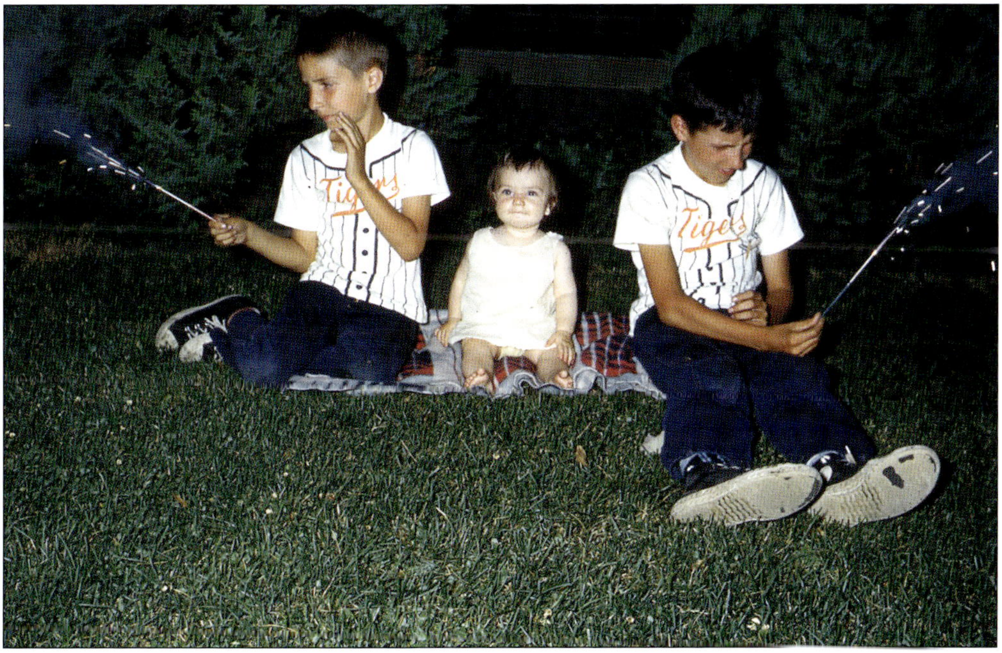

Sparklers were very popular for children during Fourth of July celebrations in the 1950s and 1960s. Of course, some kids got burned when they put their fingers on the hot wires. One child's uncle on Winthrop Street showed others the dangers of fireworks when he displayed his hand with three missing fingers. He claimed he had mishandled fireworks and it had cost him those three fingers.

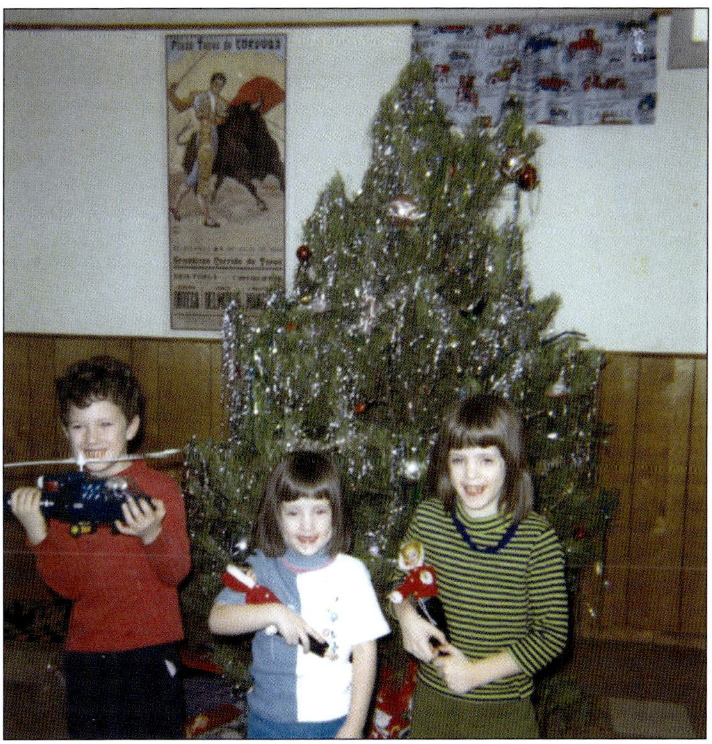

From left to right, Andy McCauley, Karin Blakely, and Linda Blakely show off their favorite Christmas toys in 1963. The Blakely-Wells family lived on Winthrop Street a few houses from Acacia Avenue, which was one block from the Grand River and Greenfield shopping district. Christmas shopping was easy with so many stores within walking distance.

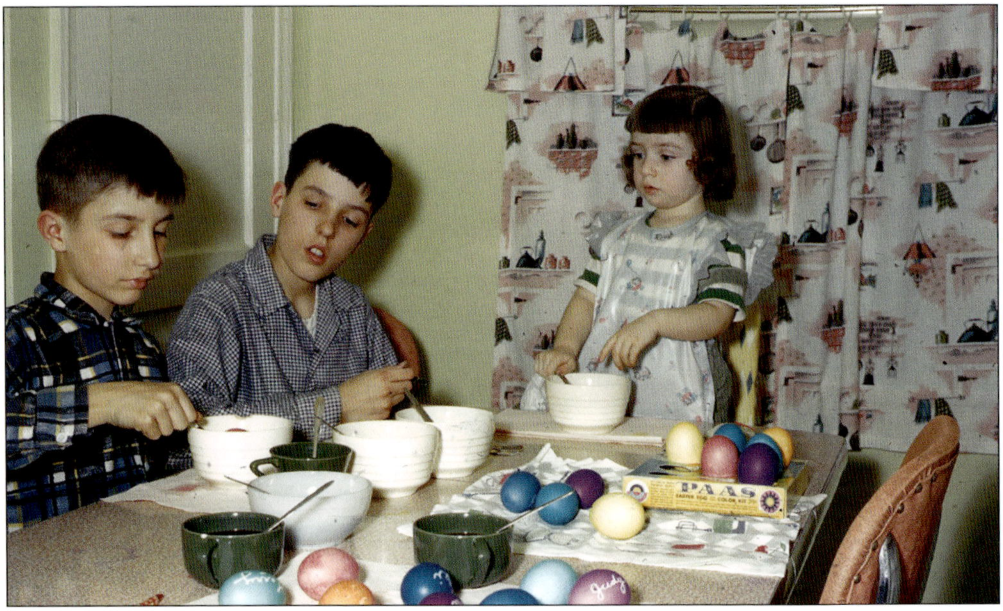

Coloring Easter eggs was a popular family activity. Kids could get different colors and personalize their eggs. Paas Easter egg dye was invented by William Townley, an owner of a Newark, New Jersey, drugstore, in 1893. Townley figured out how to concentrate dye in tablet form and created the modern Easter egg color kit. These Monte Vista Street kids are figuring out how to get the best designs on their eggs.

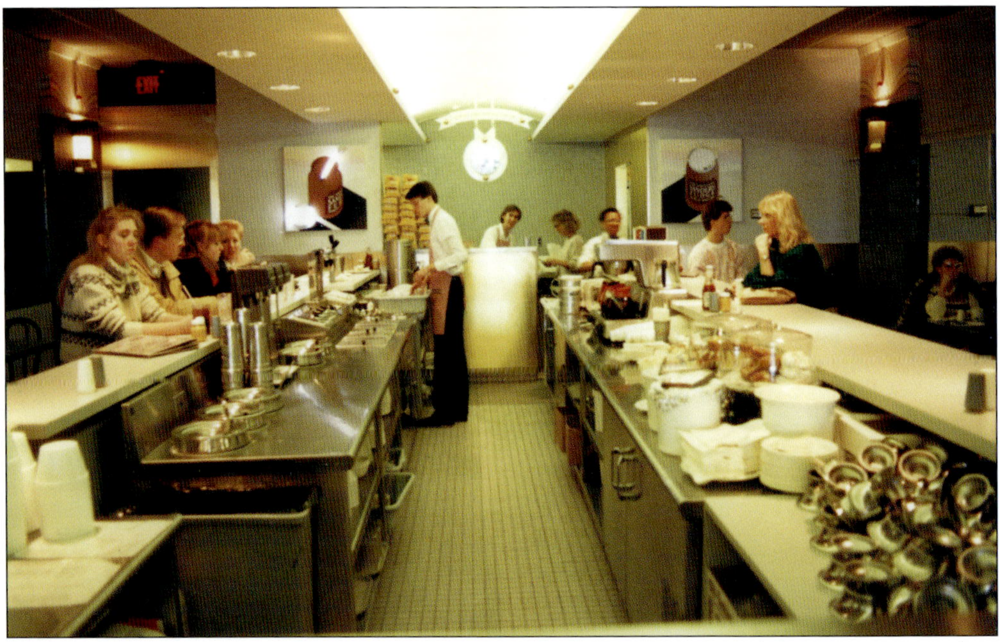

The Sanders store, at 15570 Grand River Avenue on the corner at Winthrop Street, opened on Wednesday, October 5, 1949. The Fred Sanders Company store offered breakfast, lunch, and dinner one block from the Montgomery Ward's and the new Federal store. The store featured Sanders candy, baked goods, ice cream, fountain luncheons, party services, and parcel post. The lunch counter in the back was always a busy area.

Eight

Favorite Sons and Daughters

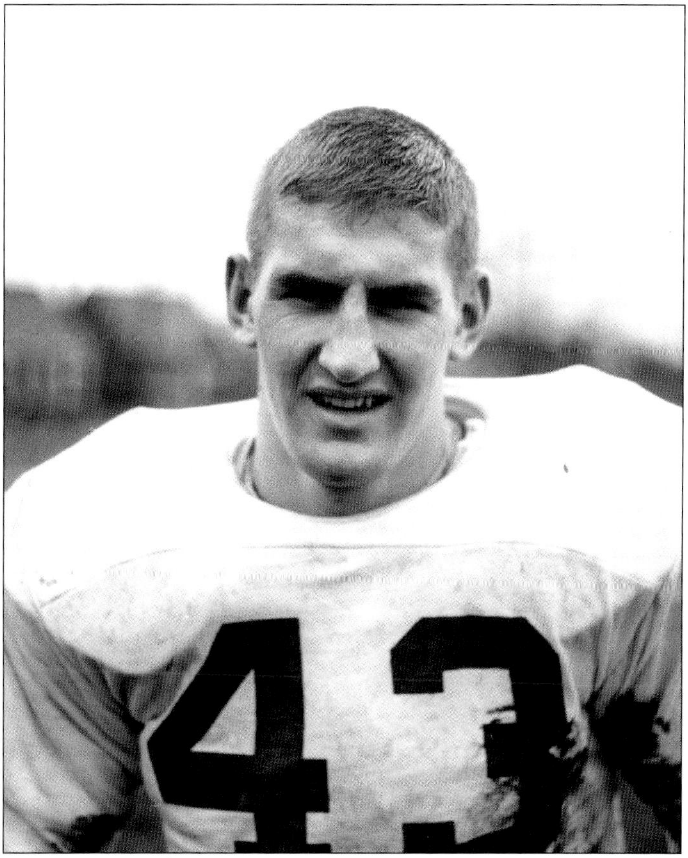

Doug Roberts (pictured) and his brother, Gordie, both played in the National Hockey League and grew up on Forrer Street. Doug played on the Cooley High School football team. Other famous locals include labor leader James Hoffa Jr.; stage and movie star Brian Mallon; beauty queen Amina Fakir; Mike Ilitch, owner of Little Caesar's Pizza, the Detroit Tigers, and the Detroit Red Wings; and actress Annette Sinclair. Many other personalities made appearances in the Grand River and Greenfield neighborhood, including Stevie Wonder, Gordie Howe, and former governor G. Mennen Williams. (Courtesy of the *Detroit News*/Zuma Press.)

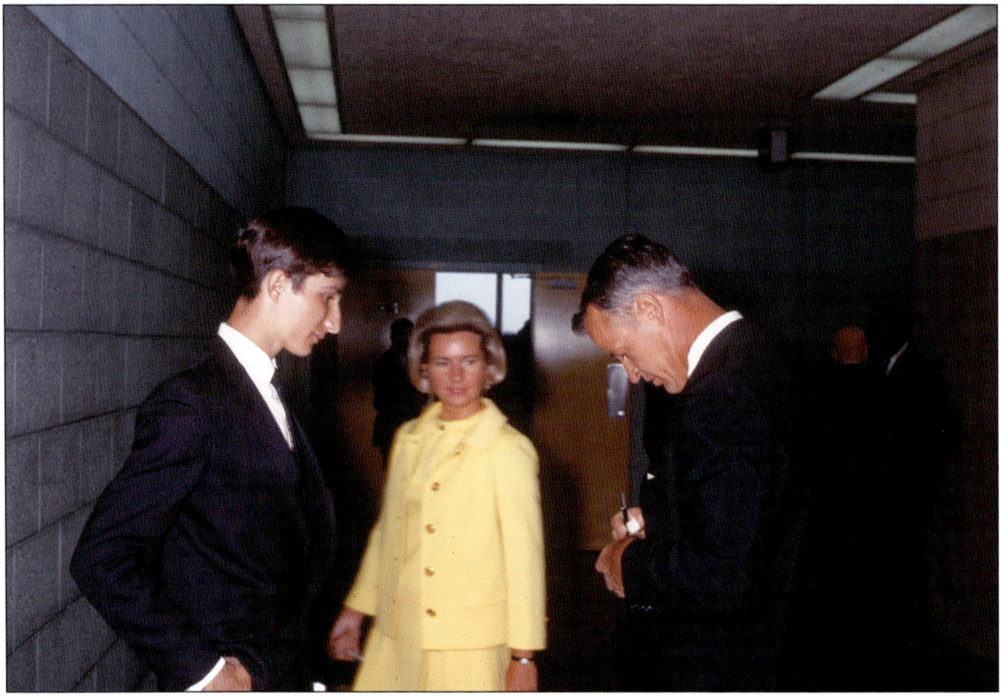

Gordie Howe (right) and his wife, Colleen, are shown with a fan getting Howe's autograph. Although born in Saskatchewan, Canada, Howe seemed like a native son, playing 25 seasons for the Detroit Red Wings. He was often seen at Jack Adams Arena at 10500 Lyndon Street by the window section near the concession stand watching his youngest son, Murray, play amateur hockey in early 1970 and 1971. Murray never became a National Hockey League player like his dad and brothers; instead, he became a surgeon.

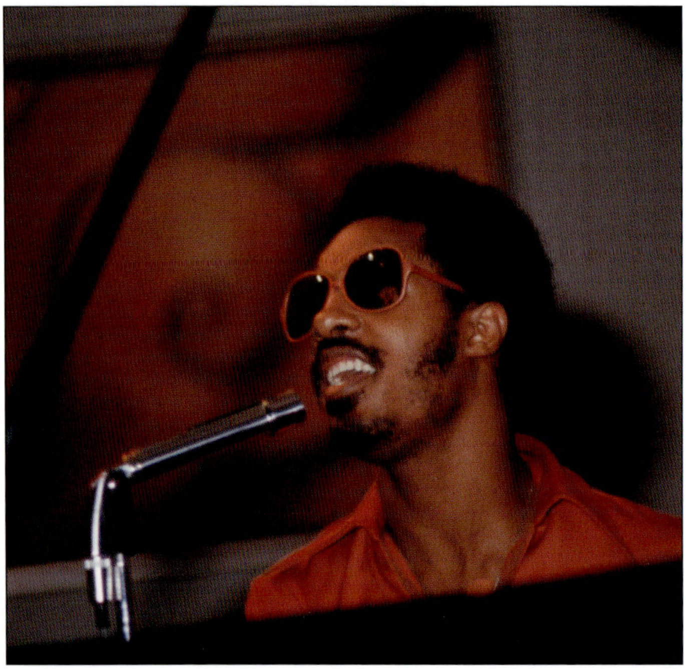

Stevie Wonder was a young teen phenomenon at Motown Records when he performed his number one hit "Fingertips Part Two" at the Arena Skate Club at 14572 Greenfield Road in 1963. Known then as "Little Stevie Wonder," he also performed at record stores and sock hops like the ones at the St. Mary's of Redford gymnasium. Leslie Gore was another star who performed there. (Courtesy of Wayne State University/ Reuther Library.)

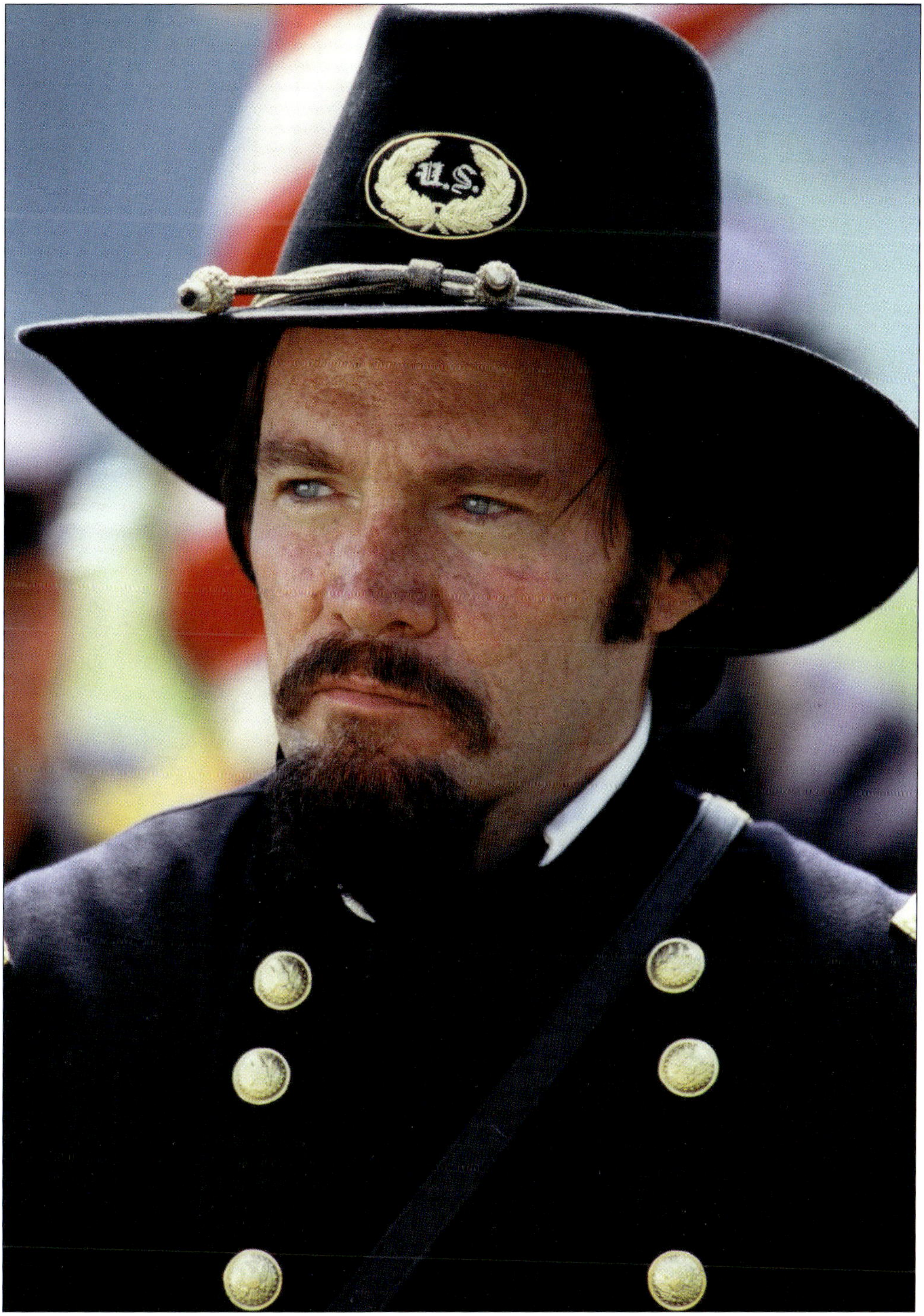

Brian Mallon graduated from St. Mary's of Redford in 1970 and has worked as a stage and screen actor for over 40 years. Mallon played Gen. Winfield Hancock in the Civil War movie *Gettysburg*. He also has starred in a one-man play about Richard Burton. In addition, Mallon authored a historical work on Ireland called *Shane O'Neil*. (Courtesy of Brian Mallon.)

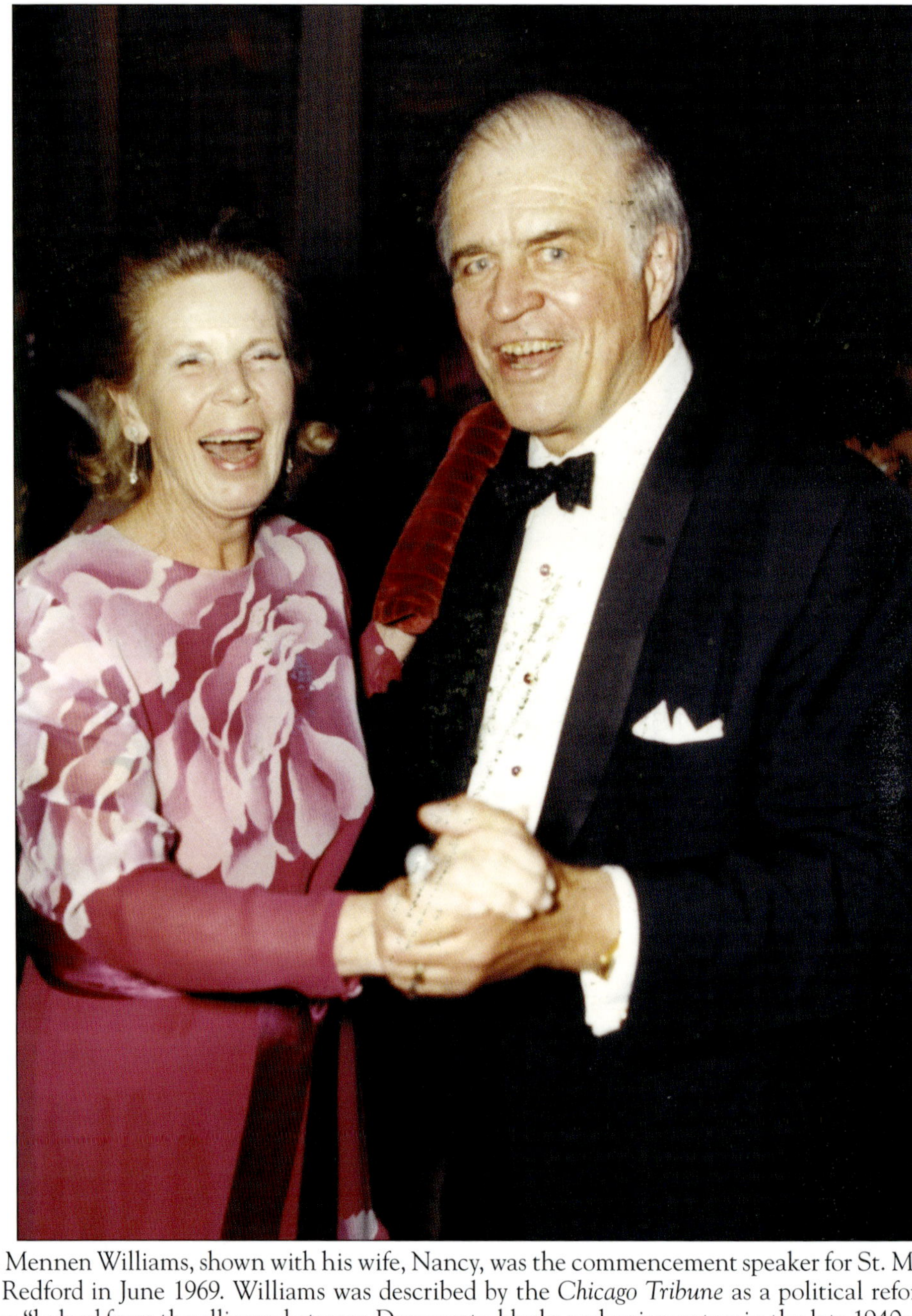

G. Mennen Williams, shown with his wife, Nancy, was the commencement speaker for St. Mary's of Redford in June 1969. Williams was described by the *Chicago Tribune* as a political reformer who "helped forge the alliance between Democrats, blacks and union voters in the late 1940s that began a strong liberal tradition in Michigan." Nicknamed "Soapy" because his mother's father was Gerhard Heinrich Mennen of the Mennen brand of personal care products, Williams often wore a green bow tie with white polka-dots. He was elected to a record six two-year terms as governor of Michigan from 1949 to 1961 and was instrumental in getting the Mackinac Bridge built in the 1950s. Williams also served during the Kennedy and Johnson administrations in the 1960s and was elected to the Michigan Supreme Court in 1970. He was named chief justice in 1983. Williams retired in 1987 and died the next year. (Courtesy of the *Detroit Free Press*/Zuma Press.)

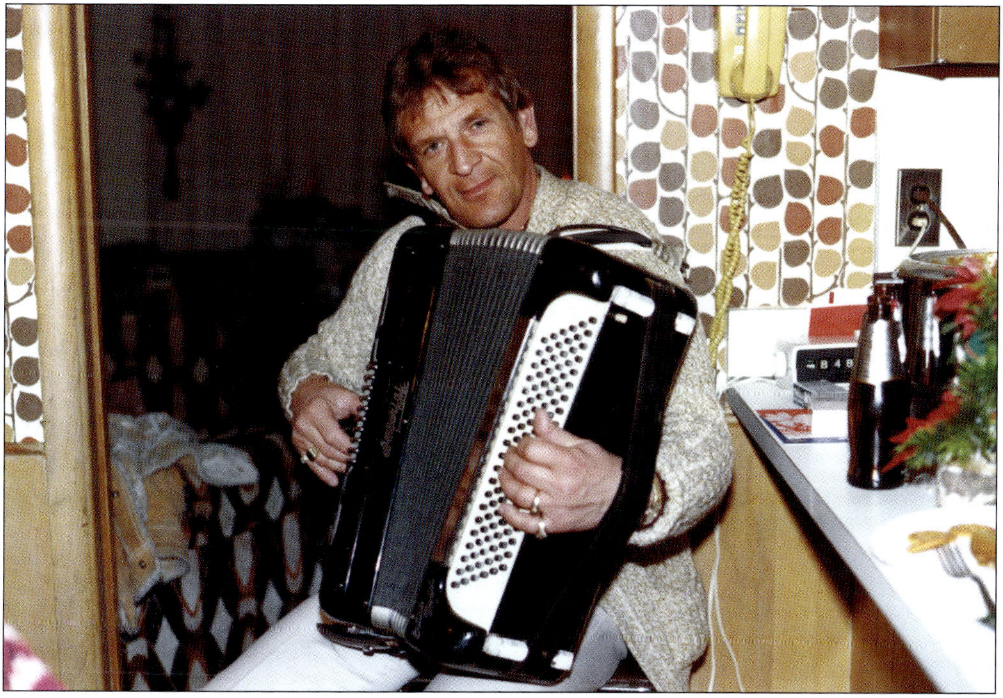

Dick Taucher was born in 1938 into a family that was originally from Yugoslavia. He attended Cooley High School and became a professional musician. Taucher played at many ethnic clubs in Detroit that his parents owned or were members of. He is shown here with an accordion, one of many instruments he played. (Courtesy of Joanne Rumford.)

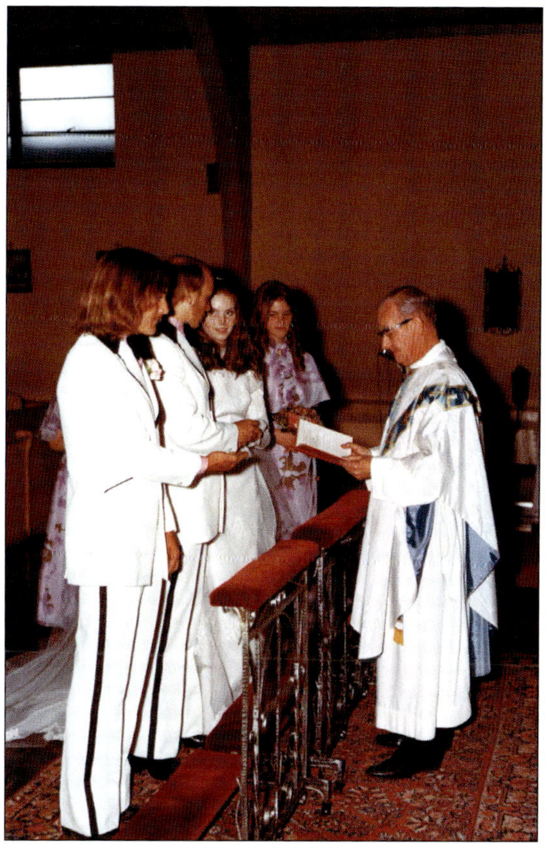

Fr. Richard Haney was born on September 31, 1907, and baptized at Holy Trinity Church. He attended the University of Detroit before entering Sacred Heart Seminary and was ordained on June 9, 1935. Haney served in a variety of assignments before becoming an assistant priest at St. Mary's of Redford from 1940 to 1946. He became pastor of the new Mother of Our Savior in 1959. He served at Mother of Our Savior for 16 years and was known as a skilled administrator who loved the Detroit Tigers, being a native of Corktown near Tiger Stadium. (Courtesy of Pam Mosteiko.)

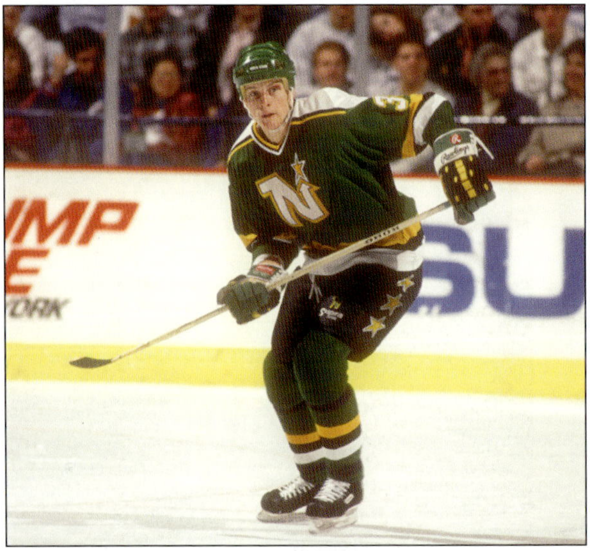

Ken Leiter, born on April 19, 1961, in Detroit, graduated from St. Mary's of Redford High School and became a professional hockey player after spending four years at Michigan State University (1979–1983). Leiter turned professional with the Indianapolis Checkers during the 1983–1984 season. He became a defenseman in the National Hockey League with the New York Islanders in the 1988–1989 season. Leiter also played for the Minnesota North Stars in 1989–1990 but had to retire due to injuries. He currently owns Laserline construction company. (Courtesy of Mitchell Layton.)

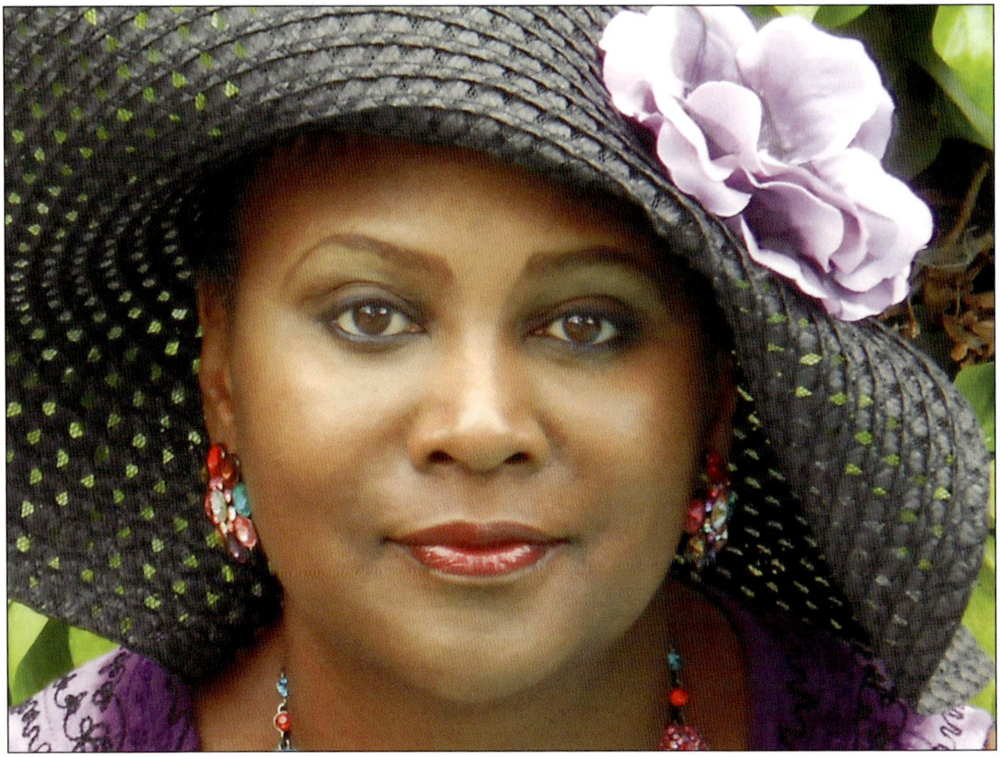

Amina Fakir used to ride her bike between Southfield Road, Greenfield Road, Fenkell Avenue, and Schoolcraft Road when she was going to school at St. Mary's of Redford High School. She was crowned Miss Black America in 1985 while she was a student at Michigan State University. She moved to Los Angeles and was an actress and producer known for *Chameleon Street* (1989), *Dominic's Castle* (1994), and *City Teacher* (2007). Fakir says she spent a decade "being a track mom and ACT/SAT tutor." She has been married to Joseph Jones for 24 years and has two grown children. She is finishing a book about her relationship with her uncle Abdul "Duke" Fakir, a founding member of the singing group the Four Tops. (Courtesy of Amina Fakir.)

Martha Griffiths served in the US House of Representatives as a Democrat for Michigan's 17th Congressional District, including the Grand River and Greenfield area, from 1953 to 1974. She was the first woman to serve on the House Ways and Means Committee and the first woman from Michigan elected as a Democrat to Congress. Griffiths has been referred to as "the mother of the Equal Rights Amendment" by *The Guardian*. She practiced law and served as lieutenant governor of Michigan from 1983 to 1991. Griffiths was inducted into the Michigan Women's Hall of Fame in 1983 and the National Women's Hall of Fame in 1993. She retired to Armada, Michigan, and died in 2003. (Courtesy of the *Detroit Free Press*/Zuma Press.)

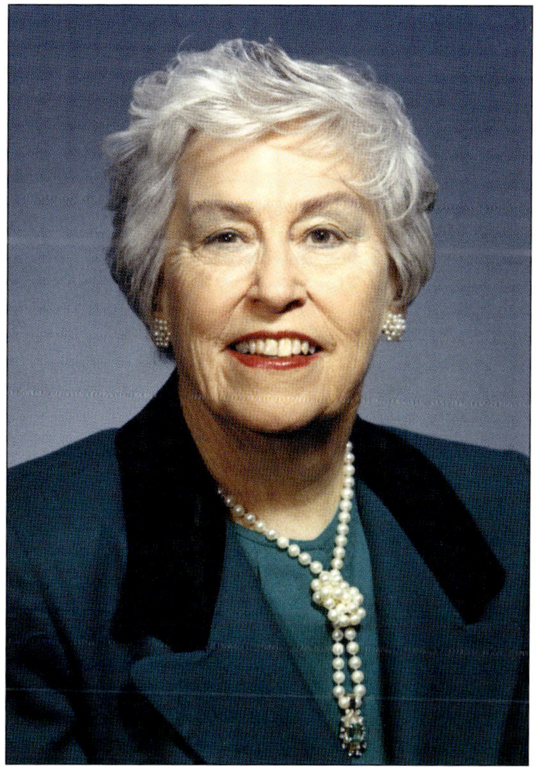

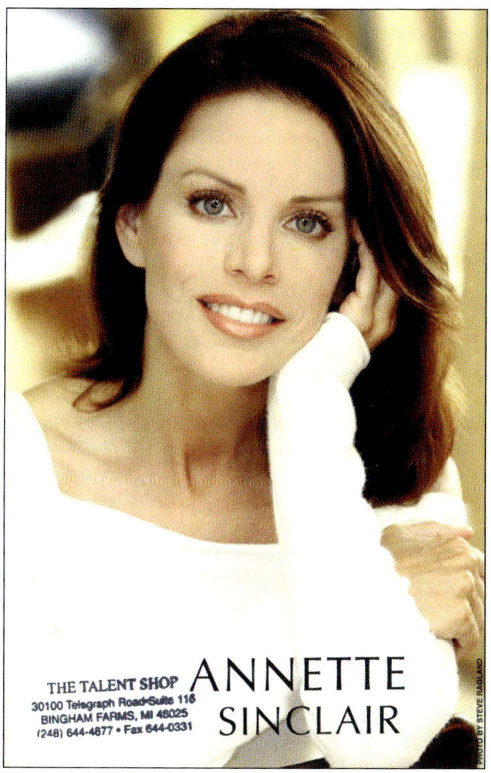

Annette Marie Szymanski Sinclair lived on Winthrop Street and Glastonbury Street in Rosedale Park while studying at St. Mary's of Redford. After graduation, she became a New York model and then a Hollywood actress. She is best known for movie roles in *Thief of Hearts* (1984), *Lunatics: A Love Story* (1991), and *The Job* (2009), plus television series like *Matt Houston*, *Finder of Lost Loves*, and *Full House*. She was previously married to rock star Bob Seger. Sinclair is now a licensed aesthetician in Michigan. (Courtesy of Annette Sinclair.)

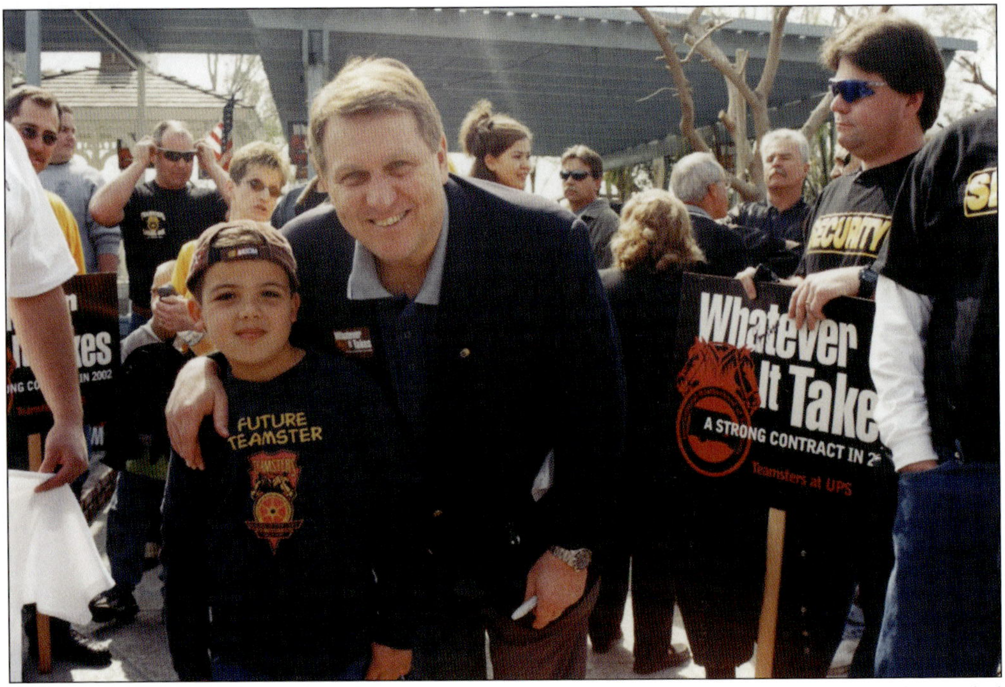

James Phillip Hoffa, the only son of Jimmy Hoffa, was born on May 19, 1941, in Detroit and attended Cooley High School. At Cooley, he became a member of the National Honor Society and an All-City and All-State football player. He earned an economics degree from Michigan State University in 1963 and a law degree from the University of Michigan in 1966. Hoffa became an attorney and the general president of the International Brotherhood of Teamsters. He has served the Teamsters since 1999. (Courtesy of the International Brotherhood of Teamsters.)

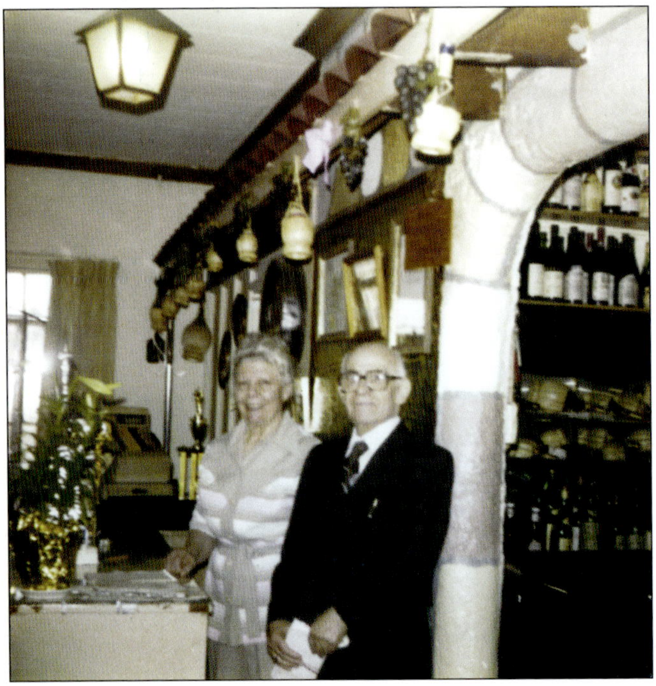

Frank Dimambro and his wife, Genuina "Jenny," stand inside their restaurant, Dimambro's, formerly Blue Ribbon Restaurant, at 13915 Grand River Avenue. Located in front of the Copco Steel Company, Dimambro's had a built-in clientele as well as neighborhood families that were introduced to Italian cuisine after World War II. Late-night sports crowds often came from the Detroit Olympia arena, as did Detroit Red Wings like Gordie Howe and Ted Lindsay. (Courtesy of Marianne Dimambro Mitchell.)

Grace Hoban Gilchrist grew up on Forrer Street and attended Mother of Our Savior Grade School and St. Mary's of Redford High School. She joined WXYZ Channel 7 in 1986 as the first female general sales manager. She was promoted to assistant general manager in 1989 and station manager in 1993. She became vice president and general manager in 1994 and retired in 2007 after 13 years in those positions. (Courtesy of David Gilchrist.)

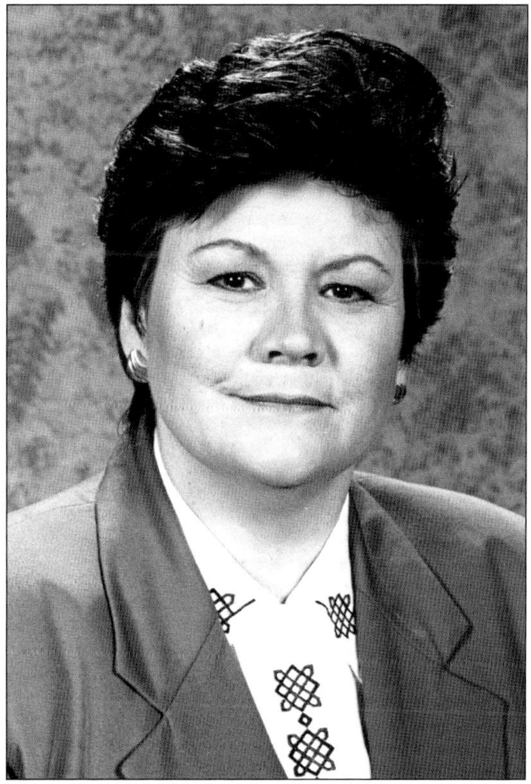

Mike Ilitch, second from left in the first row, played high school baseball for the Cooley Cardinals. Ilitch was also in the Detroit Tigers minor-league system before he left to found Little Caesar's Pizza. Ilitch purchased the Detroit Fox Theater, Detroit Red Wings, and Detroit Tigers. He is credited with helping to revive Detroit by investing in the city when it seemed no one else would. (Courtesy of Sharon Arend, director of archives and historical documents, Ilitch Holdings Inc.)

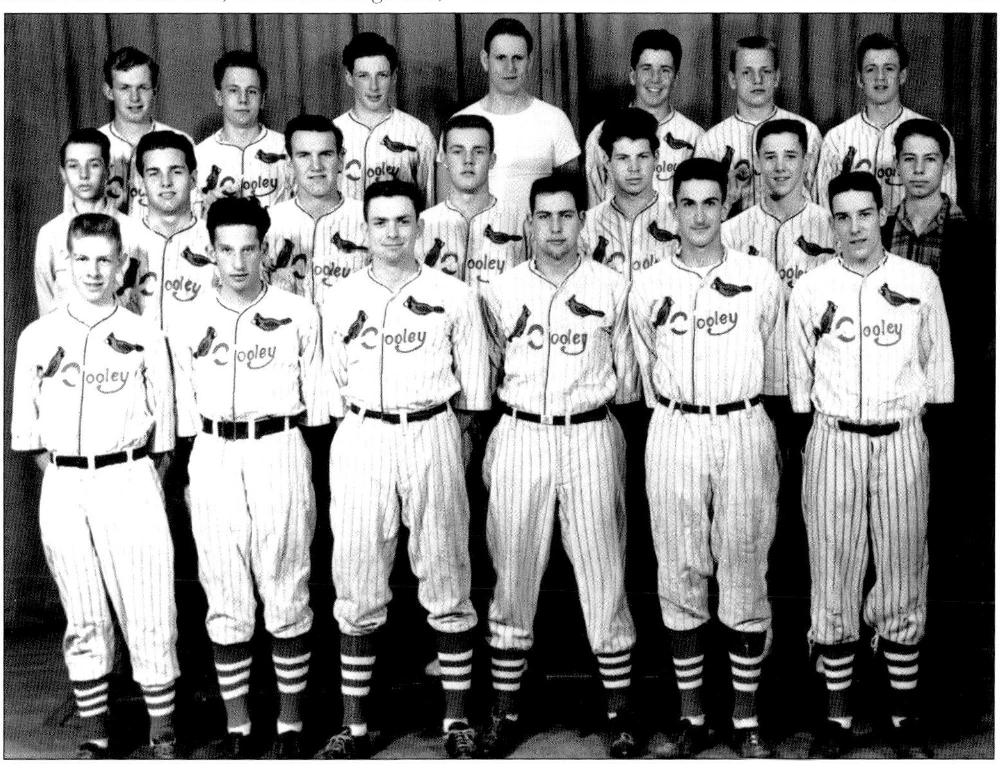

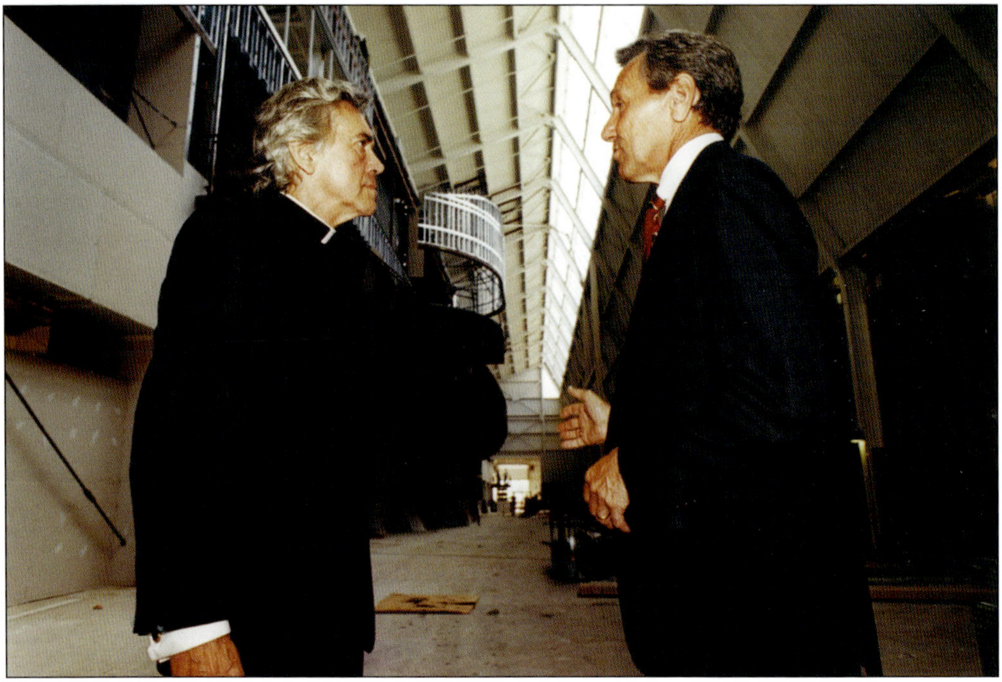

William Thomas Cunningham (left) attended St. Mary's of Redford Elementary School, Detroit's Sacred Heart Seminary, and St. John's Provincial Seminary. He was teaching English literature at a local Catholic high school when the Detroit riots began. Together with Eleanor Josaitis, Cunningham founded Focus Hope, distributing food to low-income mothers and children. Focus Hope also trained more than 1,000 youth to become engineers and factory technicians. Father Cunningham often rode a motorcycle and sparred in the ring with Muhammad Ali for charity. He died in 1997 at 67. Cunningham is pictured with Lloyd Reuss, head of curriculum at Focus Hope. (Courtesy of the *Detroit News*/Zuma Press.)

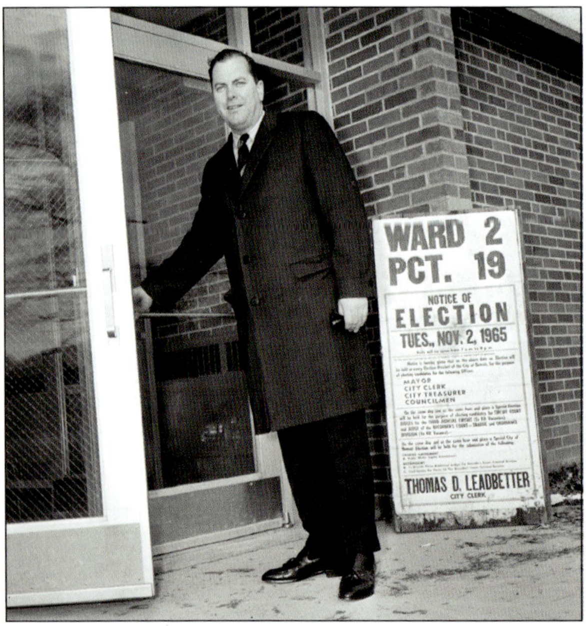

Jerome Cavanagh, born on June 16, 1928, could often be seen in the side aisle of St. Mary's of Redford receiving holy communion before going to work as mayor of Detroit. He upset the incumbent, Louis Mirani, in 1962. Known as a reformer, Cavanagh invited Martin Luther King Jr. to the March for Freedom down Woodward Avenue in June 1963. With 100,000 in attendance, King gave his "I Have a Dream" speech in Detroit before delivering it in Washington, DC. In spite of his efforts, Cavanagh could not prevent the 1967 riots. He stepped down as mayor in 1970. He returned to his law practice and died in 1979 of an apparent heart attack. (Courtesy of Wayne State University/Reuther Library.)

Artist Kim Frank Fujiwara was born and raised on the northwest side of Detroit near the Grand River and Greenfield area by O'Shea Park. He was already in advanced art classes by the first grade and was being mentored by his art teacher. Fujiwara's artwork and portraits have appeared on national ads, book covers, magazine covers, CD covers, billboards, and children's books. He has done portraits of celebrities like Arnold Palmer, Jack Nicklaus, Henry Ford II, Isaiah Thomas, George Kell, and Hillary Clinton. (Courtesy of Kim Fujiwara.)

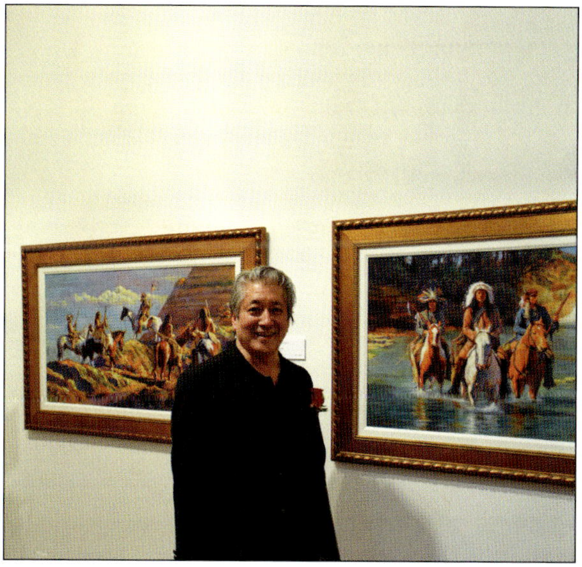

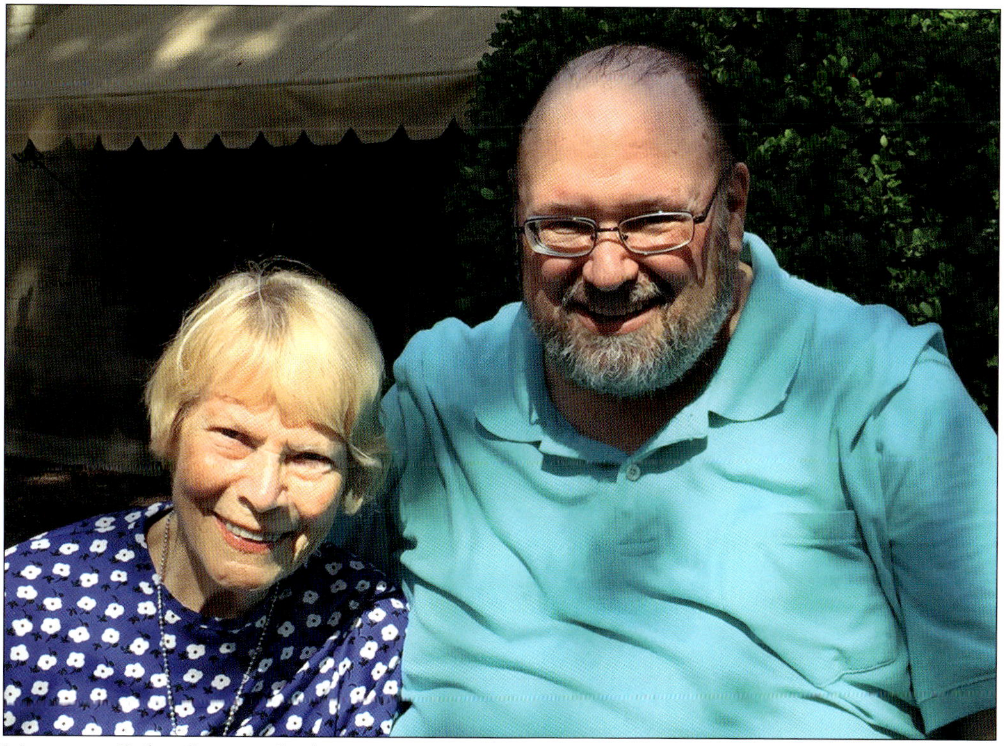

Marianne Bohn Szymanski, born in Germany, raised her family on Winthrop Street and in nearby Rosedale Park in the 1960s, 1970s, and 1980s. She escaped a German work camp in World War II only to find herself in the middle of the Battle of the Bulge when the family home she was staying at was requisitioned by Gen. Dwight Eisenhower. After the war, she worked as a tour guide and then married an American GI. She moved to Detroit, raised her family, and occasionally served as a guide and interpreter for foreign visitors to the city. In 2017, she wrote a book about her war experiences. Now in her 90s, she is an unabashed supporter of Detroit. She is shown here with the author.

DISCOVER THOUSANDS OF LOCAL HISTORY BOOKS FEATURING MILLIONS OF VINTAGE IMAGES

Arcadia Publishing, the leading local history publisher in the United States, is committed to making history accessible and meaningful through publishing books that celebrate and preserve the heritage of America's people and places.

Find more books like this at
www.arcadiapublishing.com

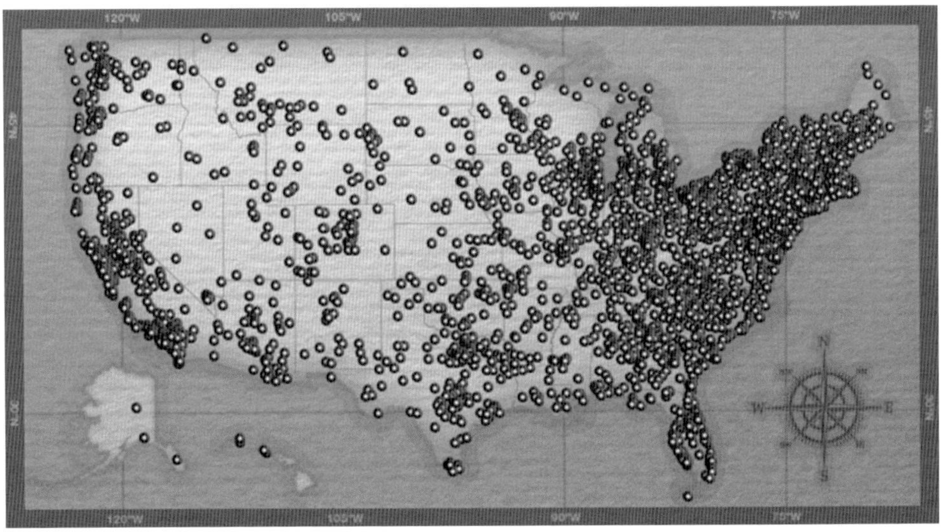

Search for your hometown history, your old stomping grounds, and even your favorite sports team.

Consistent with our mission to preserve history on a local level, this book was printed in South Carolina on American-made paper and manufactured entirely in the United States. Products carrying the accredited Forest Stewardship Council (FSC) label are printed on 100 percent FSC-certified paper.

MADE IN THE USA